UNRAVELLING
THE LANDSCAPE

An Inquisitive Approach to Archaeology

DEDICATION

This book is dedicated, with affection and respect, to
Professor Charles Thomas CBE DL
who was a member of the Royal Commission from 1983 to 1997.
He also served as Acting Chairman in 1988–9 and as Vice-Chairman
from 1992 to 1997.

ROYAL
COMMISSION
ON THE HISTORICAL
MONUMENTS
OF ENGLAND

UNRAVELLING THE LANDSCAPE

An Inquisitive Approach to Archaeology

ed Mark Bowden

TEMPUS

First published 1999

PUBLISHED IN THE UNITED KINGDOM BY:

Tempus Publishing Ltd
The Mill, Brimscombe Port
Stroud, Gloucestershire GL5 2QG

PUBLISHED IN THE UNITED STATES OF AMERICA BY:

Tempus Publishing Inc.
2A Cumberland Street
Charleston, SC 29401

Tempus books are available in France, Germany and Belgium
from the following addresses:

Tempus Publishing Group
21 Avenue de la République
37300 Joué-lès-Tours
FRANCE

Tempus Publishing Group
Gustav-Adolf-Straße 3
99084 Erfurt
GERMANY

Tempus Publishing Group
Place de L'Alma 4/5
1200 Brussels
BELGIUM

British Library Cataloguing in Publication Data.
A catalogue record for this book is available from the British Library.

ISBN 0 7524 1447 X

Typesetting and origination by Tempus Publishing.
PRINTED AND BOUND IN GREAT BRITAIN.

5403

D (BOW)

Contents

Illustrations	7
Chairman's Foreword	11
Acknowledgements	13

PART I: INTRODUCTORY

1 Introduction	15
2 Approaches and emphases	23
3 Preparation: identifying and using existing records	29

PART II: SURVEY AND INVESTIGATION

4 Analytical earthwork survey — measurement	43
5 Analytical earthwork survey — interpretation	73
6 Ground photography	97
7 Aerial survey	105
8 Other survey techniques	119
9 Special landscapes	129
10 Buildings in the landscape	155

PART III: PRODUCTS

11 Illustration and the written report	167
12 Making it all available	179
Appendix I Levels of archaeological survey	189
Appendix II Survey equipment	194

Case studies

1 Windmill Hill and West Kennet	27
2 Little Siblyback	41
3 Greenlee Lough	71
4 Yarnbury	116
5 The Royal Gunpowder Factory, Waltham Abbey	152
6 Herefordshire Beacon	177

References	202
Index	218

The illustrations

Text figures

1   Electronic survey instrument — the 'total station'
2   Traditional survey methods — 'tape-and-offset'
3   John Aubrey's plan of Avebury (Wiltshire) (1663)
4   Horsley's survey of Hadrian's Wall (Northumberland) (1732): extract
5   Dymond's survey of settlement earthworks at Threlkeld (Cumbria) (1901)
6   Herbert Toms' survey of Park Bottom field system (Sussex) (1910)
7   OS illustration card: Buckland Rings (Hampshire) (revised 1961)
8   Haystacks Hill (Northumberland): plan
9   Brougham (Cumbria): plan
10   Gerards Bromley (Staffordshire): late seventeenth-century illustration
11   Gerards Bromley: photograph (1987) replicating same view
12   Derwentcote (County Durham): OS maps 1856–1939
13   Kemsing (Kent): the park boundary
14   Cockfield Fell (County Durham): plan
15   Resectioning: schematic diagram
16   Single station control scheme: Stanton Moor (Derbyshire) control plot
17   Single station control scheme: detail control plan
18   Baseline control scheme: Burton Hall, Warcop (Cumbria)
19   Ring traverse control scheme: Stafford Castle
20   Stafford Castle: extract from control plot
21   Stafford Castle: extract from field drawing and archive drawing
22   Stafford Castle: contour plot
23   Stafford Castle: Digital Terrain Model
24   Stafford Castle: complete archive drawing
25   Taping-and-offsetting: the optical square in use
26   Taping-and-offsetting: schematic diagram
27   Graphical survey: schematic diagram
28   Sandhills Sconce, Newark (Nottinghamshire): contour plan
29   Wykeham Forest (North Yorkshire): conventional hachure plan
30   GPS equipment in use
31   Bury Castle (Devon): Digital Terrain Model
32   Example of a Rapid survey map: Middleton (Cumbria)
33   Langridge Newtake (Devon): Landscape survey
34   Chronological relationships depicted on field and archive drawings: schematic diagram
35   Stratigraphy in the landscape: aerial photograph of Braunston (Northamptonshire)
36   Church Pits (Wiltshire): plan extract showing stratigraphic relationships

37   Black Knoll, Long Mynd (Shropshire): plan
38   Stanton Moor (Derbyshire): plan
39   The Mount, Lewes Priory (Sussex): plan
40   Windmill mound, Wimpole (Cambridgeshire): monument plan
41   Windmill mound, Wimpole: as shown on landscape plan
42   Almondbury (West Yorkshire): aerial photograph
43   Ribblehead (North Yorkshire): plan
44   Haltonchesters (Northumberland): plan
45   Low Ham (Somerset): plan
46   Stow (Lincolnshire): plan
47   Carshope, Upper Coquetdale (Northumberland): ground photograph
48   Honister (Cumbria): ground photograph
49   Bodiam Castle (Sussex): ground photograph
50   The Vallum at Cawfields (Northumberland): ground photograph
51   Grimes Graves (Norfolk): ground photograph
52   Royston Cave (Cambridgeshire): photograph
53   Devil's Dyke (Cambridgeshire): ground photograph
54   Cropmarks formation diagram
55   Distribution map of specialist oblique aerial photographs held by the RCHME
56   North Oxfordshire: map showing increase in known sites pre-1967 to 1995
57   Witham (Somerset): electrical resistivity survey results
58   Coombe Down (Wiltshire): magnetometry results
59   Harbottle Castle (Northumberland): ground penetrating radar plot
60   New Farm (Hampshire): greyscale plot
61   New Farm: interpretative plan
62   Yarnbury (Wiltshire): fieldwalking results
63   Kimberley Internal Incline, Honister: photograph
64   Bailiff Wood (Cumbria): pitstead and hut
65   Micheldever Wood (Hampshire): 'banjo' enclosure
66   St Austell (Cornwall): waste heaps of china clay works
67   Newland (Cumbria): industry and settlement
68   Beckton gasworks (Greater London): aerial photograph
69   Stoke-on-Trent (Staffordshire): OS 1-inch map 1836/1879
70   Sneyd Colliery, Stoke: OS 1:2500 map 1925
71   Hamil Colour Works, Stoke: OS 1:500 map 1879
72   Chipping Campden (Gloucestershire): plan
73   Croxby (Lincolnshire): plan
74   Low Ham (Somerset): aerial photograph
75   Chipping Campden church: ground photograph
76   Avebury (Wiltshire): plan
77   Rievaulx (North Yorkshire): aerial photograph
78   Oats Royd, Midgley (West Yorkshire): ground photograph

79   Hackthorn (Lincolnshire): aerial photograph

80   Pole Moor chapel (West Yorkshire): ground photograph

81   Leeds warehouses (West Yorkshire): ground photograph

82   Newstead (Nottinghamshire): aerial photograph

83   Low Nibthwaite blast furnace (Cumbria) converted to other industrial and domestic uses

84   Luddenden Valley, Calderdale (West Yorkshire): ground photograph

85   Conventions diagram

86   Setta Barrow (Devon/Somerset): plan and profile

87   Yarnbury (Wiltshire): phase diagram

88   NMRC archive building

Case studies

1   Windmill Hill and West Kennet
         Windmill Hill
         West Kennet

2   Little Siblyback
         Aerial photograph

3   Greenlee Lough
         Excavations in progress
         Plan

4   Yarnbury
         Extract from earthwork plan
         Extract from geophysical survey
         Vertical aerial photograph

5   Waltham Abbey
         Aerial photograph of the northern part of the site
         Extract from CAD-based survey
         Component sheet for Gunpowder Press House

6   Herefordshire Beacon
         Herefordshire Beacon or British Camp, Malvern

Colour plates

1 The whin sill near Housesteads (Northumberland): aerial photograph
2 Hanging Lund, Mallerstang (Cumbria): ground photograph
3 Ingleborough (North Yorkshire): ground photograph
4 Burderop Down (Wiltshire): aerial photograph
5 Stafford Castle: aerial photograph
6 Plane tabling: taking a primary distance measurement
7 Plane tabling: taking subsidiary measurements
8 Plane tabling: the self-reducing alidade
9 Cautley (Cumbria): ground photograph
10 Munstead Wood (Surrey): relational viewpoints, related to the survey plan
11 HMS *Victory*: aerial photograph
12 Long Meg and Her Daughters (Cumbria): infra-red aerial photograph
13 Lockeridge (Wiltshire): parchmarks
14 Rollright Heath Farm (Oxfordshire): 'banjo' enclosure
15 Herberowe Bank, Lower Heyford (Oxfordshire): enclosure
16 Magnetometer in use
17 Brean Down (Somerset): ground photograph
18 Bridgwater Bay (Somerset): ground photograph
19 Minehead (Somerset): recording fish weirs with GPS
20 Hodgson's High Level lodging shop, Nenthead (Cumbria): ground photograph
21 Pendennis Castle (Cornwall): aerial photograph
22 Holne Moor (Devon): interpretation plan

The *front cover* shows the earthworks on Burderop Down, Wiltshire

Chairman's Foreword

The analysis of landscape by means of survey is a particularly valuable — and a particularly British — contribution to archaeology, and to related disciplines such as historical geography and local history. It is a tradition spanning more than 300 years, fostered by enthusiasts from John Aubrey in the mid-seventeenth century to J P Williams-Freeman and O G S Crawford in the twentieth century.

The professional inheritors of this tradition were the three Royal Commissions on (Ancient and) Historical Monuments, set up in 1908, and the former Archaeology Division of the Ordnance Survey, established in 1920. Over the years it has become increasingly apparent that there is a need for wider dissemination of the approaches to investigating and interpreting archaeological sites and landscapes that have been developed by these bodies. All too few of our professional colleagues, let alone the wider public, appreciate fully the perceptions and particular skills that Royal Commission Investigators have brought to the analysis of landscape, and yet at the same time there is great interest in methods which can produce insights and understanding of the landscape. The many training courses that we have provided over the years have highlighted repeatedly the need for an adequate textbook covering this topic.

This book draws on the expertise and enthusiasm of a large number of staff members of the English Royal Commission, past and present, in its text and in its illustrations. It covers a wide range of the activities necessary for analytical survey, and the examples chosen come from a variety of landscape types, both upland and lowland.

There is much to be gained from such non-destructive survey techniques as are outlined here, at a time when it is ever more important to emphasise that archaeology is much more than merely digging. Assessment and analysis must come first: survey provides an understanding of sites and landscapes for pure research goals, for conservation and management purposes, and for the provision of context to more narrowly focused investigations. We believe that this book will provide for the beginner, the student, and perhaps even for some seasoned, but excavation-oriented archaeologists, the first steps towards an inquisitive approach to archaeological survey. We also hope that it will introduce many to the intellectual satisfaction and the sheer enjoyment of unravelling and understanding the complexities of landscape development.

Therefore, it is highly appropriate — and it gives me great pleasure — that this book should be dedicated to Charles Thomas who has been a champion of analytical survey in archaeology, both within the Royal Commission and in the discipline as a whole, for so many years.

FARINGDON

Acknowledgements

This book is the work of many staff within the RCHME. The principal contributors are: Stewart Ainsworth, Robert Bewley, Wayne Cocroft, Steven Cole, Mark Corney, Jo Donachie, Paul Everson, Colum Giles, Amy Lax, Phil Newman, Hazel Riley, Andrew Sargent and Humphrey Welfare. Other contributions were made by: Keith Blood, Chris Dunn, David Field, Martin Fletcher, David McOmish, Paul Pattison, Simon Probert, Iain Sainsbury, Nicky Smith, Bernard Thomason, Peter Topping and Rob Wilson-North. The illustrations were worked on by Deb Cunliffe and Philip Sinton. Photographs were specially taken for this publication by Keith Buck, James Davies and Mike Hesketh-Roberts. Robin Taylor advised on arrangements for publication.

The RCHME would like to thank: Martin Bell, Stephen Briggs (RCAHMW), Brian Donnelly (Northumbrian Surveys), John Gater (GSB Prospection), Richard McDonnell, Marilyn Palmer, David Pritchard and Graham Ritchie (RCAHMS). The RCHME is grateful to the following for granting permission to reproduce illustrations: The Bodleian Library, University of Oxford (Fig 3), Northamptonshire Heritage (Fig 35), West Yorkshire Archaeology Service (Fig 54), GSB Prospection (Plate 16, Figs 57–8, 60–1), Northumbrian Surveys (Fig 59), Steve Hartgroves/Cornwall Archaeological Unit (Fig 66) and the Ministry of Defence, on behalf of the Controller of HMSO (Yarnbury case study).

PART I: INTRODUCTORY

1 Introduction

Archaeological surveys are undertaken for a wide variety of reasons: out of sheer enthusiasm for the subject, as a dissertation for part of a course, as part of a parish or regional study, as part of a larger multi-disciplinary research project, to give landscape context to an excavation, to inform conservation decisions as part of a management plan, to record in advance of damaging or destructive works, or as a combination of any of these.

Survey is often thought of as 'difficult' and overly mathematical. On the other hand, a belief has grown up in recent years, with the development of electronic survey instruments, that survey is merely a matter of learning a sequence of buttons to press on a keyboard. The truth, of course, lies between these extremes. With a little thought and application, and ideally some guidance from an experienced archaeological surveyor, the basic processes can be grasped by anyone; the message which should be given to anyone approaching a survey task for the first time is: Don't panic!

THE PURPOSE OF THIS BOOK

This book aims to provide a guide to perception and to encourage an inquisitive approach to archaeological sites and landscapes through examples of methods, procedures and best practice. It is not a technical handbook: surveying manuals are available elsewhere (eg Bannister and Raymond 1977; Muskett 1988; OS 1965; Pugh 1975; Ritchie *et al* 1977; Whyte and Paul 1997; Wilson 1971). The process of metrical surveying has become considerably easier since the 1970s, because of the development of ever more sophisticated electronic survey equipment, and many archaeologists routinely use the latest 'high-tech' instruments which are, on the whole, user friendly. However, no one should confuse the use of such instruments with the ability to see and understand archaeological remains; the second is not necessarily a corollary of the first. The purpose in this book is therefore to show how surveying techniques, both modern and traditional, can be applied most effectively to archaeological recording, analysis and research (**figs 1, 2**). As such, this book should be of use to students and to the amateur or professional archaeologist for whom survey is not part of everyday experience.

All the survey methods discussed in Part II of the book are of equal and complementary importance. That one particular method, analytical earthwork survey, is given particular weight reflects the fact that it has been relatively neglected in the literature recently. While there are many books, articles and technical papers available on surface artefact collection, geophysics and aerial photography, there is no reliable modern guide to earthwork survey.

1 Electronic survey instruments, such as this 'total station', supply a rigid and accurate control framework for survey and provide the best means of recording structural detail.

Bettess (1984; 1992) and Coles (1972) are good on the technicalities, though the latter is out of print. The admirable Taylor (1974) is now not easily obtainable, but Brown (1987, chapters 3 and 4) contains much of the same good advice. There is little else that one can wholeheartedly recommend. This complementary aspect of different survey techniques, and excavation, cannot be too strongly stressed. They can and should be used together where possible, and tested against each other where appropriate.

The sphere of interest of the investigative archaeologist is all-encompassing. It covers every aspect of human activity: domestic, economic, religious, defensive and so on. Chronologically, the sphere of interest stretches from prehistory to the present. In space, it reaches every corner of the world, including the seabed (although that is not covered here).

This book has been written by staff of the Royal Commission on the Historical Monuments of England (RCHME) and though, inevitably, most of the examples which illustrate it are drawn from England, the principles and guidance are of universal application, significance and relevance.

The idea of landscape archaeology has become increasingly popular in recent years and some genuine advances have been made in the field and in theoretical approaches to the landscape (eg Aston 1985; Fleming 1988; RCAHMS 1990; Bender 1993; Johnson and

2   Traditional surveying methods produce accurate and worthwhile results and are most effective for recording archaeological earthwork detail.

Rose 1994; Barker and Darvill 1997). It is appropriate, therefore, that the RCHME should share its experience of surveying both landscapes and the more limited areas we call 'sites'. The words 'monument', 'site' and 'landscape' are scattered throughout the book. No attempt is made to define the first two terms: the usage will become clear. 'Landscape' is used here broadly in the sense of 'the physical topography of an area' (see Olwig 1993).

Every effort has been made to illustrate the arguments and ideas presented with real examples, either within the book or through references to other publications or, in the case of unpublished sites, to National Grid References.

AN INQUISITIVE APPROACH

The spirit of enquiry and curiosity in archaeological survey is universal. The twin harbours of the ancient town of Amasra on the Black Sea coast of Turkey are guarded by the island of Boz Tepe. At the highest point of the island, close to the seaward cliffs, some very scrappy-looking earthworks were noted under scrubby undergrowth during an archaeological survey of the Byzantine defences of the town (Crow and Hill 1995). The earthworks were initially deemed to be of recent origin and of little interest, but fortunately the inquisitive approach prevailed and they were surveyed (a job which occupied two people for just one afternoon). As the plan grew, the apparently shapeless earthworks took on a symmetry and revealed the outline of a large rectangular building with an apsidal east end — a Byzantine church, clearly, and possibly the Martyrium of St

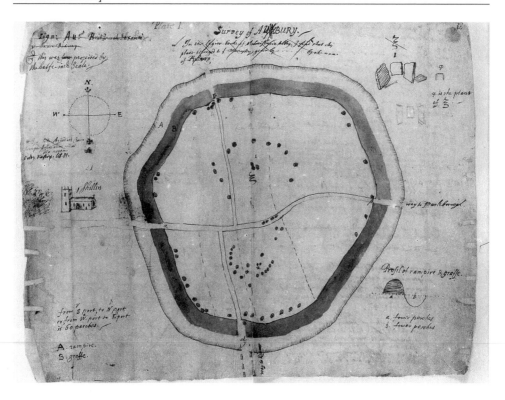

3   *John Aubrey's plan of Avebury (1663) (The Bodleian Library, University of Oxford MS Top. Gen. c24. f39-40).*

Hyacinthus, of which there are documentary records, but the exact site of which was thought to be lost (J Crow pers comm). The moral hardly needs stating. No earthwork, however unprepossessing, should be ignored. An accurate and systematic survey may make sense of an apparently hopeless jumble of 'humps and bumps'.

The inquisitive approach, however, goes beyond the discovery, recording and elucidation of individual sites. Its ultimate goal is an understanding of the development of entire landscapes, or what may be termed 'total landscape history'. A lifetime may be required for anything like the achievement of such a goal, as Christopher Taylor (1989a) suggests in his stimulating study of Whittlesford (Cambridgeshire), but that must not deter anyone from making the attempt.

The inquisitive archaeologist's first question should be: 'What do we want to know about the human past?', rather than the more negative, 'What will the available evidence, the archaeological record, *allow* us to know about the human past?' The available evidence may limit us in the end, and we will accept that, but we must not limit *ourselves* at the very outset of our quest.

Contrary to much popular belief, archaeology is not just about finding things, it is about understanding that which is found. The field archaeologist, no less than the excavator, has a duty to analyse and interpret, to further knowledge of the human past. Data collecting for its own sake is not valid and will not be found intellectually stimulating. The inquisitive approach has much to do with personal enjoyment and 'job satisfaction': there is immense pleasure to be gained from achieving some level of understanding of a site or landscape, and then drawing a plan and writing a report which together convey that story.

A BRIEF HISTORY OF FIELD ARCHAEOLOGY IN BRITAIN

Arguably, archaeological field survey in Britain began on 7 January 1649 when John Aubrey stumbled upon the earthworks and standing stones of Avebury (Wiltshire) while hunting. His subsequent survey of the site, in 1663 (**fig 3**), resulted in the first accurate plan of an archaeological earthwork in this country (Welfare 1989). Previous topographical historians, such as Camden, Dugdale and Leland, being men of their time, had produced written descriptions of antiquities, but not graphical depictions. Aubrey was an acute observer of earthworks and of landscape; his scheme for calculating the proportion of valley to downland in Wiltshire by cutting up a map and weighing the resulting paper shapes has a touch of genius. Unfortunately, he shared another, less admirable, trait with many subsequent archaeologists — an inability to bring projects to a conclusion.

Consequently, further advances in archaeological field survey did not occur until a generation later with the work of William Stukeley in the early 1720s and John Horsley in the following decade. Stukeley too was something of a flawed genius and, though his survey work was sometimes poor, his intense curiosity, powers of observation and graphical approach set high standards (Piggott 1985). One of his colleagues, Lord Winchelsea, left a description of his survey work at Julliberries Grave (Kent) (*ibid*, 57), which demonstrates a grasp of all the basic principles we now associate with the record of an archaeological monument. But Stukeley found no younger followers to train: his pupils, like Lord Winchelsea, tended to be older than himself. Horsley differed from Aubrey and Stukeley in that his principal interest was in Roman, not prehistoric, remains, which is perhaps more typical of the eighteenth-century antiquary. Horsley's monumental survey of Hadrian's Wall contained within a larger work on Roman Britain (1732) is still of immense value (**fig 4**). Not its least interesting feature is the division of the physical remains into four 'degrees' according to their state of preservation.

General William Roy carried on the work with superior survey skills in the middle decades of the eighteenth century, with his plans of Roman military works in Scotland and northern England (Macdonald 1917), and thereafter a tradition was established. This was partly sustained through the work of the Ordnance Survey (OS hereafter), established in 1791, many of whose surveyors shared Roy's interest in antiquities (Owen and Pilbeam 1992, 62–5). The county histories of the turn of the nineteenth century (eg Colt Hoare 1812) are illustrated by carefully drawn maps, plans and bird's-eye views. This achievement was carried through into the middle decades of the nineteenth century through the work of, for instance, Henry MacLauchlan (Charlton and Day 1984), but a significant advance was made by the increase in survey scale, and hence level of detail, brought about by, amongst others, the Cumbrian archaeologist C W Dymond (eg 1901) (**fig 5**). General Pitt Rivers, a surprisingly poor observer of earthworks (Bowden 1991, 121–2, 156–7), made little impact on this branch of the discipline, but his one-time

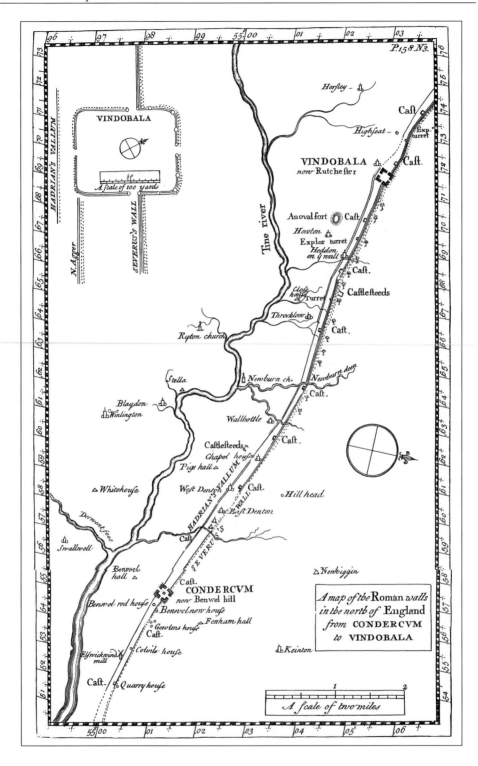

4   *An extract from John Horsley's survey of Hadrian's Wall, published in 1732.*

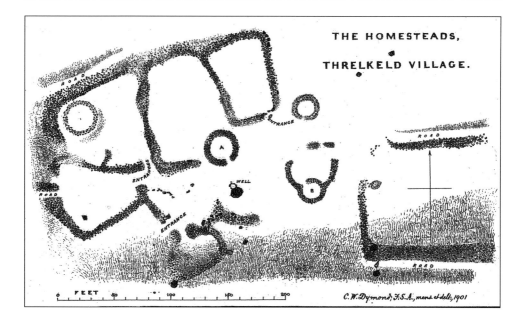

5   *C W Dymond's survey of settlement remains at Threlkeld (Cumbria), 1901.*

assistant Herbert Toms (Bradley 1989) was one of a small band, including Heywood Sumner (eg 1913) and Williams-Freeman (1915), who carried the skills of analytical earthwork survey through to the early years of the twentieth century (**fig 6**).

The establishment of the three Royal Commissions on (Ancient and) Historical Monuments in Scotland, England and Wales in 1908 set this tradition of field archaeology on a professional footing (see Dunbar 1992). An event of equal importance was the appointment of OGS Crawford as Archaeology Officer at the OS in 1922. Crawford, one of the most under-rated figures in the history of British archaeology, created a Branch and ultimately a Division within OS to deal with the depiction of antiquities, accurately located and named, on OS maps (Crawford 1955; Owen and Pilbeam 1992, 94, 152–4) (**fig 7**). The OS Archaeology Division was closed in 1983 and many of its staff, as well as its records and responsibilities, transferred to the Royal Commissions.

The boom in excavation, led by the Rescue movement from the 1960s and the rapid growth of university departments of archaeology from the 1970s, was not kind to traditional field archaeology, the skills of which were too much taken for granted. The result is that recent generations of university-trained archaeologists have been immensely skilled excavators, but rather poor surveyors and observers of landscape. Traditional field archaeology, using that term in its strict sense, has been carried forward by a tiny group of amateur archaeologists and those employed by the OS and the Royal Commissions. The growth of interest in 'landscape archaeology' and the development of new survey techniques, such as aerial photography, 'field walking' and geophysics, and new computer techniques including Geographical Information Systems (GIS), have led to renewed interest in non-excavational archaeology, but the longstanding British tradition of analytical earthwork survey still needs to be fostered.

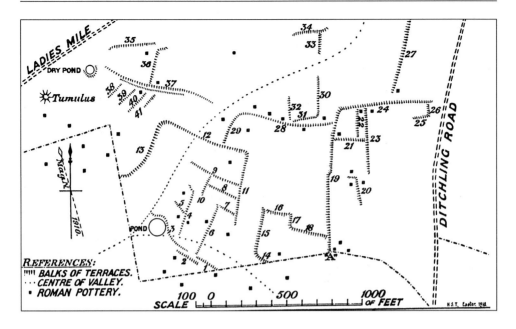

6   *Herbert Toms' survey of Park Bottom (Sussex), 1910. This suggests that Toms
         may be credited with some pioneering work in landscape archaeology (see Bradley
         1989, 38-9)*

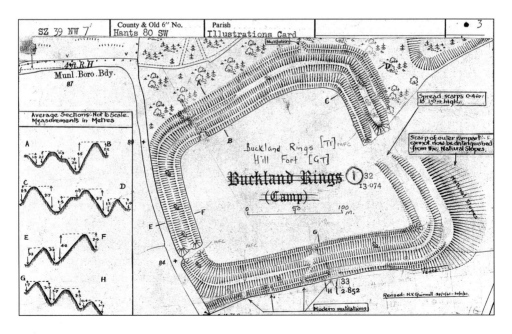

7   *OS illustration card for Buckland Rings (Hampshire), resulting from map
         revision in 1961 (extract reproduced from the 1943 Ordnance Survey map).*

2 Approaches and emphases

The task is to record the landscape, through the archaeological elements within it, in order to understand its history, development, and significance. Put so simply, the challenge may seem daunting. How can such a task be approached? The first steps are straightforward enough:

(a) Look at what is there;

(b) Consider, and try to understand, the component parts and how they relate to one another;

(c) Assess how the whole relates to its contemporary context (whether on a local, regional, or national level) and to comparable examples recorded elsewhere.

Step by step, the pieces of the jigsaw may be gradually assembled and some fragmentary information may be reconstructed. Yet some caution is necessary: if we want to understand the history of the landscape around us, tracing how it has changed through time, we must first leave aside our preconceptions and assess dispassionately what we see.

In this context, the role of the archaeologist may be compared to that of the General Practitioner in medicine. In the clinic, as in the countryside, diagnosis must be made by an examination of the surface. In most cases only one appointment is necessary and surgery (excavation) is unnecessary. An immediate problem is that the patients (the elements in the landscape) are almost infinitely diverse. Their individual histories deepen this diversity and add a chronological dimension: their ages vary, as do the complexities of their characteristics, and they bear evidence of the knocks that life has dealt them. Thus the archaeologist in the landscape must be prepared for anything, more often acting as an expert generalist, rather than as a specialist. This wide brief provides some of the excitement, heightening the intellectual satisfaction of unravelling a conundrum.

All this is a long way from the common assumption that archaeological research proceeds only by means of excavation — 'Archaeologists dig, don't they?' Sometimes, in circumstances of rescue in the face of development or erosion (the Accident and Emergency Department), they do have to. More commonly, however, excavation is — or should be — only one part of a much larger process of information gathering, analysis and assessment in which inquisitive survey has a vital role to play.

The first question, of course, is: What do we know already? Just as the GP consults the patient's records to get the background, so it is in archaeology. The first stop therefore should be the National Monuments Record (NMR) or the Sites and Monuments Record (SMR) maintained by the local authority (see pp29–30). However, a remote diagnosis, solely on the basis of the records compiled by others, may be hazardous. An informed, but open-minded examination of the surface, without any early resort to the scalpel, will achieve much.

Survey is a relatively cheap means of analysing and understanding archaeological sites and landscapes, providing a large proportion of retrievable knowledge for a small outlay. Later on in this book some consideration will be given to the wide range of equipment

8   *Haystacks Hill (Northumberland): plan showing the late prehistoric or Romano-British settlements slighted by surrounding fields of broad ridge-and-furrow, probably of medieval date. Later field boundaries in turn overlie the ridge-and-furrow. Extract from Landscape survey by air photographic transcription and fieldwork: original scale 1:2500.*

that may be used, but let us first consider the human resource required to produce work of a professional standard. Excavations vary greatly, from single-period discrete rural sites to vastly complex, multi-period urban areas with deep stratigraphy; all but the smallest require a number of roles: director, supervisors, trowellers, finds assistants, surveyors, a photographer and so on. In a survey there will usually be only two: one to carry out the metrical recording (the person using the instrument, if any), and one to select what is to be recorded (the person holding the pole, the prism, or the other end of the tape). Both will usually be involved in the analysis of the site, and possibly in the preparation of the final plan and the report, though the second will be the decision maker. Analytical survey is, therefore, supremely economical.

Does it generate worthwhile results? Survey provides useful information on the *form*, and on the *condition* of earthworks; it is also extremely good at identifying the *chronological relationships* of the elements of the landscape to one another. Are the earthworks of the settlement overlying the field system adjacent or are they slighted by it? By asking questions such as this, a *relative chronology* can be built up.

Surface examination is less good at producing ideas on *function* (while some classes of earthworks are readily recognisable, the use that others were put to may remain quite obscure), or on *absolute* dating. We may be able to see that the settlement is slighted by the

9   *Brougham (Cumbria): the medieval masonry castle and the platform of the Roman fort, the northern part of which was subsequently laid out as a garden by Lady Ann Clifford in the seventeenth century. Original survey scale 1:500.*

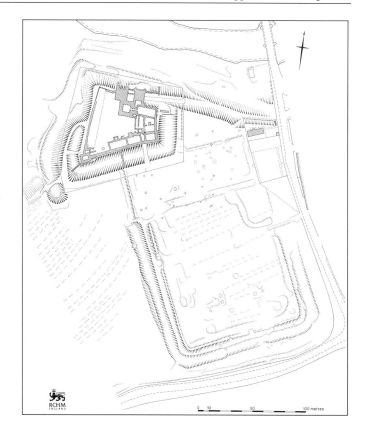

field system and that they are of types that, by analogy, are likely to be of Roman and medieval dates, respectively, but analytical survey cannot usually identify the time-slots with greater precision (**fig 8**). Nevertheless, form and relative chronology provide much of the jigsaw puzzle and will usually provide a sufficiently clear picture for the commonest purposes for which it is needed: the interpretation of the site's history and development. This information can be used in the management of the site or as the basis of its presentation to the general public.

This makes survey sound quite straightforward. To an extent this is true (everyone has to start somewhere), but experience counts. Just like the GP, the more familiar a set of symptoms becomes, the more accurate and confident is the diagnosis. The gradual aggregation of the mental inventory of site-types is a slow process, but it is one that can be accelerated by simply visiting and absorbing as many sites and landscapes as possible. The range and variety of this experience is important, not least because the 'sphere of interest' of the archaeologist in the landscape is almost infinite. Although the successful practitioner cannot be an expert on everything that may be encountered, he or she must be omnivorous. If a Roman fort has been succeeded by a medieval castle, and then by a post-medieval garden, as at Brougham (Cumbria) (**fig 9**), real understanding of their development and relationships will only emerge if all three elements are first recognised and then considered, in isolation and in combination. Undue emphasis on one element — or the exclusion of another — may seriously skew interpretation.

That said, there is always a need to decide, during the preparation for a survey, whether any particular emphasis *should* be laid. This is a hazardous course, but, for example, such an emphasis might be determined by a specific need to focus in on an area which is under threat within a wider landscape, thus necessitating a more detailed treatment. Alternatively, one particular element may be the subject of a thematic study, necessitating a plan of campaign that will address specific questions or topics. Whatever the immediate need, the archaeologist should work on the assumption that the site or landscape on which they are engaged will only be recorded and analysed this once; that being so the needs of posterity also have to be considered: these will be best served and satisfied by a balanced programme of recording and interpretation.

The record that forms the results of an analytical survey must be appropriate to the original requirement and will be dictated by the method selected. A rapid, *extensive* survey of, say, all the surviving earthworks in a given area may result in summary information and a graphical record that is limited to a locating cross or a pecked line on a map. At the other extreme, an *intensive* survey of an individual earthwork will produce a detailed textual report and a plan that depicts every discernible hump and bump. In order to illustrate and to define these different levels of detail and to assist in the decisions as to what is appropriate in any one instance, the RCHME has produced a pamphlet entitled *Recording Archaeological Field Monuments: a descriptive specification* (salient points are summarised in Appendix I).

No interpretation of the landscape, whether extensive or intensive, ever provides all the answers. Like any other method this is only a stepping-stone towards a mental reconstruction of former structures that can, at best, be only imperfectly known. However, we can come closer to the truth by adopting a holistic approach — using a variety of retrieval methods — whenever this can be justified. This is an important consideration because a normal result of any landscape investigation is a host of new questions: questions that should be much more clearly defined and articulated than hitherto, but which nevertheless remain unanswered. These may be best addressed by other techniques: geophysical survey to locate and identify levelled remains; the analysis of pollen or plant macro-fossils from water-logged deposits that would enable past environments to be reconstructed; selective excavation to untangle particular relationships or to recover material for scientific dating; and so on. The need for all or any of these may be identified as a result of an analytical survey of the extant remains. If they can be identified at the outset, this should be included in the project design — whether or not the resources exist for the ideal requirements to be satisfied. At the very least they should be included in any suggestions for further work.

In summary, the analytical investigation, interpretation and recording of an almost infinite range of extant earthworks is economical and can address subjects, for a variety of needs, at differing levels of detail. It is a key part of a longer process that will certainly include preparation by delving through existing records, and which may end with suggestions as to how and where other investigative methods — including excavation — may be applied.

Every initiative should have clear objectives, targets that — ideally — should be set out in a formal or informal project design (Darvill 1993; Renfrew and Bahn 1996, 67). One of the aims of this book is to aid the articulation of those objectives and bringing them to fruition.

BARROWS IN THE LANDSCAPE
WINDMILL HILL AND WEST KENNET (WILTSHIRE)

Some burial monuments occur in isolation, while others are paired or grouped, sometimes to form sizeable cemeteries. Round barrow cemeteries may be linear, nuclear or dispersed (Ashbee 1960, 34). The focus of these cemeteries was sometimes an earlier monument, such as a long barrow, as at Winterbourne Stoke crossroads (Wiltshire) (RCHME 1979a, x-xi). Barrows cluster around major ceremonial centres. Stonehenge alone has about 400 round barrows grouped around it (RCHME 1979a, ix; Woodward and Woodward 1996).

In the field it is essential to examine the relationship of barrows and cairns both to their topographical setting and to other archaeological sites; observations may suggest associations and manipulations of the natural or 'eternal' landscape (Bergh 1995, 157). On Bodmin Moor (Cornwall), the higher ends of two of the three long cairns point to impressive Tors. It has been suggested that the construction of the cairns formalised the cultural significance of these natural features (Tilley 1995, 14). Natural rises or hillocks were sometimes used to give burial mounds greater prominence and artificially to increase their size, as possibly at High Park (Lancashire) (SD 645 785). The fact that such features were visible and chosen says something about the openness of the landscape at the time and their symbolic significance. Equally important to consider are areas which lack barrows and cairns; on Bodmin Moor, many eminently suitable locations were not chosen for cairn sites (Johnson and Rose 1994, 41).

It is not uncommon for barrows and cairns to be sited on false crests which give panoramic views over low-lying land that may have been the settlement areas of the barrow builders. This very specific siting was a deliberate device to enhance the visual effect of barrows, so that from lower land they appear as prominent features on the skyline. At Windmill Hill (Wiltshire), the visual focus from the hilltop changed during prehistory. The Neolithic multiple enclosure complex is false-crested on the northern

Aerial photographic transcription of Windmill Hill; original scale 1: 10,000, north to top.

0   500m

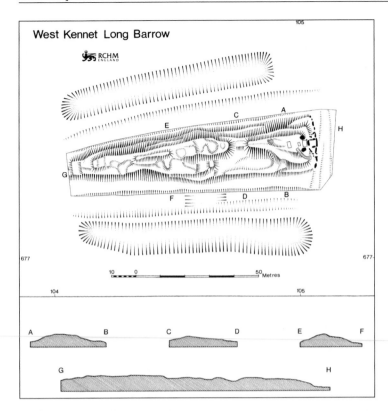

West Kennet Long Barrow

RCHM
ENGLAND

10 0   50 Metres

West Kennet long barrow: plan and profiles in combination demonstrate evidence for the theory that the barrow consisted originally of two contiguous mounds; original scale 1:500.

edge of a chalk ridge, both to overlook and to be seen from the upper reaches of the Thames Valley. The Bronze Age round barrows, however, are set back from this edge to overlook the ceremonial monuments at Avebury to the south-east, from which the barrows are clearly visible on the skyline. In valleys, barrows were often built on the edge of a terrace right above the river. This peripheral location may have been chosen either to emphasise the importance of the river as a boundary, or a routeway, or to leave the main area of the terrace free for farming and settlement (Dunn 1988, 37).

It is often sufficient to survey the position of barrows and cairns at 1:2500. However, large-scale surveys should be contemplated for long barrows and for sites containing structural elements such as chambers and kerbs. Profiles should be produced for barrows exhibiting marked changes in slope. When carefully used, contour surveys also have their value, especially when combined with hachured plans to depict barrows which have been reduced by ploughing (RCHME 1979b, 35). Notebook measurements must include length together with maximum and minimum widths and heights for long barrows, and diameter and average height for round barrows and cairns. If present, ditches should be measured and their depth recorded; features such as cists and external banks also require individual measurement and description. Geophysical survey and aerial photography may aid the discovery of buried features, such as graves and infilled ditches.

The observer must be open-minded as to date and aware of the possibility of confusing burial mounds with windmill mounds, small mottes, prospect mounds, clearance cairns and so on.

3 Preparation: identifying and using existing records

Background research should begin before or concurrently with field reconnaissance. At this stage all that may be necessary is a check of the standard archive sources, listed here, and a cursory reading of the main published references. Detailed study of maps, air photographs and other sources is often better done at a later stage. The desire to know as much as possible in advance about a site or landscape which is to be the subject of survey has to be balanced against the wish to see that site or landscape with fresh eyes and without prejudice; this is further discussed later.

ARCHAEOLOGICAL DATABASES

Archaeological survey has a long history and archaeological databases contain a wealth of existing records of the sort that the activities described in the following chapters set out to create. These include antiquarian drawings, plans and reports, as well as OS Archaeology Division records and excavation-related documents. Some of these have inherent problems, such as a lack of firm locational information, but careful study may nevertheless reap substantial rewards.

A number of organisations compile consolidated indexes to sites and other information which might be relevant in the planning stages of a survey project. These are mostly available in computerised form and are accessible to the public. Access may be restricted for reasons of security, though once an individual has established their credentials, greater levels of information may be made available.

The addresses of archaeological organisations in Britain can be found in the yearbooks and directories published by the Council for British Archaeology (CBA) and the Institute of Field Archaeologists (IFA). Similar publications are available in many other countries.

National Monuments Record

The first point of entry for users of heritage data in England, to establish what is known about a site or area, is the National Monuments Record (NMR), maintained by the RCHME. Similar national records are curated by the Royal Commissions on the Ancient and Historical Monuments of Scotland and Wales. The Northern Ireland Monuments and Buildings Record is maintained by the Environment and Heritage Agency.

The NMR, like many other archaeological records, was originally based on the OS Archaeology Division record cards and antiquity models. It provides a national overview of England's archaeological heritage, holding information on monuments, archaeological events and archive collections:

> (a) The NMR Monument Inventory provides an index to archaeological sites and historic buildings, including records on county SMRs and the results of the RCHME's own fieldwork and aerial photographic survey.

> (b) The NMR Excavation Index records all the excavations, evaluations, watching briefs and topographic and geophysical surveys (event) which have taken place in England. For each event, the location of the finds and documentary archive is recorded, where known.

> (c) In addition, the NMR maintains an index to collections of documentary archives which contain an archaeological element — including the RCHME's own archive holdings, with its extensive aerial photographic library and the results of surveys undertaken by the RCHME.

Information can be supplied for a specific site, event or area, examples of similar sites can be identified for comparative study and enquirers can be 'signposted' to archives held by other organisations which deal with their area and/or topic of study. This information will help to direct further research and planning for a project.

Sites and Monuments Records

At the local level, the Sites and Monuments Record (SMR) is a register of all known archaeological sites within an administrative area, often supported by files of documentary material. Its primary purpose is as a management tool in the planning and development control system, although most SMRs also serve a secondary function as a source of local archaeological information for amateur and professional research.

An SMR is maintained for every county in England, as well as many towns, districts and national parks, the majority under the auspices of the relevant local authority. Most Scottish Regional authorities maintain an SMR, while in Wales the four archaeological trusts are each responsible for the SMR for their own region. The National Trust and the National Trust for Scotland each maintain an SMR for their own properties.

Museums and Record Offices

Archaeological finds and documentary archives should be deposited in museums or County Record Offices. Whilst the databases discussed above can provide some information about museum and record office holdings, no comprehensive detailed listings are available. It is therefore necessary to direct specific enquiries to museums and record offices which are likely to hold relevant documentary material.

HISTORICAL SOURCES

Strategies for documentary research

In emergency situations, such as threatened destruction or damage, archaeological field remains can be surveyed without preliminary documentary research of any type. In most cases, however, some level of documentary research should be considered.

The potential range of strategies for documentary research is great. Some sites, such as pre-medieval sites in upland locations, can perhaps even routinely be tackled in the field with minimum documentary preparation. Here, the sum total of previous archaeological recording may be encapsulated in monument records held in the NMR or local authority SMRs. It may amount to little or, in the case of new discoveries, nothing. At the other extreme lie complex industrial and military remains. Documentary research into site and factory plans, buildings drawings, historic photographs and company records, which can survive in voluminous quantity, is commonly the essential preliminary that gives structure to fieldwork by providing standard building numbering and functions, and knowledge of processes and flowlines (see Waltham Abbey case study). Such industrial and military documentation may not lie in the public domain, but in company or departmental archives, or even (in the case of newly redundant industries) on site among uncurated working materials (eg Atterbury 1995). Its survival in these circumstances is at best doubtful and can depend on the interest and goodwill of individuals. Access to and use of such documentation can then be an equal or greater priority than fieldwork, as well as an essential preliminary to it.

Between these two extremes there is broad variation from site to site, between consulting documents before survey, and following up and consolidating insights that emerge during survey. There may be variation, too, with the experience, the grasp of contextual background, and the time and resources available to the individual or group.

The danger of 'full' prior documentation is of seeing only what you therefore expect to see, of operating within a framework that acts as a straight-jacket, and ultimately therefore of reducing archaeological fieldwork to a process of illustrating what is otherwise documented, rather than a process of recording and understanding original evidence that has its own weight and validity. A good example of this is the treatment of medieval monastic sites, whether earthworks or standing remains, which has concentrated on describing them only in those terms to the exclusion of the fact that the form of the visible earthworks and standing fabric are commonly the remains and result of the presence of a post-Dissolution country house and its setting (Everson *et al* 1991, 46-7; Everson 1996a; see pp148, 163).

Conversely, the danger of limited prior documentation is uninformed field observation, not alert to the understanding that may be available, and results that are liable to be a heap of unstructured, undigested and therefore unintelligible information.

There is a balance to be struck. In most cases, there are some sources that can give *information* relevant to the survey task and to the time and opportunity of being in the field, looking directly at the original evidence represented by the field remains. They can raise

10   *Gerards Bromley (Staffordshire): illustration from Robert Plot's* Natural History of Staffordshire, *privately published in Oxford (1686).*

11   *Gerards Bromley: photograph (1987) replicating the same viewpoint.*

questions which fieldwork may have the potential to answer; they can *direct attention* to important features or anomalies, real or supposed; and they can help *understanding* of field remains during the process of recording. For example, an anomalous linear ditch may be shown by an estate map to be an early road or hedgeline. In addition to that direct interpretation, this may provide a fixed point within the site's stratigraphy or relative chronology that encourages understanding and analysis to develop during fieldwork.

Primary sources

The most useful group of historical sources in preparation for fieldwork are therefore those that give a direct or indirect topographical or visual access to the field remains. They most obviously include: air photographs, topographical drawings (Barley 1974) (**figs 10, 11**), antiquarian accounts (especially those with supporting drawings or sketches, though care has to be taken over biases of perception and contemporary frames of reference), historic photography, county, estate, tithe and enclosure mapping and historical OS maps (Harley 1972; Hindle 1988; Oliver 1993). For the latter, County Record Offices are the key, both to their own holdings and to material held elsewhere. Some produce hand-lists of their holdings, and other printed aids are available but inevitably become outdated in detail (eg PRO 1967; Tate and Turner 1978). For Tithe Awards, the Inland Revenue set held by the Public Record Office at Kew provides a national one-stop source, complementary to local holdings. Large-scale OS mapping of various dates from the later nineteenth century onwards will certainly be available (Harley and Phillips 1964; Harley 1975). For post-medieval or modern sites, such as the industrial complex at Derwentcote (Co Durham) for instance, such mapping may show the site in use and changing through time (**fig 12**); for earlier sites they may show residual remains, but otherwise a topographical framework for their survival and later land-use. Earlier, small-scale OS mapping can be useful in the 1-inch series reprinted by David and Charles, and has behind its first edition a fine set of original surveyors' drawings at 2 inches to the mile, but earlier county maps generally have less utility for site-specific detail (Rodger 1972).

Occasionally, early OS and tithe maps provide the only reliable evidence for features of archaeological interest which subsequent development has almost wiped from the landscape and, therefore, from modern maps, as in the case of the medieval park at Kemsing (Kent) (Bowden 1996a) (**fig 13**).

In the mid-nineteenth century, the OS compiled a register of all the place-names to be included on the maps with brief descriptions of what was being labelled, as well as a record of who had authenticated the spelling. The *Name Books*, as they were known, for England and Wales were largely lost when the OS Southampton headquarters were bombed during the Second World War, but the Scottish *Name Books* were held in Edinburgh and provide an important complement to the 6-inch and 25-inch maps. They can be consulted on microfilm at the Scottish NMR.

A valuable guide to record sources for England and Wales is provided by Riden (1987). For Scotland many original documents, including an extensive collection of estate plans, are held by the Scottish Record Office (SRO). The SRO has published a guide to available resources (Sinclair 1994). Local libraries and archives also hold primary documentation, and early maps are available in the Map Library of the National Library of Scotland.

The Royal Commission on Historical Manuscripts maintains the National Register of Archives, an index to finding aids supplied by record offices and museums. This can be interrogated by subject, by personal name or by company name. It can offer a point of entry to relevant archive materials, such as estate maps, and it is a useful source for industrial records; archaeology as a specialism is not well covered, however.

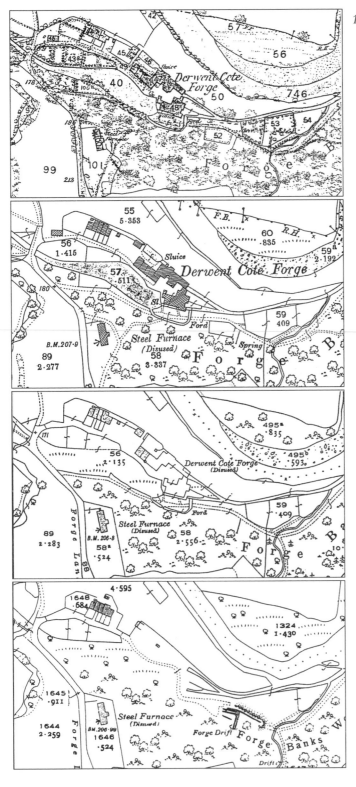

12 The changing
    landscape of
    Derwentcote (County
    Durham), as mapped
    by the OS at 1:2500
    scale in 1856, 1895,
    1915 and 1939
    (reproduced from the
    1862, 1895, 1920
    and 1947 Ordnance
    Survey maps).

13 *The medieval park at Kemsing (Kent): A — the park pale represented by field boundaries as shown on the 1st edition OS 1:2500 map (1861); B — remaining fragments of the park boundary in the 1990s after the construction of a railway and a motorway, and the removal of several field boundaries; the recognisable 'signature' of the park has been lost.*

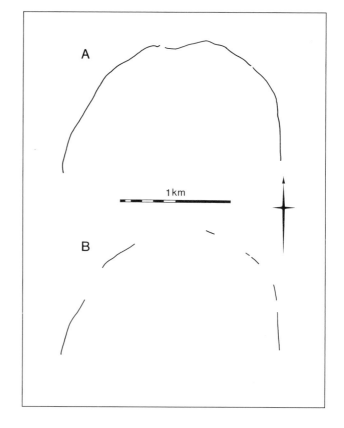

Secondary sources

Readily available resources such as the Pevsner *Buildings of England, Ireland, Scotland* and *Wales* volumes or the statutory Listed Buildings lists, accessible through local planning authorities or as a national, one-stop service in the NMR, offer authoritative if not infallible information at a relatively low level. These sources belong to a secondary group in preparations for fieldwork, offering derivative or ancillary information, though in specific cases they may carry more weight.

Further input to preparation can come from published specialist scholarship and the opinions of what in OS terms were known as 'authorities', from thematic local, regional or national studies of monument types, from local history studies of a parish or topic, or from local information or opinion. There are risks: they can bring with them a blinkering effect of received opinion which inhibits a clear-eyed assessment of what the field remains actually reveal. Mis-identifications and mistaken correlations of sites do occur, and re-interpretation of field remains is part of the fieldwork process, but it is a serious, substantial and sometimes problematic matter (Everson 1988; 1989a).

Substantial research into original historical documentation is rarely a part of fieldwork preparation. Some English localities are fortunate enough to have a mine of information available through traditional county histories (Currie and Lewis 1994), through the modern volumes in the Victoria County Histories (VCH) series or in the *History of the*

King's Works, for example. A less uniform set of county histories exists in Wales. Core documentation for special monument types like monasteries and castles is to hand in Knowles and Hadcock (1971) and King (1983) respectively, for instance. For other medieval and post-medieval sites, documentary research is best focused on interpretation and publication. Even then, original documents represent potentially a bottomless pit; their use in normal circumstances needs to be purposefully selective and relevant, rather than merely accumulative.

Among the more relevant specific historical sources for England are:

(a) The county-based volumes of the English Place-Name Society, a rich and reliable source (especially recent ones), though by definition they can only indicate the earliest date when the name of a village, hamlet or farm is documented; they cannot comment on the form the named settlement took, whether nucleated or otherwise, or how it may have changed through time.

(b) Sources nominally listing locations nationally for taxation and other purposes, eg *Domesday Book*, 1316 *Nomina Villarum* and 1428 Parish Tax (PRO 1899–1921), 1334 Lay Subsidy (Glasscock 1975), 1676 Compton Census (Whiteman 1986), nineteenth-century census returns (locally specific sources can augment this range considerably (eg Everson *et al* 1991, xviii–xix)) — the approach is most effective in zones of predominantly nucleated settlements: elsewhere the more complex and dynamic circumstances of dispersed settlement demand more detailed study (eg Dyer 1991), though personal names can be one source of clues (Aston 1983).

(c) For churches, 1291 *Taxatio* (Ayscough and Caley 1802) and 1535 *Valor Ecclesiasticus* (Caley and Hunter 1810–34), while in some areas the more difficult complementary listing of medieval chapels has been undertaken (eg Owen 1975).

(d) For medieval parks, Cantor (1983) and for post-medieval parks and gardens, English Heritage (EH) non-statutory County Registers (available in the NMR as well as in County Record Offices).

(e) For industrial sites, listings by individual special-interest groups and through the developing coverage of the IRIS recording project (AIA 1993; Trueman 1995).

Three overviews known as the *Statistical Accounts* prepared by the parish ministers with descriptions of topography, antiquities, civil history and industry provide a valuable source of information about the state of each parish in Scotland. *The Statistical Account of Scotland* was compiled by Sir John Sinclair between 1791 and 1799, *The New Statistical Account of Scotland* dates from 1845 and *The Third Statistical Account of Scotland* was published between 1951 and 1993. The first two in particular offer snapshots of local conditions and often contain descriptions of antiquities that have subsequently been destroyed.

Historical context

An over-riding consideration is that most documents were not created for the use to which archaeological surveyors put them. It is both desirable and rewarding for those who do use them to acquire at least a minimum understanding of why, how and when they were created. Without it, both their relevance and their limitations of scope and bias cannot be appreciated.

Indeed, at least as important as site-specific documentation in preparing for fieldwork and interpretation is a grasp of the wider historical context and current scholarly understanding of any given site type. The primary responsibility of the fieldworker — and this may serve to define the appropriate focus and limits to documentary research — is sensibly to provide sufficient information to enable the context and relevance of fieldwork results to be recognised by interested external parties. This may in the case of a moated site, for example, be no more than the approximate documented date range and ownership or social/functional context, or, in the case of a deserted settlement, a name and a population profile that allows the approximate date of desertion to be identified.

Whatever level of documentary research is undertaken, it must not detract from treatment of the field remains as a valid independent source of evidence, which have the strength of reflecting something actually done, not just planned, desired or reported. Yet the field remains do not stand alone. If archaeology is a dialogue with the physical remains of the past, that dialogue needs to be informed by a grasp of the historically documented context.

THE GEOGRAPHICAL CONTEXT

Some appreciation of the natural background of 'solid' and 'drift' geology must be achieved by anyone seeking to understand archaeological sites or landscapes.

In Britain, the 1:50,000-scale maps and regional handbooks produced by the British Geological Survey (BGS) provide all the information that will normally be required, and they can be found in many libraries. In exceptional circumstances, such as when dealing with the relict landscapes of the extractive industries, much higher levels of detail may be required in the form of the 1:10,000 maps that are available from the BGS for a few areas of the country. Some of this geological information will have direct relevance for the interpretation of the landscape, most obviously in understanding the sources of raw materials for industry (**fig 14**). More commonly, however, the effects of the underlying geology will have been less direct, governing, for instance, the drainage or the ease of cultivation of a hillside. Even in terms of the use of mineral resources, relationships are far from straightforward: human agency has to be taken into account as well as the natural landscape (Alfrey and Clark 1993, 8).

The solid geological structure has been shaped by time, and the field archaeologist has to be conscious of the resulting geomorphology of the area being studied. This is especially important when distinctions have to be drawn between the natural and the artificial elements of the landscape (see pp89–90). Beyond this again is the symbolic significance of natural features highlighted by Tilley (1994).

A little research in a local library should provide adequate sources for the local geomorphology. After that, there is no substitute for looking at the landscape itself. The present or former whereabouts of poorly drained areas that will have been unattractive for settlement, or the way in which the forward edge of an escarpment provided conspicuous

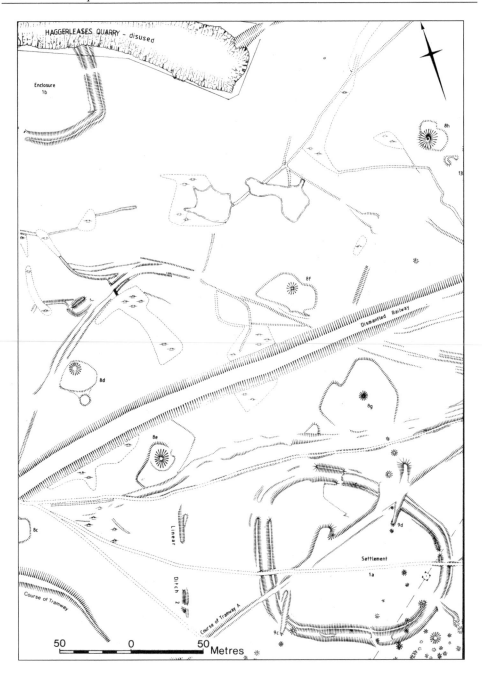

14   Cockfield Fell (County Durham): extract from the RCHME 1983 archive plan (not
        redrawn for publication: original scale 1:1000). The survey recorded sandstone quarries on
        the summit of the hill (not shown on this extract) and the deep trench of a dolerite quarry
        on the lower ground, while coal pits and consequent areas of subsidence are scattered across
        the landscape. All these features cut or overlie prehistoric and medieval enclosures, linear
        ditches, fields and tracks and are associated with tramways and the railway of 1863.

situations that the builders of Bronze Age cairns often preferred, will quickly become apparent. The investigative archaeologist needs to develop a thorough familiarity with the landscape, onto which archaeological questions can be posed. The ideal is to enter the minds of those who lived there in the past; such empathy is the basis of much of the most successful archaeological intuition, as long as it does not develop into the straightjacketing notion that people in the distant past thought and acted 'just like us'.

The land is continuously subject to natural forces: one of the most powerful is erosion, a key effect of which — as far as the archaeologist is concerned — is the creation of soils. The field archaeologist does not usually require the detailed analysis necessary to the excavator (Renfrew and Bahn 1996, 219–23 *et passim*), but there should be some appreciation of the way in which the soils have affected the agricultural potential of an area. Fertile soils will develop over softer, soluble, sedimentary rocks (like limestones), whereas the soils that form over hard, impervious volcanics (such as the Whin Sill (Northumberland) (**plate 1**)) are easily exhausted. Agricultural technology and agricultural regimes have changed through time, as has the climate, however, so the rich agricultural lands of today have not always necessarily provided the same relative levels of cropping. For example, in Wessex the downs were extensively ploughed in later prehistory, but in the medieval period much of the land was turned over to sheep-pasture, and it was only in the later twentieth century that the 'prairie-buster' ploughs came in, converting downland sward into huge fields for the production of grain. Where this has not happened, the 'Celtic' fields still survive (see **plate 4** and **fig 36**). In the hill country along the Scottish border, late prehistoric fields have survived high up the valleys; on the lower slopes the ridge-and-furrow of medieval and later arable has also been abandoned and most of the area would now be classed as poor pasture (Foster and Smout 1994) (see **fig 8**). In some areas, the soils themselves have changed; for instance, loess deposits on the southern chalklands, now largely eroded, may have had a significant effect on the agricultural potential of patches of clay-with-flints in the Neolithic (Fisher 1991).

In the lowlands, where the landscape is less dramatic, the shapes of hills and valleys have still influenced the location of settlements and field systems. The most obvious factor is aspect: the direction in which a site faces. South-facing hillsides are the warmest, but elsewhere shelter may have been sought from the prevailing wind. North-facing slopes, which may not see the sun at all in winter, have always been less attractive. If the remains of settlements and fields are found on north-facing slopes, there may be inferences to be drawn about population pressures in the area in the past. The very frequent re-use of favoured locations may suggest an element of symbolic and social choice.

In most cases, the field archaeologist is looking at the remains of settlements and structures that have, ultimately, failed. A good deal can be learned by considering the position of the 'successful' settlements, the existing ones. In a few areas, such as the Howgill Fells in south-east Cumbria, the earlier archaeology is almost invisible, apparently because much of it is buried beneath the few sites available for settlement or agriculture which, almost by definition, are still in use today (Bowden 1996b, 3, 5) (**plate 2**). In that particular area, choice is restricted by the very steep slopes of the valley sides which leave only the valley bottoms available. Elsewhere, the gradient of a hillside may well dictate the form of the earthworks: whether settlements have had to be terraced into the hillside, or whether lynchets have developed through arable farming, for instance. The slope of the hills is, therefore, a factor that always merits consideration.

Those exploring the potential of an area of upland also have to bear altitude in mind. Within normal patterns of distribution the incidence of settlements — at any period — begins to fall off over about 300m OD, and above 400m they are comparatively rare. Particular needs — including that of defence — have drawn people onto the hilltops at various times throughout history, but any extreme choice may provoke a particularly inquisitive reaction. Thus the hillfort on the summit of Ingleborough (North Yorkshire) was constructed at an inhospitable 723m above sea level (Bowden *et al* 1989) (**plate 3**). At that height, can it ever have been permanently inhabited? Was it built to make a point: to claim territory, or to flaunt prestige? Where settlements or field systems are encountered especially high in the hills, there may be inferences to be drawn about the climatic conditions that prevailed at the time which may be a pointer to their date. Moving away from purely utilitarian considerations, hilltops of all shapes and elevations have always attracted the spiritual side of the human character, and ritual and religious needs inform other aspects of daily life. The prospecting archaeologist should always study the contours to identify likely positions for, say, a burial cairn sited on a hilltop or on any false skyline that is a prominent natural feature.

At the other extreme, those investigating very low-lying areas will need to consider more subtle variations in topography. In former wetlands, the slightest elevation, of no more than a metre or two, may be enough to have made human activity possible, just as a very shallow, possibly water-logged, depression may have prevented it.

Finally, the investigative archaeologist who has considered fully the natural background is often well placed to identify the opportunities within the landscape for environmental sampling. This may take various forms: phosphate analysis, the investigation of the differential patterns of the deposit of alluvium through time (providing information on the intensity of arable agriculture), taking cores from peat deposits in search of plant macro-fossils or pollen, or even the dating of boundaries by applying dendrochronology (Renfrew and Bahn 1996, 224–32, 128–31) to the trees growing on them. These specialist techniques can be expensive, but this should never deter the field archaeologist from making suggestions for further research of this kind.

CHANGING PATTERNS OF AGRICULTURE
LITTLE SIBLYBACK (CORNWALL)

The detailed study of field systems can build a chronology of changing land use. A good example can be seen at Little Siblyback on the eastern edge of Bodmin Moor, where a multi-period field system is located upon the east-facing slopes of Newel Tor at about 300m OD. A prehistoric field system was laid out, comprising irregular fields, some of which contained stone-built roundhouses; most of the fields show abraded narrow ridged cultivation which appears to be broadly contemporary. Subsequently, in the medieval and post-medieval periods, settlements and field systems were constructed over parts of the prehistoric fields, and in some cases prehistoric field walls have been re-used in the later period to create the new boundaries. The later fields have been much levelled

Aerial photograph of Little Siblyback.

and stone clitter has been removed, flattening the earlier ridges (though they are still visible as faint striations on aerial photographs). The post-medieval settlement is located in a series of regular paddocks within the fields (see Johnson and Rose 1994, 59–60).

This example illustrates the ways in which earlier field systems can be 'fossilised' by later land-use patterns, but through careful observation the stratigraphy can be untangled and some idea of landscape development gained, even before documentary sources are consulted.

Any analytical investigation of a field system has to proceed through a detailed record of the relationships and association of the system, to distinguish not only the phasing of agricultural episodes, but also to gain an understanding of the development of associated settlements and other sites, before it proceeds into further, possibly multi-disciplinary research to elucidate the chronology of the field system in its landscape setting.

Field systems are often extensive but can generally be adequately surveyed at relatively small scale (1:10,000 – 1:2500), except where they meet other monuments, where large-scale windows may be required to record crucial relationships. Cultivation remains should always be recorded and plotted. Ridge-and-furrow is conventionally depicted by broken lines (see **fig 85**). However, at scales smaller than 1:2500, it is sufficient to delineate the area of cultivation and use an arrow to indicate the orientation of ridge-and-furrow (see **fig 32**). Field boundaries can take the form of lynchets, walls, hedges, banks and ditches in any combination and should be depicted accordingly.

PART II: SURVEY AND INVESTIGATION

4 Analytical earthwork survey — measurement

The activities of measurement and interpretation in earthwork survey form a seamless whole in practice. Their division here into two chapters is for the sake of clarity.

PRELIMINARIES

Permissions and local contacts

Obtaining permission to enter private land is a time-consuming, but vital process. It is important to identify sensitive areas or times to be avoided and to abide by any agreements reached. (In different parts of the world different situations apply: in some countries, the permission of the authorities may be at least as important as the permission of a landowner.) Apart from obtaining permission to work, contact with the landowner or tenant will often result in the acquisition of valuable information about previously unrecorded sites. The importance of involving the community in the survey cannot be over-emphasised. If the project is likely to run for an appreciable length of time, publicity in the local newspaper and a talk to a farmers' group reap much goodwill and useful knowledge, although oral information must, of course, be treated as critically as any other source.

Maintenance of good relationships with landowners and other interested parties should be a prime object at all times; other archaeologists will want to visit the site in the future and their reception will depend to a large extent on the impression you have made.

Health and safety, and insurance

There are now a number of booklets and guidance documents which can help identify the main areas to consider in fieldwork (eg NERC 1997; TUC 1988). Employers and employees have legal obligations in this area, in undertaking formal Risk Assessments, for instance. Solo working should be avoided for health and safety as well as professional reasons, especially in remote areas. Field surveyors should carry first-aid kits and, in remote areas, survival kits; ideally everyone involved in field survey should be a qualified first aider. Anyone working in upland terrain would be well advised to read a standard text on mountaincraft, such as Langmuir (1995). Basic preventative measures, such as anti-tetanus inoculations, should always be taken. Among animals to beware of in Britain are cattle (not just lone bulls but bullocks, and cows with young calves), horses, rams, goats, dogs and adders, as well as gamekeepers, and any tenant or owner of whom you have not asked permission.

Professional archaeological organisations will have their own insurance schemes. Amateur archaeologists in Britain can arrange insurance through the CBA.

Seasonal considerations

Slight earthworks can be difficult to see at the best of times. Light conditions and the state of vegetation are crucial considerations for the archaeological investigator (**plate 4**). Archaeological field survey is therefore, to a large extent, a seasonal occupation. Autumn, winter and spring are generally more productive than the summer months when vegetation is high. The ideal time to undertake field survey is early spring when days are getting longer: the weather is often favourable, vegetation and crops do not hinder observation and farming activity is relatively quiet in many areas.

Some areas of moorland may only be accessible at certain times of year due to inclement weather and the constraints of lambing, and gamebird rearing and shooting seasons. Woodland can only be surveyed in winter (see pp 138–9). Bracken areas are best surveyed in late winter and spring, between snowfall and new growth.

SURVEY TECHNIQUES

At the outset, it should be said that while *measured* survey is desirable, it is not always possible or necessary. Where time and resources are very limited, observations, simple field notes, sketches and ground photography can adequately convey the identification, location and interpretation of a site or monument. This approach demands little more than a notebook, pencil, a map at an appropriate scale and a camera. At the other extreme is the 'high-tech' survey equipment considered below.

The process of archaeological field surveying and plan production, at any scale, can be broken down into three distinct tasks: Reconnaissance, Observation and Measurement, and Depiction.

Reconnaissance

Reconnaissance ('recce') is the process of preliminary inspection. This is without doubt one of the most important, yet often inadequately carried out, processes of field survey. It is critical to the success and cost-effectiveness of a proposed survey that appropriate resource is invested in recce at the correct time. This would normally be before any project design is prepared and certainly before any survey is undertaken or any resource committed. Too often recce is approached at the level of a 'quick look round' instead of being undertaken with the same intellectual thoroughness as would be applied to the analytical survey itself. Time spent on recce is rarely wasted and should be proportionate to the size and extent of any proposed survey. There are no hard and fast rules for this, but clearly a significantly higher level of recce time would be needed for a large area with many unknown archaeological parameters, such as a tract of moorland or afforested landscape, than would be needed for a single site in pasture. For the former, recce and setting-up time will repay dividends in the long run by identifying the unknown factors at an early stage and allowing them to be quantified, rather than emerging as surprises later. However, even a small site will benefit from applying basic principles of reconnaissance and planning.

Whatever the size of a survey, the recce belongs within the earliest operational stages. It is desirable, however, that before venturing into the field the fieldworker undertakes a preliminary 'desk-top' appraisal of the site or landscape, so as to get the best value from the time spent on the field recce (but see Chap 3). Armed with this material, the fieldworker can assess the quality of information for any site or landscape and thus identify gaps or weaknesses in the record; recce time can then be targeted at specific sites or questions as necessary.

The archaeological quality and value of a survey, as well as the metrical accuracy and recording methodology to be applied, is likely to be determined during the field recce. Perceptions of a site or landscape acquired through desk-top information gathering process are often radically altered once the ground evidence is examined. During the recce itself the fieldworker should address the site from three main perspectives, Archaeological Assessment, Survey Strategy and Site Logistics.

Archaeological Assessment

One objective of the recce is to identify the archaeological significance and extent of a site or landscape. This may result in the first identification of previously unrecognised earthworks, the re-interpretation of known features or confirmation of existing knowledge. It is not, however, necessary to make detailed observations about archaeological interpretation at this stage; understanding of the archaeological remains may only come during, and because of, the survey. It is good practice to perambulate not only the site itself but also the area surrounding: this will ensure that its full extent can be confidently determined, and its landscape context established. Background information gathered during the desk-top survey can play an important part in this process. The archaeological hinterland can often reveal as much evidence for the interpretation of a site as the site itself. Factors affecting the modern landscape and land-use, which may have influenced the physical form of a monument, as well as the historical and archaeological influences, need to be considered as part of this process.

Survey Strategy

Having determined the form and extent of the site or landscape, the choice of survey strategy will come into consideration. That choice can range from a simple line or dot on a map with the briefest of notes, to a large-scale measured survey and detailed report. A number of factors will have to be taken into account:

(a) The purpose of the survey. Is it a detailed survey for management purposes or a rapid identification survey? However desirable large-scale surveys are, the time and cost has to be justifiable against the need. The Level (see Appendix I) may have been specified by a client, but flexibility of approach has to be built into the recce as field observations may change the initial desk-based perception and lead to re-definition of the brief.

(b) Size of area. This is often the biggest single influence on the choice of surveying methodology. If the area is large, but adequately covered by large-scale OS maps (1:2500 or 1:1250), surveying within mapped detail such as field boundaries may be the most cost-effective method; any of the surveying techniques described later can be applied to recording the archaeology within a map base. Where there is no large-scale map detail to work from, surveys of large areas become more demanding in terms of maintaining accuracy. Surveys undertaken independently of a map base are referred to as 'divorced surveys'.

(c) Survey methodology and equipment. What are the most appropriate techniques and equipment to suit the proposed task? Will traditional survey methods suffice or is a control scheme involving electronic instruments desirable? The methodology may be dictated by the available equipment, but one of the tasks at the recce stage is to identify the most appropriate survey equipment to undertake the task defined (see Appendix II). The position of control stations (see pp54–7) can be identified, and possibly ground markers inserted, at this stage.

(d) Scale of survey. Many archaeologists, more used to excavation than to earthwork survey, and used to planning and section-drawing at 1:10 or 1:20, find it difficult to adapt to the very different scales of field survey. Scale will be influenced mostly by the purpose of the survey. If the survey is intended to be used as a management document and has to include fine detail of earthworks and structures, then the largest scale practical is required (1:500 is commonly used for an individual site in this context and occasionally 1:250). A scale which is particularly suited to earthwork portrayal and provides a happy compromise between the ability to show detail and to cover large areas sensibly is 1:1000; this is the mainstay of RCHME field recording. If the purpose is less geared to detail and more to wide coverage, identification and basic interpretation, OS large-scale mapping at 1:2500 in rural areas and 1:1250 in urban areas offers a solution. Assuming that maps are available, very large landscape projects can be undertaken at 1:2500 scale, whilst still allowing the salient details of individual monuments to be portrayed. Very large area landscape recording, particularly in the upland zone where no 1:2500 mapping is available, is best addressed at 1:10,000 scale, the largest map scale available in these zones; alternatively air photographic transcription provides a method of supplying custom-made, accurate large-scale maps in such areas. When deciding on the scale of survey, it is worth remembering that doubling the scale generally means quadrupling the number of measurements needed and therefore the time taken. As a rough guide, at 1:1000 scale it is possible for an experienced team to survey 1ha of open ground in a day. The use of electronic survey equipment does not absolve the surveyor from thinking about scale at the recce stage, because the scale of the final product dictates the level of detail to be recorded and therefore the number of measurements that must be taken (see pp48–50).

(e) Metrical accuracy. The plans produced must be accurate to the scale at which they are surveyed, ie there must be confidence in the plan to enable measurements to be scaled and alignments as portrayed trusted.

(f) Personnel. Identification of the number of people required to undertake the survey: do they have the right skills and will training be required?

(g) Timescale. Time is always likely to be limited and this can be a significant influence on the choice of methodology. It may be subject to external factors over which the fieldworker has no control. It may be more efficient when dealing with large areas to undertake rapid surveys to identify the nature and extent of archaeological remains, followed by more detailed survey of specific areas, rather than attempting large-scale survey at the start.

Site Logistics

Fieldwork is often unpredictable, as anybody who has tried to survey in a field occupied by horses will know. However, some of the unpredictability can be eliminated by assessing the following items:

(a) Ownership and access. Identify landowners and negotiate permissions and access arrangements. Will 4-wheel drive vehicles be necessary to get equipment onto site? Will keys be needed for gates? It is important to sort out these things in advance.

(b) Health and safety. Is the site safe to work on?

(c) Legal constraints. Is the site a Scheduled Ancient Monument (SAM) or a Site of Special Scientific Interest (SSSI), or is there any other constraint on the land? Special rules and procedures have to be followed before undertaking work in these areas — it is necessary to have Scheduled Monument Consent even to hammer a survey peg into a SAM.

(d) Other potential problems. Is the site frequently used by the general public? Will there be grazing animals on site? Adopting simple measures, like using discreet markers (eg golf tees) and not leaving equipment unattended, can forestall any potential problems.

Observation and Measurement

All surveying depends on relative positions, expressed as angles and distances. If that sounds as if it might be complex, think of the simple statement, 'Edinburgh is 330 miles NNW of London'; the angle and distance fix the positions of the cities relative to one another. If we add that 'Belfast is 310 miles NW of London and 150 miles SW of Edinburgh', we have a rock-solid piece of surveyor's geometry.

Surveying, the physical process of measuring features on the land, determining their relative positions and portraying these on a plan or map, can be divided into two main areas, *plane* and *geodetic* surveying. In the majority of cases, the archaeological field surveyor is working within the parameters of plane surveying (ignoring earth curvature) particularly when dealing with an individual site or small landscape area, but it is important to recognise when the task in hand will fall outside these parameters and become subject to geodetic (including earth curvature) considerations; this boundary is usually crossed when surveying very large areas, and when trying to incorporate those surveys into the OS large-scale map base or within the National Grid triangulation control framework (see pp50–1).

Whatever the surveying task, whether it be plane or geodetic, the *principles* never change though the *practice* does. If the fieldworker can grasp and apply the principles, then some of the mystery which surrounds surveying, especially in this technology-dominated era, can be unravelled.

Principles of surveying

The main principles of survey are listed below; they apply to archaeological survey ranging from the simplest traditional techniques to the use of the most sophisticated electronic instruments. These principles should be applied to all surveys whatever the extent or final scale of plan: (1) Control, (2) Economy of accuracy and consistency, (3) The independent check and (4) Revision and safeguarding.

The maxim 'Work from the whole to the part' is as appropriate in the planning of a small burial mound, as it is to the recording of an extensive landscape. Work should always proceed from control to detail — making sure the whole framework is accurate before surveying individual components within that framework.

1 Control

Control is a term used to define an accurate framework of carefully measured points within which the rest of the survey is fitted. Survey of detail between these control points may then be carried out by less elaborate methodology or equipment. Control can take the form of a network of points on the ground, such as pegs, telegraph poles, or fence junctions, whose relative positions are carefully measured using a number of techniques, from a taped baseline to an electronic instrument survey. The principle of control applies regardless of the scale of survey, although generally the larger the scale the more carefully control has to be measured. The accuracy of the finished plan is determined by how carefully this control is surveyed, and the larger the scale, the more errors become identifiable.

Topographic detail depicted on OS maps, such as walls and buildings, can also be used as control. These features are a ready-made control framework to which archaeological detail can be related, but only at the scale at which they were originally surveyed by the OS; any enlargement of a plan may lead to errors which will be difficult and time-consuming to resolve (*pace* Brown 1987, 49, whose remarks on this subject should be disregarded). Control can also be established by the mathematical network of ground-marked points, usually triangulation stations, Global Positioning System (GPS) points and other OS co-ordinated surveying frameworks. OS agents have details of these, but they are expensive. From these points, National Grid co-ordinates can be established on sites or within project areas using electronic instruments.

2 Economy of Accuracy and Consistency

This applies to both *linear* and *angular* measurements. As a general rule, the higher the standard of metrical accuracy, the higher the cost in terms of time and money. It is important therefore to decide at the planning stage what standards of accuracy are required. In determining accuracy requirements, the main considerations are: the best method of presenting the survey information, the scale of final plot or maps and possible re-use of data (such as co-ordinate values). Accuracy will also influence the choice of techniques and equipment, as high standards of accuracy can only be achieved with the appropriate methodology and equipment while, conversely, time and effort should not be spent trying to achieve a higher level of accuracy than the scale warrants.

Accuracy is usually quoted as a representative fraction which shows the ratio of the magnitude of the error (the difference between true value and measured value of a quantity) to the magnitude of the measured quantity. If, for example, the error over 1000m is 0.10m then the accuracy is 1/10,000 — high accuracy, of an order that would not show on the majority of map and plan scales; the same error over 100m would result in an accuracy of 1/1000, which would still be acceptable for most archaeological surveys. To achieve 1/10,000 over large areas requires precise techniques and equipment, whereas 1/1000 can be achieved with careful tape measuring and basic equipment. Because accuracy is a relative term, it is important to define the context of its use in relation to archaeological survey. There are three areas of accuracy which the archaeological surveyor needs to be aware of:

(a) Accuracy of measurement. This is governed by technique, ie care and consistency in reading measurements.

(b) Accuracy of equipment. This is ensured by choosing the type of equipment which will give the results required, eg not measuring very long lines with fibron tape-measures when an electronic instrument would be more appropriate.

(c) Accuracy of portrayal. Equivalent care and precision is required in drawing technique and employing methods of depiction appropriate to the scale of survey, to ensure that the final plan reproduces the field observations faithfully.

In addition to understanding accuracy, the archaeological surveyor should be aware of three categories of error which are likely to affect it:

(a) Gross. These are eliminated by care in observing, measuring, booking and drawing. One source of such an error would be failure to take account of the difference between slope and horizontal distance.

(b) Systematic. Caused by a constant factor such as a stretched tape or poorly maintained theodolite, which produce measurements which are always too great or too small, these errors are cumulative, so their effect will increase throughout the survey. These are usually prevented by standardising and maintaining equipment.

(c) Random or Accidental. Less quantifiable errors may still occur, even though all effort has been made to eliminate (a) and (b). They may result from such sources as personal bias, changing climatic conditions, etc. Their effect is usually to cancel each other out.

Working from the whole to the part, it follows that the standard of accuracy can change with each stage of the survey, but it can never be more accurate than the control. Standards at each stage of survey must be *consistent*. Therefore, economy dictates that accuracy at all stages is of the necessary standard to achieve consistency and that time and resources are not wasted trying to achieve a higher standard of accuracy than any particular stage demands.

3 Independent check

It is advisable to build into any survey a checking process. This should ideally be undertaken at each stage, so that any errors or problems are solved before moving on to the next (surveying textbooks will help in identifying the methods of checking appropriate to different equipment and techniques). Some methods are self-checking, such as mathematical solutions when computing co-ordinates; others may be more mechanical, such as checking regularly that a plane-table is correctly aligned. Clearly it is important to ensure that the control is right before moving on to detail survey, and detail survey itself can become a check on the plotted control when ground measurements are checked against plotted measurements as the survey progresses. It might be thought worthwhile at the end of survey to take some random measurements between features to see how they scale with the plan. At the absolute minimum, the surveyor should walk over the ground with the finished field plan in hand to see if it 'looks right' and to make sure that nothing has been missed.

4 Revision and Safeguarding

It is usually possible to plan and execute a survey so that it can be added to or revised at a later date, thus increasing the value of the original investment in time and resources. This process can be aided by simple procedures, such as recording the positions of ground markers in relation to nearby permanent features by measurement and photography, so that they can be found again and re-used, or ensuring that topographical detail which is likely to have permanence, such as walls and buildings, forms part of the control and appears on the final plot.

Plane surveying

For the vast majority of surveying scenarios within an archaeological context, the surveyor is working on a *plane* surface, ie the earth's curvature can be ignored. In practice, areas up to 300 sq km can be regarded as plane surfaces.

Geodetic surveying

Allowing for the curvature of the earth becomes important:

> (a) When survey areas are very large and are being surveyed for the first time. This is unlikely in the UK as all surveys of such large areas (over 300 sq km) should be surveyed to fit within the OS National Grid network.
> (b) When surveying into an existing map base, such as that provided in the UK by the OS. In the case of surveys of archaeological landscapes on large open moorlands, for instance, whether they be ground or air-photogrammetric

surveys, they should be tied to OS National Grid wherever possible; they must therefore take account of the same geodetic and cartographic principles embodied within the grid itself. If a large area of landscape was to be recorded as a 'divorced survey' on a plane surface, the resulting plan would not fit the OS large-scale maps of the same area. This is because the OS maps have been surveyed on a geodetic surface to take account of earth curvature, reducing the curved surface to match a particular mathematical map projection (Transverse Mercator). In practice, any measurement or network of measurements over 1km would have to be adjusted to take account of this reduction by consulting a table of Local Scale Factors published by the OS. Similarly, any surveys using GPS to provide control or detail survey will have to take account of this adjustment in data processing to match OS base mapping. This is a complex area which is dealt with comprehensively in various publications (eg Harley 1975, 6–9, 19–23; OS 1968; Whyte and Paul 1997, 23–4, 201; Wilson 1971), and any fieldworker who is considering projects over large areas, particularly where OS mapping or provision of National Grid co-ordinates is involved, should acquaint themselves with this subject.

Surveying Equipment

It is not within the remit of this book to detail individual types of surveying equipment or their use; there are numerous specialist textbooks and handbooks which more than adequately cover these areas (eg Whyte and Paul 1997, *passim*). Appendix II provides a guide to the general categories of surveying equipment.

Surveying is simply about measuring two main components, *angles* and *distances*. All surveying equipment is designed to measure one or both of these. What usually differentiates equipment, and consequently the cost, is the accuracy attainable. Despite the 'high-tech' functionality and appearance of modern electronic equipment, such as co-axial Electronic Distance Measurers ('total-stations') and GPS, they are still fundamentally only measuring angles and distances.

It is quite possible to produce surveys with very basic equipment and without expensive instruments, though when the area is large and there is a requirement to preserve accuracy, more sophisticated equipment may be necessary; it may well be most cost-effective to hire instruments for a short period to put in control and then complete detail survey using basic equipment, rather than to buy. This is particularly applicable when the requirement for high-specification control or survey is infrequent. Also it may be possible to negotiate with colleges and universities, particularly those with surveying departments, to have control established on an archaeological site as part of a surveying project. Sometimes it is worth talking to the manufacturers of surveying equipment who are usually more than eager to demonstrate how their particular instrument works: persuade them to demonstrate how effective their equipment is by putting control on your site. Lack of access to modern electronic surveying equipment should be no barrier to undertaking even large surveys. It is important to remember that before the 1970s *all* surveying was undertaken with manual theodolites, plane-tables and chains, to accuracies far beyond those necessary for most archaeological surveys; as stated above, the principles never change, only the practice. Surveys of almost any size can be achieved with a combination of a theodolite, plane-table and tape measures. Small to medium-sized areas can be recorded, even at large scales, using a plane-table, optical squares and tapes. Compass and pacing alone may be perfectly adequate for small-scale (1:10,000) surveys.

It is useful to maintain a basic survey kit, a store of items which may be needed on any measured survey, and which can be kept in a bag and carried at all times. Such a kit might comprise some of the following: two 30m tapes; compass; pocket level; pencil case with drawing kit; notebook; surveyor's chalk; degradable survey spray paint; golf tees; survey nails; wooden/plastic/steel pegs; hammer/mallet; brass rivets and hand drill; fluorescent tape or material; masking tape; camera; binoculars; hard hat, gardening gloves, safety goggles. Items which will not fit into the bag, but which should always be to hand, are a pair of ranging rods or bamboo canes.

Personnel

All instrumental survey, optical or electronic, requires a team of two, or occasionally three. Tape-and-offset can be done by a single person, but the advantages of working in teams must be considered: solving problems in survey and in archaeological interpretation benefits from dialogue, and working alone can be a health and safety risk.

Usually one person, who is going to be responsible for drawing up the plan and writing the report, will take the lead. This is because there is no single 'right' way to survey any site or landscape; decisions have to be made at every stage and it is better if those decisions are made consistently. It might appear that the leader would take the instrument, but this is not the case because all modern surveying instruments are relatively easy to use and with practice the work becomes mechanical; the part of the job requiring skill and thought is knowing *what* to record, ie positioning the prism or staff, and consequently the team leader takes this role. If survey is protracted, however, the observer may become bored and/or cold; the leader should be prepared to change places for a while.

The Process of Surveying

At small scales (1:10,000–1:2500) archaeological detail can be added to existing map bases by taping or pacing, and the use of simple angle-measuring instruments such as optical squares and compasses. In remote areas, where local map detail is sparse, archaeological features can be supplied by resectioning or traversing. Resectioning involves taking bearings to three distant mapped objects (preferably at about 120° from each other) and drawing these bearings out on the map; the point, or more often the small triangle of error ('cocked hat'), at which they meet, shows the position of the observer (**fig 15**). A traverse is a series of movements, starting from a known point, of given distance and bearing (see below).

After reconnaissance, the process of measured survey at larger scales (1:2500 and larger) can be broken down into two main tasks: (1) Control Survey and (2) Detail Survey.

1 Control Survey

The importance of providing a rigid framework of control, from which detail can be supplied, has already been explained. Where this framework is not provided by map detail,

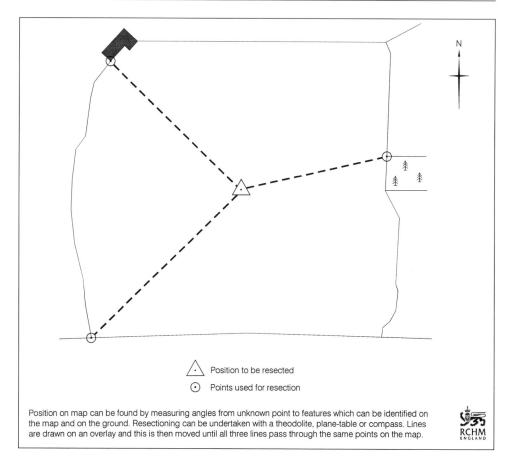

Position to be resected

Points used for resection

Position on map can be found by measuring angles from unknown point to features which can be identified on the map and on the ground. Resectioning can be undertaken with a theodolite, plane-table or compass. Lines are drawn on an overlay and this is then moved until all three lines pass through the same points on the map.

RCHM
ENGLAND

15   Resectioning: schematic diagram.

it must be supplied from scratch. Factors identified at recce stage such as the size of the area, accuracy, scale and equipment required will all influence the most appropriate methodology to put this control in place. There are two main types of survey control, *regular-grid* and *irregular-grid*.

Archaeologists are familiar with a rectangular grid of pegs as control for an excavation, from which archaeological features and finds can be planned using tapes and graduated frames. This is a good example of a *regular* grid. The technique can be used to produce plans of earthworks on small open sites, but it is not recommended.

The *irregular* or mathematical grid is defined by an opposite methodology to the regular grid, in that detail control is observed from control stations and is placed on or near to archaeological and topographic features at the will of the surveyor; the grid is invisible and exists only as a mathematical background when computing co-ordinates, though it may be shown on the final plan. This is the type of grid system used by most surveyors and mapping organisations, such as the OS and the RCHME. The concept is easily visualised by looking at any OS map: for example, on a 1:2500 scale map there is a 100m grid interval printed over the features depicted on the map, but this grid is not physically marked on the ground. The large number values printed with the grid (from which grid references are taken) actually indicate horizontal metres east and north of the origin of the grid, which is off the Scilly Isles.

The mathematical grid used by the OS is known as the National Grid. If an archaeological survey project utilises the same system of co-ordinated control points established by the OS, this will ensure that it can be fitted to existing mapping. Although this is desirable for large landscape projects, it is not necessary for small, discrete archaeological surveys, though sufficient immovable detail must be surveyed to 'fix' the site, so that the survey can be related to OS mapping for location and the establishment of grid references. These 'divorced surveys' can be referenced to a site grid with a false origin. Positive values should be given to the false origin, to ensure that negative numbers are not generated for points 'west' and 'south' of this point. In practice, values of 1000m for both x and y axes are suitable for areas of up to 4 sq km; for larger surveys, 10,000m for each axis would be more suitable. Although convention expects surveys to be oriented to the north (OS National Grid is oriented to Grid North), this is not necessary with divorced grids as the control is laid out to suit the site; to avoid any confusion a dated magnetic north arrow should appear on all field plots and grid north on finished drawings. Mathematical or divorced grids are purely a means of computing co-ordinates of the control points to form the basis of the survey. It is not necessary that the grid appears on the final plan, although if site grid references are used for identification purposes, the grid should, of course, appear.

It is outside the scope of this book to discuss co-ordinate computation. Numerous textbooks (eg Muskett 1988; Wilson 1971) cover this subject and most modern electronic survey tools have on-board co-ordinate displays and calculation facilities which allow divorced grids to be defined, and most will accommodate OS National Grid calculations on site, as well as via computer software. Values read from any angle measuring instrument and any linear measurement technique (together referred to as *polar co-ordinates*) can be converted to *rectangular co-ordinates* for plotting on a grid system with a simple hand calculator with trigonometric functions, the calculations can be done arithmetically using log tables, or they can be plotted manually on graph paper; it is not necessary to have electronic instruments to establish this type of grid system for a site.

Control is made up of two parts, *Control Stations* (where instruments are set up during control survey) from which *Detail Control* (points from which the detail will be surveyed) is supplied. The control scheme should also include 'hard' detail (see below). Surveying techniques are well documented in the various surveying publications listed in the bibliography (Bannister and Raymond 1977; Muskett 1988; Whyte and Paul 1997; Wilson 1971). A brief explanation of some basic procedures (particularly for divorced surveys) will provide a guide to fieldworkers and illustrate some of the techniques which can be employed.

Control Stations
The complexity of a control scheme will depend on the size and nature of the site; the aim is always to use the simplest possible scheme. Control is now normally supplied using electronic instruments. For divorced surveys, three basic control station techniques can be

16   *Single station control scheme*
— Stanton Moor
(Derbyshire): control plot.

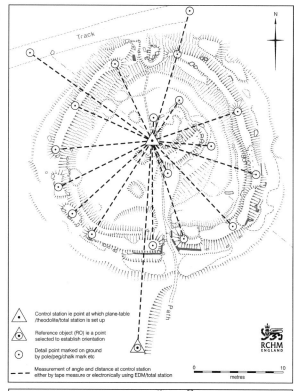

17   *Single station control scheme*
— Stanton Moor: detail
control plan showing tape
and offset used for detail
survey.

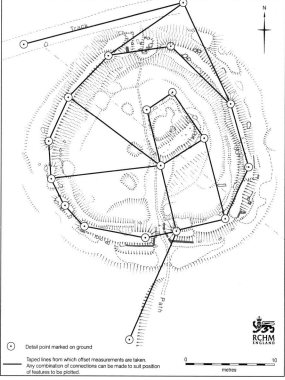

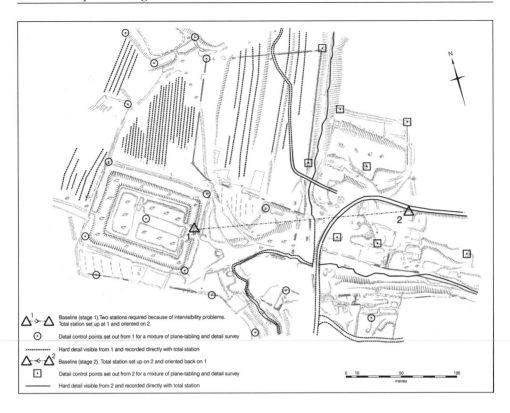

18   *Baseline control scheme — Burton Hall, Warcop (Cumbria).*

applied to almost any circumstance:

(a) Single Station. A surveying instrument is set up on one station from which the whole site can be seen and all necessary measurements can be taken from this point. Orientation is related to a single reference object, such as a peg or building corner (**figs 16, 17**).

(b) Baseline. Where all the necessary measurements cannot be taken from one station, two survey stations are established, one at each end of a measured straight line. Both stations will be occupied by the instrument in turn. Each station provides the orientation for the other, and detail control points are established by angle and/or distance measurements from each station (**fig 18**).

(c) Ring Traverse. Three or more stations are connected by angle and distance measurement beginning and ending at the same station, each observed station becoming the orientation for the next; returning to the first station automatically checks the accuracy of the whole ring. Ring traverses are used for large sites where observation to detail and visibility are difficult (**plate 5** and **figs 19–24**). This is where a third team member is valuable, to carry and set up the third tripod which will be required. On some sites, such as in woodland or large building complexes, the ring traverse alone may not be sufficient. This scenario is usually addressed by running a series of *closed traverses* between stations on the ring

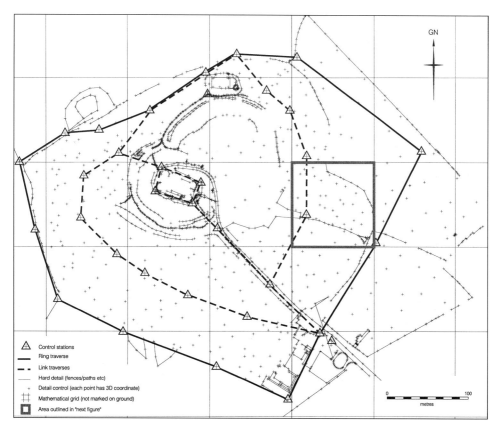

19   *Ring traverse control scheme — Stafford Castle: control plot.*

traverse (**fig 19**). Due to the greater number of stations and related observations accuracy can only be maintained by disciplined measuring technique; even so errors occur and these have to be adjusted either mathematically or graphically. These methods of adjustment are covered in most surveying textbooks. There is a further type of traverse known as an *open traverse* which is not closed on a known point as above but is simply a set of stations connected by angle and distance, used for long linear earthworks through woodland, for example. However, because they are not self-checking, open traverses should be avoided wherever possible. An open traverse can be converted to a 'flat' ring traverse by returning to the first station, occupying the same intermediate stations on the return leg.

All control survey stations should be marked on the ground by appropriate survey markers (see Appendix II) and their locations recorded by measured sketches and/or photography.

Detail Control
Detail control is the network of points marked on the ground, positioned on or close to archaeological and topographic features, so that they can be measured and drawn on a plan (**fig 20**). Detail control is supplied from the control stations, usually by angle and distance

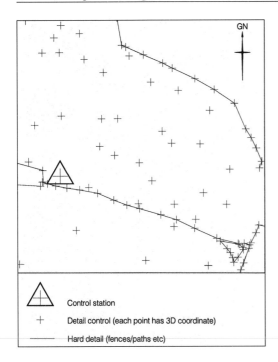

20   Stafford Castle: extract from control plot showing hard detail (fences, path edges) and detail control (pegs). The sides of the square are 100m.

△ Control station

+ Detail control (each point has 3D coordinate)

——— Hard detail (fences/paths etc)

measurements or, if necessary, by measuring angles alone (intersection) or distances alone (trilateration) from two or more stations.

'Hard' and 'soft' detail

'Hard' detail consists of objects where there is no question as to the point to be measured, including modern landscape features, such as buildings, walls and telegraph poles, but also any masonry elements of the archaeology. Many natural features such as rock outcrop, boulders and cliffs are often best treated as 'hard' detail, as is well developed and distinct ridge-and-furrow. 'Soft' detail includes all other archaeological earthworks where the points to be measured are a matter for subjective judgement.

The control plot

However control survey is undertaken, and whether it is plotted by electronic plotter or by hand, the final result will be a control plot (see **fig 20**) showing all the positions of the stations, detail control and 'hard' detail, on drawing film for stability and ease of use. This plot will then be taken into the field to form the basis of the detail survey.

2 Detail Survey

Having established the accurate framework of control, the next stage is to survey the archaeological features so that their morphology and relationships can be portrayed in plan-form by conventions, such as hachures, on the control plot (**figs 21, 24**). This detail survey process is the essence of analytical survey — using the measuring process to examine slopes, their forms and patterns, and to examine relationships and compare with analogous examples.

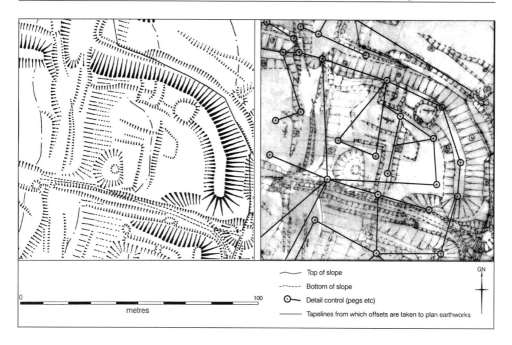

Top of slope
Bottom of slope
Detail control (pegs etc)
Tapelines from which offsets are taken to plan earthworks

GN

0 ———————————————— 100
metres

21   *Stafford Castle: comparative extracts from archive drawing and field drawing.*

22   *Stafford Castle: computer-produced contour plot derived from 3-dimensional co-ordinates of detail control.*

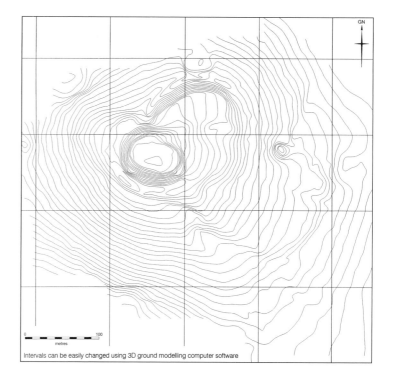

GN

0 ——————— 100
metres

Intervals can be easily changed using 3D ground modelling computer software

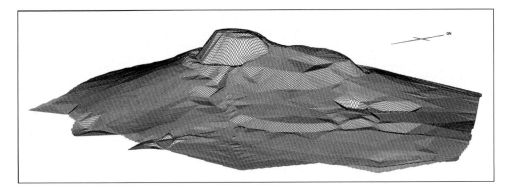

23   *Stafford Castle: Digital Terrain Model derived from 3-dimensional co-ordinates of detail
control.*

While control and 'hard' detail are now often supplied electronically, by 'total-station' or GPS, 'soft' detail is best supplied by traditional methods, usually tape-and-offset or plane-table with self-reducing alidade (see below and Appendix II). The reasons for this division of surveying techniques are that each technique has its own strengths which are appropriate to the different parts of the task. Electronic instruments supply a rigid and accurate framework but produce too mechanistic a portrayal of 'soft' detail. The advantages of traditional methods for supplying 'soft' detail are:

(a) Speed: an experienced team can survey detail at least as fast with traditional equipment as with a total-station;

(b) Quality: the end product is superior because traditional techniques entail a close observation of the ground and allow the fieldworker to treat archaeological and topographic features as complete entities rather than as series of lines to be chased; surveying earthworks by traditional techniques forces the archaeologist to look at them properly in a way which electronic survey does not;

(c) Instant checking: drawing in the field instantly identifies any errors or omissions (this is now also true of electronic drawing boards);

(d) 'Batteries not included': electronic systems are prone to breakdown and battery failure — there is less to go wrong with simpler equipment.

It can be argued that a totally electronic survey is digitally stored, with all the advantages that gives in terms of downloading, plotting and copying, but the disadvantages of digital drawings are that they are usually aesthetically challenged and that digital media are not archivally stable.

The detail control points which have been positioned close to archaeological features now become the points from which measurements are taken, so that earthwork remains are portrayed in their correct relationship to these points and to each other. The process of measurement and drawing of each section of earthwork, as well as ensuring that a good and accurate plan is being made, also facilitates critical observation, so that surface stratigraphy is perceived and thus the relationship and function of earthworks can be understood. This is a dynamic process, each part of a site being carefully examined and

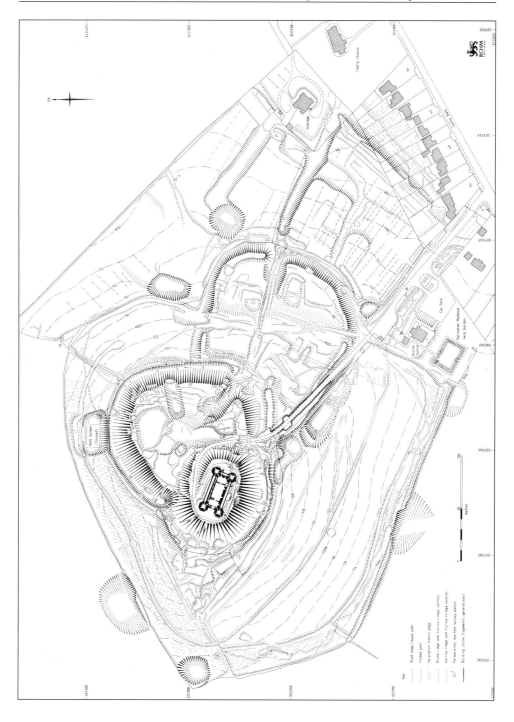

24   *Stafford Castle: complete archive drawing; original scale 1:1000.*

25   *Taping-and-offsetting: using an optical square to raise a right-angle from the baseline.*

measured in a systematic way. If accurate control has been established, confidence can be placed in emerging patterns, such as alignments which might not otherwise be obvious, on opposite sides of a wood, for example.

The main techniques used for detail survey are tape-and-offset and plane-tabling. The first technique is simple to learn and demands very little equipment: some tape measures, ranging poles, optical square (or cross-head (Brown 1987, 51–2)), pencil, scale and setsquare. It involves laying a tape measure between two control points and at measured intervals along this line setting out right-angles (offsets) and measuring along these offset lines to tops and bottoms of slopes, changes in direction and so on (see **fig 2**). Offsets are best kept as short as possible to avoid errors. If an offset is longer than about 3m, an optical square should be used to obtain a right-angle (**fig 25**); if an optical square is not available, there are techniques using the tapes themselves to raise right-angles from the baseline (see Brown 1987, 49–50). Offsets are taken when considered appropriate; too many waste time and effort, while too few will not depict the detail fully and will preclude careful observation of the earthworks. The placing of offsets comes with experience (**fig 26**). The resulting measurements are plotted on the plan with a scale and setsquare. Tops and bottoms of slopes can then be joined to produce an accurate portrayal of the earthworks which can be constantly checked and analysed as the survey progresses. Although this technique works most efficiently with two people, one measuring and one plotting, it can be done singly. If undertaken by one person, it is sensible to book measurements for each line and plot these as one operation before moving on to the next line. This method allows

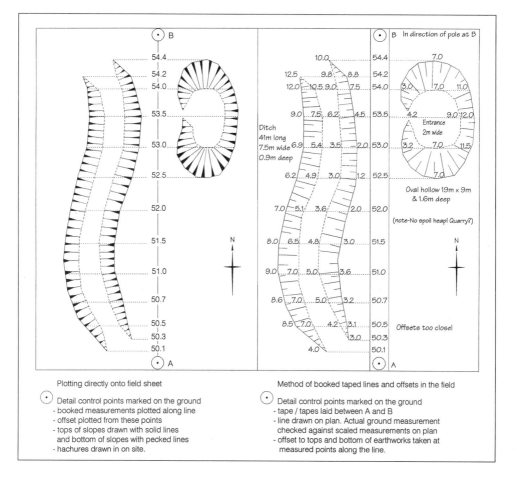

Within the figure:

B

In direction of pole at B

Ditch
41m long
7.5m wide
0.9m deep

Entrance
2m wide

Oval hollow 19m x 9m
& 1.6m deep

(note-No spoil heap! Quarry?)

Offsets too close!

N

A

Plotting directly onto field sheet

- Detail control points marked on the ground
  - booked measurements plotted along line
  - offset plotted from these points
  - tops of slopes drawn with solid lines
    and bottom of slopes with pecked lines
  - hachures drawn in on site.

Method of booked taped lines and offsets in the field

- Detail control points marked on the ground
  - tape / tapes laid between A and B
  - line drawn on plan. Actual ground measurement
    checked against scaled measurements on plan
  - offset to tops and bottom of earthworks taken at
    measured points along the line.

26   *Taping-and-offsetting: schematic diagram.*

tops and bottoms of slopes to be depicted in such a way that the level of detail portrayed is commensurate with the scale of the final plan (for the conventions of field drawing, see Chapter 5).

Lines other than right-angle offsets can be used. Gaps can be filled by running tape lines from a point measured along a baseline in direction of another control point; building alignments ('straights') can be taped along and extended; alignments of other points can be extended or 'pulled back'; intersections can be established with the optical square and taped from (**fig 27**). As long as the control is accurate, the resulting plan will be accurate. By checking that the ground measurement and scaled measurement between points agree ('tie out'), the possibility of errors will be reduced. If an error occurs (and this is often the case when surveying directly into OS 1:2500 scale maps), it is important to resolve the problem before continuing, as its effects will become cumulative and cause bigger problems later.

Alternatively, detail can be surveyed with instruments such as plane-table and alidade, using a staff or tape for distance measurement, and plotting on site. Experience has shown

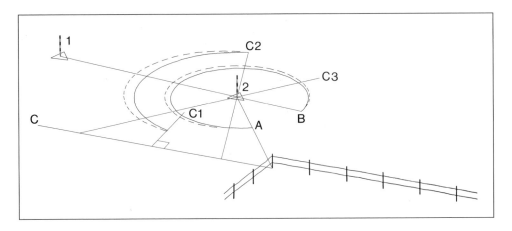

27   *Graphical survey: schematic diagram. From detail control point 2 —*
        A is a measurement in direction of *the fence corner post*
        B is a measurement pulling back *Station 1*
        C is a line established by extending the straight *of the fence for* offsetting *and* shots
        through point 2 (C1, C2, C3).

that detail surveying with plane-table and self-reducing alidade is very fast and accurate. This is a task for a team of two; one works the instrument and draws the plan while the other positions the staff (**plate 6**) and takes subsidiary measurements with staff or tape (using 'pull backs', etc, as above), calling the results to their colleague who plots them immediately (**plate 7**). The slight disadvantage that the plan is drawn at a fixed position away from the features being measured is minimised by the fact that this distance is rarely more than about 50m, the comfortable range of the instrument; it is very easy for the team members to converse and for the plotter to walk over to the features to check any uncertainties.

The plane-table is one of the oldest surveying instruments and is still probably the best tool for the archaeological fieldworker to acquire and learn how to use, especially with the self-reducing alidade (**plate 8**). It is ideally suited to small teams and is an essential tool for teaching the principles of surveying. Most surveys, at whatever scale, can be undertaken with a plane-table, tapes, optical square and ranging poles. Plane-tabling is a technique worth learning, teaching and practising.

Because the recording technology of 'total-stations' (see Appendix II) allows large numbers of points to be recorded accurately and rapidly, and computers can plot these with lines, colours and text annotations, they are very efficient for detail survey at small to medium scales where subtleties cannot be portrayed anyway, but, for the reasons mentioned above, they are less efficient in terms of detail survey at larger scales where the requirement to observe and plan subtle and complex relationships is greater. The demands of recording the necessary computer codes in the field to draw complex slopes can detract from the observation of the archaeological nuances themselves; it is more important to spend time looking closely at earthworks and thinking about the archaeological interpretation, rather than running round with a surveying pole, trying to remember

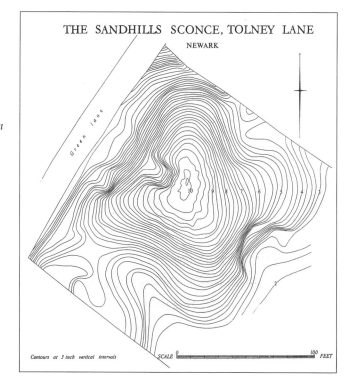

28   *Sandhills Sconce,*
      Newark-on-Trent
      (Nottinghamshire):
      a severely eroded,
      single-phase
      earthwork (a Civil
      War gun battery) on
      relatively level
      ground, this is an
      ideal candidate for
      contour survey.

which slopes have been done and whether all the lines will join up as computer instructions. Nevertheless, total-stations can be used for detail survey on sites where earthworks are simple and easily understood; if a small percentage of the area is complex, one can put in some detail control and survey this part with traditional methods.

Detail Survey — the third dimension

In the majority of cases, the artificial slopes of archaeological earthworks are best represented by hachured plans. This is a tradition which is long established and understood by most archaeological practitioners. On many sites, natural slopes are also of archaeological interest and can reveal much about the form and siting of a particular monument. These must therefore be included in the detail survey. In some cases simply depicting them with a different style of hachure ('natural hachure' — see p170) may convey all that is necessary, though this may be inappropriate for more complex inter-relationships; where this is the case, contouring the natural topography at a suitable vertical interval to show the landform may be necessary (see **figs 22, 28**). The decision to embark on contouring would normally have been made at the recce stage and therefore the appropriate equipment and methodology would have been used to cover the site with spot heights. Interpolating contours from these is one of the most tedious and time consuming exercises in surveying and, although it is quite feasible to achieve this by manual methods, electronic data recording and computer-based interpolation and plotting should be used wherever possible. Otherwise contouring should not be undertaken lightly. GPS equipment and digital ground-modelling software present the most efficient

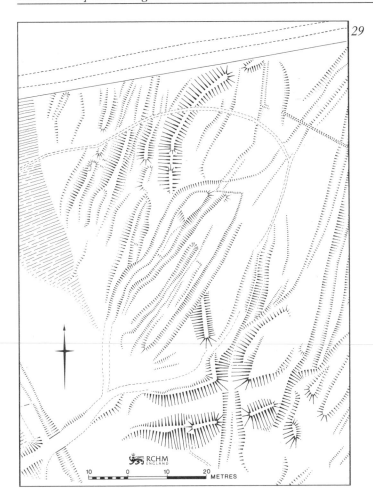

29 *Wykeham Forest (North Yorkshire): a series of braided hollow ways on a south-facing slope cutting an earlier bank and overlain by more recent tracks and paths. Contour survey could not show the chronological complexity demonstrated in this hachured survey diagram. Extract from field survey archive plan, original scale 1:1000.*

way of gathering and processing large amounts of 3D co-ordinate data for depiction of contours, but this will not be available to all.

The value of contouring *archaeological* earthworks for analytical purposes is extremely limited and best restricted to depicting simple sites and very low spread monuments, such as ploughed-out barrows and single-phase fieldworks (**fig 28**). The advantages of hachured survey over contour survey for earthworks are broadly that contour survey cannot:

    (a) distinguish between natural and man-made slopes

    (b) show chronological relationships between features (**fig 29**)

    (c) give a consistent depiction of features as they turn across or along slopes.

Contour surveys are sometimes said to be 'objective'. This claim can be questioned: judgements have to be made, for instance, about horizontal and vertical intervals. The desirability of 'objectivity' is another question; the corresponding 'subjectivity' of hachured survey is its strength, because that is where the fieldworker's judgement, experience, knowledge and interpretative skill can be deployed. The best solution is to show archaeological earthworks by hachures and natural slopes by contours (see **fig 24**, for instance).

Recording height values around a site in the form of spot heights at strategic points can also enhance the value of the detail survey. This can be particularly relevant on sites, for example, where waterflow management may form part of the interpretation; in the case of a major linear feature, such as an aqueduct, this may involve a complex levelling survey (eg Mackay 1990). Measured profiles across earthworks are an effective means of conveying changes in height, where vertical differences are dramatic, and also help to illustrate interpretations (Brown 1987, 54–5).

However, precisely levelled heighting information is not always necessary, when a sufficiently accurate estimation of height above sea level can be read from an OS map; before setting off on a long levelling traverse, the fieldworker should consider whether it matters if a particular hut circle is at 270m or 272m OD.

Depiction

The depiction of hard detail is subject to systems which have been developed by cartographers and draughtsmen and which meet with general acceptance; these are sets of symbols, lines and annotations known as conventions. The depiction of archaeological features is also subject to conventions, such as those used by the Royal Commissions (see **fig 85**) and the OS; many individuals and units have developed their own in response to individual sites and projects. It makes sense if conventions, such as those used by the Royal Commissions, form the core of any survey and site-specific conventions are added where appropriate. It is always worth looking through journals and other publications to see how other fieldworkers present their surveys. Conventions vary according to the scale and purpose of the plan being drawn.

Any convention or symbol should aim to look like what it is trying to portray, eg tree or marsh symbols. Some conventions can be used to convey a feeling of depth or height, eg the slope hachure, quarry or cliff symbol, and at large scales (1:2500 and larger) conventions should aim to allow accurate depiction of detail. For small-scale surveys (1:10,000 and smaller) a combination of lines, schematic symbols and colours is usually adequate. Whatever set of conventions is used, it should be clear, unambiguous and consistent throughout the survey.

Many convention sets for topographic features such as fences, hedges and buildings ('hard' detail) have already been defined by bodies such as the OS. Also surveying textbooks and manuals frequently contain examples from civil engineering and other surveying disciplines which can provide a guide for developing project conventions. Most surveying software packages have a range of computer linestyles and symbols embedded in their drawing capabilities which can be coded in the field with data-loggers. Annotations and notes on the drawing can be used to good effect as an alternative to developing large numbers of conventions: time in the field is better spent looking at the archaeological detail than producing a 'pretty' plan. However, drawings should always be kept as clean as possible and detail drawn clearly — always draw in the field in order that the final drawing could be done by somebody who has never seen the site (though this should never be the case). Before leaving, check unclear elements and make any necessary notes; this is easier than having to return to site later because you cannot remember what a particular line represents.

30 GPS survey equipment in use: single frequency differential GPS 'rover' equipment, consisting of an antenna and controller mounted on the staff, and receiver and battery in the backpack.

Advanced survey technology

The principles of surveying never change, though the practice does. Today, surveying equipment and techniques of recording have become more and more automated. The main advances have been in speed and accuracy of measurement, automated computation and drawing, as well as coding and categorisation of information, so that it can be accessioned electronically into databases. This section will provide a brief guide to the types of new and emerging technology which have applications today in archaeological surveying and recording. It must be remembered though that, however advanced this technology is, none has yet been developed which can emulate the human skills of observation and analysis of archaeological earthworks.

Global Positioning System (GPS)

High-precision National Grid co-ordinates for control in a site or landscape survey can be achieved with GPS (**fig 30**) by using a network of three or more OS control points around the site, the accurate co-ordinate position of which can be purchased from the OS. (It must be borne in mind that linking a site survey accurately to the National Grid in this

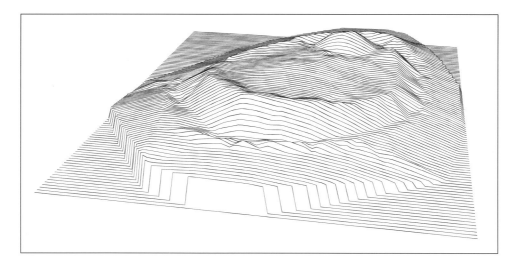

31   Bury Castle, Brompton Regis (Somerset): Digital Terrain Model

way may mean that its relationship to local map detail may be incorrect.) Detail survey can be completed by the methods outlined above.

Besides being a powerful tool for providing survey control, GPS is increasingly in use as a flexible, rapid way of planning archaeological features, particularly suited to scales from 1:2500 to 1:10,000. In kinematic (constantly moving) mode, the system accurately records its three-dimensional position at a preset interval. Thus, a surveyor carrying a GPS receiver in a backpack can record the position and shape of archaeological features by walking around them. Textual tags recording the significance of particular points can be added to the data. Feature codes can also be inserted by the surveyor at the time of the survey, so that when the data is processed in the office, modern features are clearly distinguished from archaeological features by virtue of their line-type and colour. GPS also provides a simple way of collecting three-dimensional information across an archaeological landscape in order to construct a Digital Terrain Model (DTM) (**fig 31**). DTMs can be manipulated so that subtle features can be more easily seen; these digital models can then be rendered to provide images of the site upon which interpretative reconstructions can be built. An example of GPS and CAD in Level 2, 1:10,000 scale recording of the upland landscapes of Dartmoor is given in **plate 22**.

Electronic drawing boards
A technical advance in portable computer design which has benefits for the surveyor is the pen computer. Rather than a computer keyboard with an attached screen, this design places the emphasis on the screen; in some models the keyboards are completely detachable. The computer software is controlled using a stylus with which the user points and clicks in similar fashion to using a mouse on a desktop computer. Survey software has been written for these pen computers that allows the surveyor to use digital maps in the field. Data can be collected electronically, but the surveyors can see the survey growing as

they work and are able to adjust it graphically. Thus this system combines the benefits of digital data recording with the immediacy of using a plane-table or other hand-drawn method. They can be directly linked to electronic theodolites, so that when a point is recorded, instead of numeric data being stored for later computation, the result appears directly as a point in the appropriate position on the computer screen. The surveyor can tag each surveyed point with textual information. Taped measurements can be incorporated and all the data can be organised by colour and layer for transfer to a CAD package for finishing and plotting.

Computer-Aided Drawing (CAD)

Computer-aided draughting software has the same relationship to technical drawing as word processing has to written text. It can describe lines, arcs and other vector elements accurately in three-dimensional space. The user can identify elements by using different colours and line-types and by grouping them together in various ways. One of the most powerful of these is by using layers, which compares with the traditional use of tracing paper overlays. Different groups of elements can then be turned on and off at will; for instance, if a distribution map showing sites of different periods is prepared with a layer for each period, relative distributions can be readily illustrated. It is possible to plot CAD images at any desired scale or to pass the images on to computer graphics or desk-top publishing software. Where height information is available, 3D models can be constructed and manipulated beyond the presentational range of free-standing modelling software.

Geographical Information Systems (GIS)

Geographical Information Systems have been developed from the functionality described above for CAD systems. They are a specialised application with tools developed for the manipulation and display of spatially referenced database information usually against the background of digital mapping. An example of a straightforward use of a GIS for archaeologists is the display of distributions of sites or finds against the geology or topography of an area. Relative densities of sites or finds can also be shown graphically by means of symbols or by selecting colours to represent different densities. Depending on the complexity of the sets of data available to the system, far more complex analyses can be carried out, for instance to find the effect of the rise and fall of water levels on defined categories of site, or to find intervisibility between sites.

A MULTI-PERIOD LANDSCAPE
GREENLEE LOUGH (NORTHUMBERLAND)

The landscape at Greenlee Lough, on a south-facing dip slope 1.5km north-west of the Roman fort at Housesteads, displays features of many periods. The underlying geology consists of limestone and sandstone, the division between them apparently marked by a series of solution hollows lying in a gully running from east to west. A small, circular settlement was built above Jenkins Burn at some point in the later prehistoric period and a small hillfort, overlooking the Lough to the north. The dwellers in these two settlements seem to have cultivated the intervening ground, dividing it with earth banks and raising narrow ridges of the type known as cord-rig. A Roman camp was subsequently built over these fields: this chronological relationship, observable on the surface, has been confirmed by excavation (Welfare 1986). To the north of the solution hollows, peat has developed over the sandstone, reducing the definition of the camp's earthworks in this area. Subsequently, at some point in the medieval period or even later, transhumant farmers built a number of shielings and sheepfolds over and around the remains of the hillfort and within the Roman camp. Later still, probably in the nineteenth century, the area was divided by stone walls and cultivated once again, though the resulting straight ridge-and-furrow is poorly developed and has failed to obliterate traces of the earlier fields or of the prehistoric trackway leading eastward from the circular settlement. A modern track crossing the area is contemporary with, or later than, these stone-walled fields.

Excavations in progress, revealing cord rig and ploughmarks under the rampart of the Roman camp.

Field survey plan of Greenlee Lough: original scale 1:1000

5 Analytical earthwork survey — interpretation

ARCHAEOLOGICAL RECORDING

The RCHME has divided archaeological recording into four broad Levels (see Appendix I) and has adopted surveying methodologies which broadly complement these Levels of record. In all cases, the principle of establishing control for the survey is the first stage (either providing it with new survey or by using map detail), followed by a second stage of detail survey (depicting archaeological remains).

There are three basic methodologies, *Rapid Survey, Landscape Survey* and *Large-scale Survey*. These methodologies, when studied with the *Principles of survey* in Chapter 4 and *Surveying equipment* guide (Appendix II), can be used as a basis for planning and executing any archaeological survey.

Rapid Survey (Level 1)

A Rapid survey of the archaeology of a large area can be a productive method of obtaining an audit of the quality, quantity, identity and distribution of the archaeological resource. Reasons for undertaking a Rapid archaeological survey include: the identification and inclusion in a database of sites not previously recorded, the assessment of change to the archaeological record, the creation of an archaeological overview in advance of development or positive management, and the promotion of the understanding of the archaeological and historical nature of the landscape. Rapid survey ideally incorporates a balanced input of desktop research utilising readily available sources, including maps and air photography, complemented by fieldwork. By the definition of Rapid survey, however, field input will be restricted to a single visit to any location.

Because field action is limited, a disproportionate amount of time is spent travelling and gaining permissions for access in Rapid survey. For this reason the cost-effectiveness of such projects must be carefully monitored: having taken the trouble to get to the site, might it be worthwhile to undertake a higher Level of recording?

Preliminary assessment
The parameters of a Rapid survey must be carefully defined at the outset of the work. These will include the following:

(a) Cost/benefit analysis. A rapid overview of the available evidence will result in the acquisition of a broad range of data at a fairly superficial level.

(b) Determining intensity of survey. Whether each hectare is to be systematically quartered or a selective sampling strategy is to be adopted — for instance focusing the investigation on areas of ancient woodland and grassland. The decision to visit known sites during the survey, or to concentrate exclusively on a search for 'new' sites, will depend on the stated aims of the particular survey.

(c) Determining the scope of survey. For instance, whether sites of every period will be recorded.

A Rapid survey will almost always reveal the need for further archaeological work in the area, consequently posing new questions.

Scale and Methodology

The most appropriate surveying scale for Rapid survey is 1:10,000, using the OS mapping at this scale as the base document in the UK. This mapping scale covers a large area (25 km²) on one manageable sheet for use in the field and shows the majority of landscape detail necessary for positioning the archaeological detail to a tolerably accurate standard. Equipment required for the survey includes a board with 1:10,000 field sheet covered by drawing film, notebook, drawing kit, tape measures, ranging rods, a compass or pocket sextant, binoculars and possibly a camera.

Information gleaned from any preliminary desktop survey should be added to the fieldsheet before fieldwork commences. This can be augmented by notes of field names and cartographical changes obtained from old OS maps or tithe maps, for instance. Colour-coded conventions can usefully be adopted. Marks visible on air photography can be depicted as seen; new sites can be sketch-surveyed (**fig 32**) or indicated by a cross, and large-area features delimited by a pecked line. Ideally, a second set of 1:10,000 sheets covering the area should be maintained to which extra information, such as the areas actually visited, can be added as an aid to future work.

A new site can be positioned from map detail using an optical square or prismatic compass survey — pacing distances is adequate at this scale over short distances. An adult pace is about one metre in length, but individual variation can be tested by pacing along a 20m tape. This sketched siting on the 1:10,000 map will result in the production of a 6- or 8-figure grid reference (ie to an accuracy of 100m or 10m respectively), acceptable for location records. Each new site should be separately recorded. The range of information to be collected should be clearly defined to avoid data overload. A pro-forma recording sheet can be devised which incorporates the data required by the SMR and NMR and by the individual project, if required. The use of the RCHME/EH *Thesaurus of Monument Types* (1998) will ensure the adoption of standard classification terms. New sites must be classified if possible, though period and type may not be apparent until a higher level of survey (or more invasive investigation) has been carried out; the requirement to classify rapidly on the basis of one field visit demands considerable skill and experience — Rapid survey is not an easy option.

As at all Levels of survey, the project specification must include an adequate time allowance for archiving the information, as well as the production of the final report.

*32   Example of a Rapid
survey map: part of
an overlay to OS
1:10,000 map SD
68 NW, showing an
area around Hollins
and Beckside Hall,
Middleton
(Cumbria). The
hard lines represent
earthworks of
prehistoric and
medieval settlements,
field systems and
tracks; the dotted lines
represent the
boundaries and the
arrows the alignment
of ridge-and-furrow.*

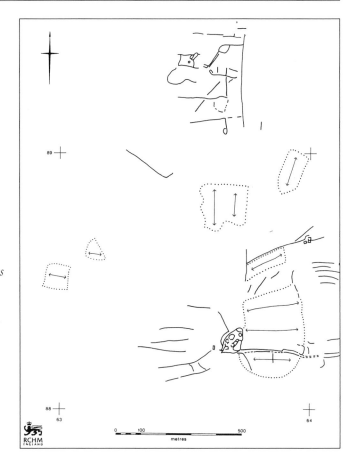

Landscape Survey (Level 2)

The purpose of Landscape survey can be defined as the mapping and preliminary analysis of an area, often quite large, containing many archaeological sites and components. Consequently, it differs in two respects from Rapid survey: it is both metrically accurate and analytical. Landscape survey also offers the possibility of multiple field visits with consequent advantages in terms of varied directions of approach, and different climate, light and ground conditions (see Fleming 1988, 39).

This type of approach is usually adopted in those areas where there is an outline knowledge of the archaeology, whether that in itself is a product of random cumulative record or of Rapid survey. During Landscape survey it is not the intention to map and record each individual archaeological component in *detail*, but to survey each element accurately at 1:10,000 or 1:2500 scale in *outline*, produce a short written description and attempt an overview. The spatial relationships between archaeological features can be determined and, in some cases, a relative chronology established. In turn, this can enable preliminary analysis of how the area has developed through time. Moreover, the sites are depicted in their real landscape context, a base from which further study can proceed: a common important outcome is the identification of smaller areas within the whole which,

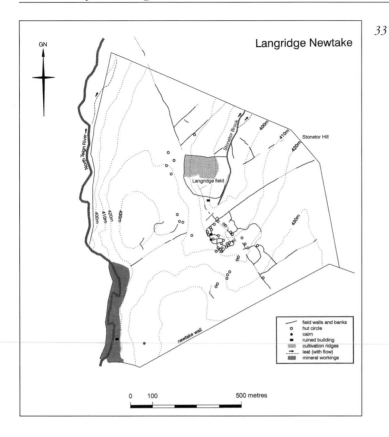

33   Landscape survey at Langridge Newtake (Devon) (reproduced from Ordnance Survey mapping with the permission of the Controller of Her Majesty's Stationery Office © Crown Copyright. RCHME Licence GD03133G/4/98).

for particular reasons, are significant enough to be considered for future Large-scale survey or other forms of archaeological work. In **figure 33**, for example, a goal might be to clarify the relationships in the complex cluster of hut circles and enclosures south of Langridge Field, notably how they relate to the rectilinear reave system.

Reconnaissance

As already stated, this is an important stage in any survey, when the exact area is carefully defined and decisions made about an appropriate survey method, equipment, access, time of year for survey and so on. Extended reconnaissance at this stage can also effectively eliminate parts of the area from the survey, if there happen to be no visible surface features, although some fieldworkers prefer to look at these areas during the actual survey, when they have begun to establish an understanding of the landform and the archaeology.

If map detail is to form the survey control, then the map should be visually checked for overall accuracy of depiction, using the most recent revision available. If instrumental survey is envisaged, then the positions of the survey control stations should be identified.

Scales

The appropriate scales for Landscape survey are between 1:10,000 and 1:2500, but preferably the latter. In the UK 1:2500 is the OS basic scale in rural areas, except in large expanses of upland, where it is 1:10,000. In both cases, there is a ready-made control framework within which an archaeological survey can fit. Both scales also offer the ability to depict the main archaeological components in a simple and uncomplicated fashion, as a series of carefully chosen conventions, usually a combination of hachures, line types and small symbols. Because of this simplicity of depiction, inter-relationships can be effectively articulated in plan. However, 1:2500 gives much greater scope for depicting detail 'as seen' rather than relying on the use of map symbols.

Methodology
1. Using OS map control
This approach will often be preferred where the OS map control is available and reliable. OS maps can be obtained from OS agents in digital format or as hard copy from a digital database (Superplan). The use of this data is, however, governed by OS copyright and potential users should familiarise themselves with the rules: most data can be used under licence. For use in the field, the map detail should be penned on the reverse of polyester film for durability, stability and high resistance to moisture. Such sheets are available by National Grid map sheets or to National Grid co-ordinates as defined by the user. The latter enables maps tailored to the survey to be obtained, avoiding purchase of whole maps which contain only a small part of the survey area, although the option is more expensive per unit area; the cost-benefit should be assessed individually for each case.

With an OS map plot secured to a light drawing board, mounted on a tripod if desired, it is possible for a single surveyor to plan archaeological features into the control provided by the map using tapes and an optical square, applying appropriate checks in the process. Measurements should be carefully recorded in a survey book and plotted onto the map base in manageable blocks: plotting should be done while it is fresh in the surveyor's mind. With two surveyors recording by tape-and-offset in this way, or by plane-tabling, large areas can be covered quickly and more effectively; surveying and plotting keep pace with each other.

2. Using instrumental control
In areas where there are very few 'hard' features and therefore a lack of map control, for instance in remote moorland, the establishment of independent survey control using electronic instruments is the preferred method. Where rapidly changing environmental conditions dictate that survey should be accomplished quickly, for instance in coastal and estuarine locations, it is also an effective method.

For Landscape survey, instrumental control involves the establishment of a series of survey stations linked in a geometric framework, from which detail control, or the archaeological features themselves, can be located directly and accurately. In the former case, the detail control points form a network from which the archaeological features are plotted using tape-and-offset or plane-table. In the latter, the theodolite and EDM can be pre-programmed with a series of set codes for the different line types and symbols representing the archaeological features, and which a computer uses to process and plot an accurate plan. The landscape shown in **figure 33** was surveyed with theodolite and EDM.

3. Computer-aided air transcription for enhancement by ground survey

In areas covered by high-quality stereoscopic air photography, it is possible to produce accurate transcriptions via computer showing hard control, archaeology and even apparently ephemeral landscape features such as sheep tracks and vegetation changes, which can be extremely useful for location in open moorland. These transcriptions are taken into the field for checking and completion. This method has been used to great effect by the RCHME in large upland areas on Bodmin Moor and in the Cheviots (see **fig 8**). It is described in the section on Photogrammetry in Chapter 7.

Large-scale Survey (Levels 3 and 4)

The purpose of a Large-scale survey is to provide a detailed analytical record of a monument, site or landscape for management or academic research purposes. This would comprise an accurate survey recording all features, archaeological and topographic, in their correct relationship, as well as an interpretative written report.

Scales and methodology

A Level 3 survey must be accurately located, measured (either map-based or divorced) and at a scale which adequately represents the form and complexity of the site or monument; this would normally be at a scale between 1:1250 and 1:500. In some cases, 1:2500 (using OS map base where possible) is sufficient. The survey might be enhanced by measured profiles and selected 'windows' of larger scale survey to illustrate specific aspects of the site. Large-scale archaeological survey, especially of complex earthwork sites, is relatively time consuming and therefore costly. It should have a specific purpose, whether that be management or research, and is best suited to individual sites and monuments.

All large-scale survey is undertaken following the sequence of Reconnaissance, Control survey and Detail survey already described, using, wherever possible, electronic instrumentation for control and traditional techniques for the detail.

Depiction

An accurate interpretative large-scale plan of a site must be drawn and presented in such a way that it can be used by the compiler and others who perhaps have never visited the site. An archaeological surveyor is attempting to portray a three-dimensional ground surface on a flat piece of paper or film in such a way as to convey to the eye and mind of the plan user exactly what has been seen on the ground and how it has been interpreted. It is essential that any system is as simple as possible and readily understood. Over the years, map conventions and some specific conventions for archaeological portrayal have evolved.

Conventions can be divided into two main categories, those used in the field and those appearing on the final plan — the two are not necessarily the same.

Field Conventions

Drawing earthwork slopes ('soft' detail) on field plans, particularly complex ones, is much more difficult than depicting 'hard' detail and is a skill which has to be developed. The

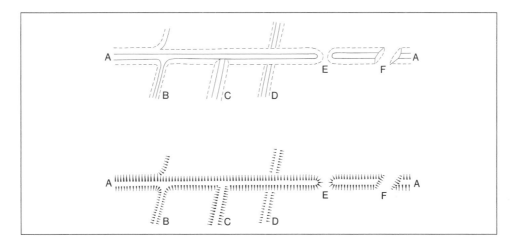

34   *How chronological relationships are depicted on field and archive drawings.*
        Bank A-A:
        - has no discernible relationship with B and is probably contemporary
        - is overlain by, and is therefore earlier than, C
        - overlies, and is therefore later than, D
        - has a gap, probably original, at E
        - has been cut by a later breach at F.

reason for this is that in analytical survey not only are you trying to position the top and bottom of a slope on a plan, you may also be conveying the relationship between one slope and another to record their relative stratigraphy (**fig 34**). You may also be aiming to indicate relative heights and steepness of slopes (see **fig 85**), or which slopes may be related because they have similar morphology. This sort of information will form the basis of your interpretation of the site and therefore some conventions and annotations have to be used to record these observations. On RCHME field drawings the tops of slopes are represented by hard lines and bottoms by pecked lines; on the final plan, these lines are omitted, being replaced by hachures which indicate the extent, relative steepness and direction of the slope. Again it is not necessary to draw hachures in the field, except where they may clarify complex areas, but it helps to annotate slopes according to their relative steepness as 'o' (open), 'm' (medium) or 'c' (close), or a similar code. On large-scale surveys even the most intricate pattern of slopes can be shown with a sharp pencil and a keen eye by this method.

It is always wise to add a key to the field drawings and to include details of location, site grid reference, north arrow, scale, date of survey and staff involved. Where the survey is based on a grid (either physical or computational), grid values should be recorded around the edge. The RCHME uses field sheets with title boxes printed on them to ensure relevant information is recorded with each drawing (see **fig 64**). The field plans should be viewed as archive material and retained along with all other site information. For the process of drawing up the field plan for the archive and publication, see Chapter 11.

Noting

The final act in most large-scale surveys is noting, though this may be done in the course of the survey if preferred. Noting gives the investigator a final opportunity to look around the site, to check that nothing has been missed and that the survey represents the site fairly; it should not be rushed. The notes to be taken will include the heights of scarps and depths of hollows, the all-important chronological relationships, and any other details (such as the presence or absence of stone) or broader observations (such as intervisibility with distant sites) that will be valuable in writing the site report. Whether notes are made on the plan, in a notebook, or on a voice recorder for subsequent transcription will depend on the preference and circumstances of the individual and on the requirements of the particular site.

INTERPRETATION

Stratigraphy in the landscape

Survey drawings form 'windows' of the wider landscape in much the same way that an archaeological excavation forms a window onto the sub-surface deposits of a site. For this reason they are normally presented framed, like any printed map sheet, with the topographical details extending to and cut off by the frame, and with all features within the framed area depicted as encountered during fieldwork. This practice emphasises the continuity and change inherent in most landscapes, which may aptly be described as a palimpsest, up to and including the recent past. It affords the opportunity to observe and record relationships of chronological priority, which can give otherwise undated features a secure — if sometimes very broad — context.

Such stratigraphy is inherent in the landscape. It appears in any mapped depiction or photographic image of that landscape and can be read as a sequence of events. For example, motorways and bypasses of the later twentieth century slice through existing field and communication patterns, frequently creating redundant fragments. Railways in the mid-nineteenth century did the same, and the canals before them (**fig 35**). If, for example, a furlong of ridge-and-furrow survives as earthworks on either side of a canal that cuts through it, that is clear field evidence that the cultivation pre-dated the canal and was abandoned before (or because) it was driven through. Late eighteenth-century field and road patterns resulting from parliamentary enclosure typically have a similarly clear stratigraphical relationship to medieval ridge-and-furrow cultivation that is observable in the landscape no less readily than in the plans attached to an Inclosure Award; this contrasts with earlier enclosure, piecemeal or by agreement, which characteristically followed the tenurial structure of the medieval strips and furlongs. Air photography and excavation in turn reveal ridge-and-furrow overploughing pre-medieval sites. Early coaxial field systems fossilised in current or recent field patterns in East Anglia are seen to be of pre-Roman date from the relationship of a Roman road slicing obliquely through them (Williamson 1987).

35   *Stratigraphy in the landscape — Braunston (Northamptonshire): fields of ridge-and-furrow associated with the deserted medieval settlement of Braunstonbury have been cut by the old canal which curves in an arc from the top right-hand corner to bottom right of the picture. The canal in turn has been blocked by the railway, now itself disused. The earthworks of the settlement, centre and left, are cut by a modern minor road which also slices through the ridge-and-furrow beyond. The Grand Union canal and main road at the top of the picture are also truncating blocks of ridge-and-furrow (copyright Northamptonshire County Council).*

Such forms of argument by *stratigraphy* are logically stronger than considerations that rely only on *morphology* or *analogy*. But beware: they rely for their strength on the valid identification of the fixed elements. In a case at Heronbridge (Cheshire) superficially similar to Williamson's example, a modern road on the line of the Roman road south from Chester clearly slices through a complex earthwork landscape of ridge-and-furrow furlongs and enclosed fields (SJ 411 636), but they are not therefore pre-Roman in date. Closer study shows that the road is a nineteenth-century re-creation closely matching the ancient alignment, but the Roman road and landscape lie completely buried below the changing medieval and later cultivation patterns. In another case, where a section of Offa's Dyke appeared to slice through a similar complex earthwork landscape of cultivation remains, thereby post-dating them, detailed study proved it to be the ostensible relationships that were problematic (Everson 1991); in every instance the Dyke was shown to be the earliest feature visible.

Juxtaposition is sometimes taken in a facile way to indicate contemporaneity. In such cases, detailed observation of crucial points in the landscape where features meet will often reveal evidence of chronological relationships. At Haystacks Hill (Northumberland)

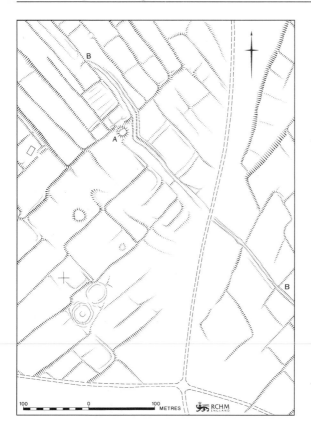

36   Earthwork chronology at Church Pits, Orcheston (Wiltshire): extract from field survey drawing, original scale 1:1000. The earliest component is a small barrow cemetery, around which a co-axial field system has been laid out. Although this respected the barrows, the lynchetting resulting from cultivation has encroached on the northernmost mound (A). Still visible, however, this mound subsequently acted as a marker for the alignment of a linear ditch. (B– B). This ditch cuts through the fields, including the lynchet encroaching on the barrow, but respects the barrow, curving to avoid it. Later re-use of the field system in turn obscures the linear ditch, though it re-emerges from the fields a little over 200m to the north-west. The field system saw intensive, but evidently intermittent use for perhaps as long as 1500 years, the final phase relating to a Romano-British village situated 200m to the north-east. During this time there was much modification, the boundaries, for example, between many of the original square plots being levelled to form larger rectangular fields.

the stony foundations of late prehistoric or Romano-British settlements (NU 005 152) are surrounded by extensive broad ridge-and-furrow, but the ploughing can be seen to clip and truncate the settlement boundaries, showing them to be earlier (see **fig 8**).

Stratigraphy in site surveys

It has been said (eg Clarke 1984, 27) that earthwork survey can only reveal the final phase of a site. This is untrue. Chronological depth and sequence are always sought, and frequently found, in survey. Most survey diagrams, though 2-dimensional, have stratigraphy in them. This has the same evidential strength and value as stratigraphy in excavation or in building analysis. It must be recognised, correctly depicted as a matter of record, and used in interpretation. As in excavation, it represents the key original form of evidence that fieldwork can contribute; interpretation can turn on it. In its strongest and most readily recognisable form, it might be termed *vertical stratigraphy* (**fig 36**).

Stratigraphy occurs equally in both complex and simple situations. In West Lindsey, a small circular embanked earthwork, sometimes described as a Roman signal station, was

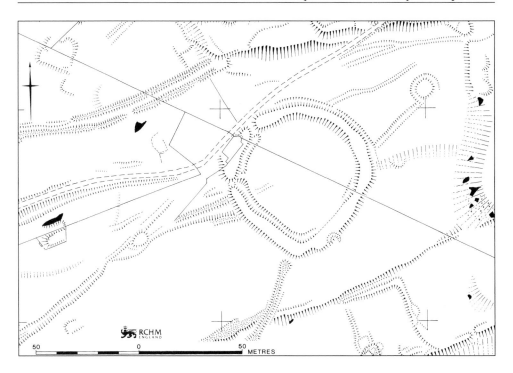

37   *Black Knoll, Long Mynd (Shropshire): extract from field survey drawing, original scale*
        1:1000.

given a secure post-medieval context (and a probable interpretation as a tree-planting ring)
by being shown to be situated on top of earthwork ridge-and-furrow (Everson *et al* 1991,
127); at Stainfield, embanked closes overlying deserted medieval village earthworks were
the outer parts of a post-medieval formal garden attached to a lost post-Dissolution
country house on the adjacent monastic site (*ibid*, 175–7).

At Quarrendon, near Aylesbury (Buckinghamshire), a moat, ostensibly a manorial site
(part of the adjacent deserted village), actually cuts and blocks the village's main street. It
is more plausibly, therefore, the site of the great sixteenth-century house whose elaborate
formal garden earthworks lie on the side opposite the village, which is also shown by the
relationship to have been deserted by that date (cf Beresford and St Joseph 1979, figs 19,
47). At Black Knoll on the south end of the Long Mynd (Shropshire), a circular enclosure
previously recorded as a late prehistoric settlement site can be observed to overlie and
block earthwork packhorse trails of medieval and later date. Whatever the function of the
enclosure, therefore — and that is uncertain — its date must be post-medieval or early
modern (SO 389 878) (**fig 37**). Within the parkland of Attingham Park, also in Shropshire,
a previously unrecorded linear earthwork sliced through ridge-and-furrow. It too, must be
of post-medieval or early modern date (Everson and Stamper 1987; and see below). The
instances that could be cited are endless.

However, an example from Stanton Moor in the Derbyshire Peak District emphasises
the strength of such field relationships in curious circumstances. A line of stony cairns

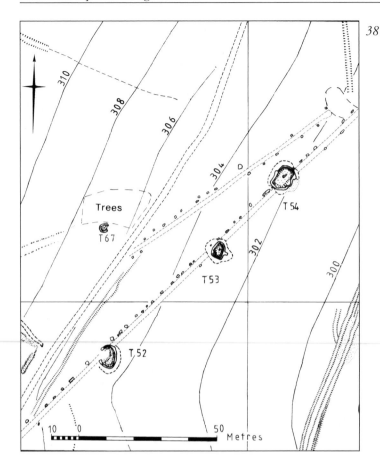

38   *Stanton Moor (Derbyshire): extract from field survey archive drawing (not redrawn for publication), original scale 1:1000. Bronze Age cairns rebuilt after excavation in the 1930s and 40s and in consequence overlying the linear bed of a First World War tramway.*

conventionally identified as Bronze Age funerary monuments in fact overlies and cuts into a slight linear causeway, part of a network observable in various parts of the moor which local oral information identified as a First World War tramway (**fig 38**). The observed stratigraphy appeared topsy-turvy, yet it must be correct; the cairns now visible result from piecemeal excavation during the 1930s and 1940s and the rebuildings that resulted (Everson 1989b).

A stratigraphic relationship can contain significantly more information still. In West Lindsey, earthworks at Legsby show an enclosed chapel site inserted into the end of a furlong of ridge-and-furrow. But they also show the arable lands continuing to be ploughed to a new shorter length against the inserted boundary. The chapel is therefore both later than and contemporary with that arable (Everson *et al* 1991, 126 and see also 63–4). The observation is critical for a site otherwise effectively undocumented. In a similar example at Ingram (Northumberland) a field of broad ridge-and-furrow is overlain by a wall (NU 034 136) which now marks the parish boundary with Alnham; on the north side at least, the ridges seem to have continued in use after the construction of the wall.

A further tool of analysis is what may be called *horizontal stratigraphy*. This is most simply observable in circumstances where the core of a site has a formal coherence or completeness and there are other elements of a different plan form, of a different scale, lying at a different angle that manifests itself in some form of disjunction, any of which individually or together may suggest that they are additional to and therefore later than the core. Examples abound in medieval village and urban studies, where such essentially morphological analysis has been highly developed (Conzen 1969; Roberts 1987). It can be applied to existing or historically mapped plan forms, to recorded earthworks and to a combination of the two. Simple cases might lie in the contrast of regular and irregular blocks of village properties, perhaps with a regular element added to an earlier irregular nucleus, or *vice versa* (eg Everson *et al* 1991, 211–3). The observation, like vertical stratigraphy, may be relevant in the simplest fieldwork situation, yet provide critical information. On Hadrian's Wall the traditional view is that the Vallum is later than the forts, except Carrawburgh (Johnson 1989, 57); yet observation of the horizontal stratigraphy at several sites suggests a more complex relationship, with the surveying and construction of the Vallum chronologically interleaved with the laying out and construction of the forts (eg Bowden and Blood 1991, 29–30). A further example can be seen at Church Pits, Orcheston (Wiltshire) (see **fig 36**), where some of the fields to the east are on a slightly different alignment from those in the main block, suggesting a chronological dislocation.

A related consideration is the *congruence* or *coherence* of remains either within themselves or with other features in the landscape. It may indicate the associations of a site or specific features and therefore their date. This may be a matter of function within a system, like the header reservoir for the formal water gardens at Old Madeley Manor (Staffordshire) (SJ 7730 4229). A different example is provided by the abandoned water features surrounding the late fourteenth-century castle at Bodiam (East Sussex) (Everson 1996b) (see **fig 49**). In form they might be of any medieval or later date, but they lie so conformably with the castle itself, and can be understood as working so successfully in manipulating access to it, that they may reasonably be taken to be contemporary with the well-documented standing structure; this is bolstered by the absence of any evidence or context for their later addition. At Tupholme Abbey (Lincolnshire), it is the coherence of the whole pattern of rectangular embanked closes representing garden compartments with the square of the former monastic cloister (converted into a post-Dissolution house) that carries the conviction that the visible earthworks indeed represent that post-Dissolution conversion rather than monastic remains (Everson 1996a).

Quite minor *anomalies* in the detail of field evidence can be a further clue to aid interpretation, both of chronology and identification. At Kettleby near Brigg (Lincolnshire), a moated manor site retains earthwork traces of a small formal garden within it (Everson *et al* 1991, 70–1). The fact that this fails either to achieve a good geometric layout or to sit tightly with the moat shows that the formal garden remains were added, together with a new house of perhaps early seventeenth-century date, into the pre-existing irregular-shaped moat, rather than being a contemporary original feature. Similarly, among the prehistoric field remains of the moorlands of the Derbyshire Peak District, anomalies in Bronze Age field clearance banks in the form, for example, of a curving arc within an otherwise straight alignment reveal the sites of contemporary settlement remains, that have long been thought to be absent from the area (Ainsworth forthcoming). This in turn sets a new framework for thought which can be tested by other means, such as excavation.

Wider considerations of *context* may also have a contribution to make to interpretation that calls for the fieldworker to look beyond the immediate remains under survey. At High Stones on the western Pennine fringe of Derbyshire, for example, a small rectangular earthwork which might be a medieval or later farmstead has also been interpreted as a Roman fortlet (Hart 1981, 90). There is nothing sufficiently distinctive in the site itself to afford a clinching argument between the two, but the surrounding landscape shows no signs of abandoned field boundaries such as might be expected to accompany a farmstead. This absence makes the Roman military interpretation more likely.

Other wider land-use circumstances may establish a *terminus ante quem* of abandonment and perhaps its cause. The most commonly encountered may be eighteenth- and nineteenth-century emparking. Village earthworks within parkland, as at Wimpole Hall (Cambridgeshire) (RCHME 1968, 210–29) or Nuneham Courtenay (Oxfordshire) (Batey 1968), are likely to have been abandoned in advance of the creation of parkland. Beresford (1971, 198–203) affords a classic study of the process at Milton Abbas (Dorset). Exceptions may occur in cases, as suggested at Shugborough (Staffordshire: SJ 990 220), where for a period some form of rural settlement formed part of the parkland design in the manner of a *ferme ornée*. Not only settlement remains may be affected, as shown at Attingham Park (Everson and Stamper 1987).

It would be wrong to give the impression that each of these factors commonly and individually give a clear-cut basis for interpretation. Each is frequently present in the process of field recording to some degree and needs to be sought out and recognised as part of a truly archaeological approach to material information. But most frequently it is a combination of observations that is at play, and a probability of interpretation that has to be teased out, giving due weight to each factor.

Form and Function

Morphological categorisation is often seen as the principal tool of field archaeology. It is indeed often the most direct method; but the argument-by-analogy implicit in it is in practice a relatively weak one compared with site-specific stratigraphic and associative observations, and it is the source of many misinterpretations and false trails. A large mound like The Mount within the site of Lewes Priory (Sussex) or a smaller one at Kinderton (Cheshire) have both been identified as possible castle mottes on general morphological grounds (King 1983, 69). That at Kinderton, a truncated pyramid in form, has been recognised as a garden mount, initially because of its shape and secondly from survey of associated earthworks, showing its relationship with a lost post-medieval house; at Lewes, it is its setting centrally within a square plot combined with its place in a sequence of land use that make it clear that the Mount, though different in scale, is also a prospect mound of early post-medieval date (**fig 39**). These examples emphasise that field archaeology is not a process of collecting discrete items capable of pigeon-holing in record systems, but of recording and understanding fragments of landscape of diverse sizes.

Nevertheless, details of form and function do contribute critically to understanding.

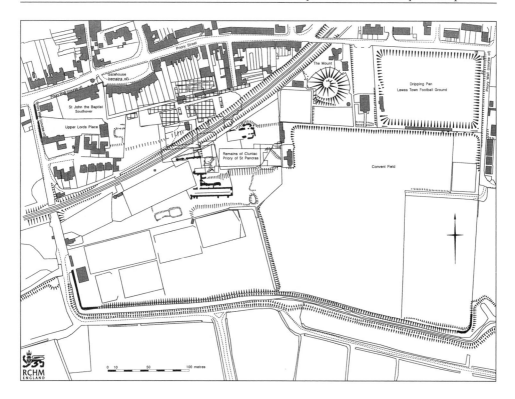

39   *The Mount lies within the former precinct of Lewes Priory (Sussex), which is still clearly picked out by the street pattern following its boundary on the north, east and west. It stands centrally within a square plot fossilised in modern property boundaries. To its east, a second compartment — 'the Dripping Pan' — is itself surrounded by massive earthwork terraces. These post-date the dissolution of the monasteries. These are the most obvious surviving components of a formal garden associated with the house called Lords Place, which formerly stood to the south of St John the Baptist, Southover (reproduced from the Ordnance Survey mapping with permission from Her Majesty's Stationery Office © Crown Copyright. RCHME Licence GD03133G/4/98).*

Ditched round mounds superficially not greatly different from the two just mentioned can with confidence be interpreted as windmill mounds, if they have a causewayed break in the ditch leading to a ramp up the mound, and especially with a hollow or disturbance in the top, as at Wimpole (Cambridgeshire) (RCHME 1968, 225–6) (**figs 40, 41**). The motte at Huntingdon castle (TL 2409 7145) has precisely these details because it was converted into a windmill mound. The linear feature in parkland at Attingham Park (mentioned above), shown to be post-medieval by its relationship with ridge-and-furrow and made redundant by inclusion in an early nineteenth-century extension to the park, in form is a broad flat-bottomed ditch with an equal flanking embankment to either side, ruler straight and dead level. This engineered form points to a function as a canal, albeit unfinished in this case (Everson and Stamper 1987).

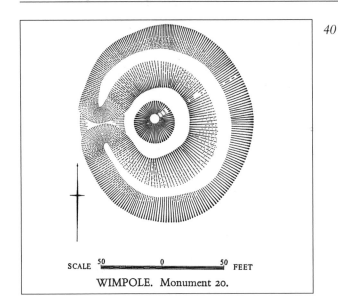

SCALE 50 0 50 FEET

WIMPOLE. Monument 20.

40   *Windmill mound,*
      Wimpole
      (Cambridgeshire)
      (RCHME 1968, 225).

It is sometimes said that interpretation of extensive *complex* earthworks is the most difficult problem in fieldwork. The grasp of such situations may be difficult and the skill in articulating resulting understanding may be considerable, but the presence of relationships and associated information at least gives something to work with. A different and often more severe difficulty is actually found in assigning function and date to very *simple* forms of field monuments, because their very simplicity gives few clues. A small circular earthwork, especially when found isolated, might be a prehistoric hut circle, a sheep-fold, a sow kiln for burning limestone, a tree-planting ring, a stack-stand, a charcoal pitstead or any of a number of other features. Without a context or other information, there may be no way of deciding definitively, from form alone.

Sites which are unique or rare in any respect also present particular problems. A feature which appears to be unique, such as the stone avenue extending from the entrance of Maiden Castle, Swaledale (North Yorkshire) (Bowden and Blood forthcoming), is by definition, not explicable or datable by analogy.

Topographical location

Topographical location is a further factor inherent in every site. The preference of pre-Roman settlements on upland moors for locations on sloping shelves of land with deeper soils and avoiding north-facing aspects may help to confirm a new identification or condemn a doubtful one. The established common preference of early burial monuments for skyline locations or grouping around the heads of valleys can be a factor in interpretation and analysis of those monument types.

A phenomenological approach to landscape must also be considered. Natural features may have taken on a significance over and above their 'functional' use for past societies (Tilley 1994). At Cautley in the Howgill Fells (Cumbria) a late prehistoric enclosed settlement has been placed, so that it is intervisible with a (possibly earlier) round cairn, but

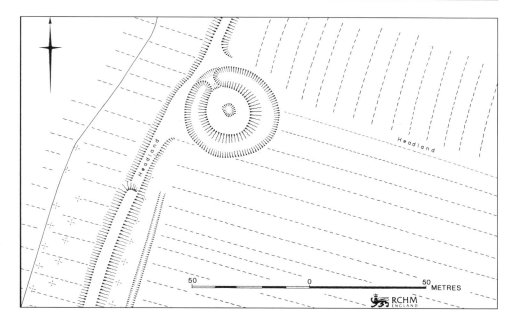

41   *Windmill mound, Wimpole, shown as a component in a wider landscape, demonstrating that it is overlying ridge-and-furrow: extract from field survey drawing, original scale 1:1000.*

it also has an optimum view of the spectacular waterfall of Cautley Spout, tumbling over the dark, lowering mass of Cautley Crags (**plate 9**). This somewhat tenuous relationship is perhaps given more concrete expression by the existence of a well-made track leading from the settlement's western entrance directly towards the Spout and apparently with no other destination beyond the confines of this enclosed valley (Bowden 1996b, 3).

Aspects of visibility and intervisibility, though mainly discussed in a prehistoric context, are factors in ritual and designed landscapes of all periods up to and including the present. An example illustrating both strands is offered by the earthworks at Stanwick (North Yorkshire), where the extensive views presented by the Iron Age ramparts were appreciated by the eighteenth-century park designers who laid out carriage drives, paths and viewing points along their crests (Bowden 1998). A consideration of form and topographic location *in combination* is also particularly rewarding: it led to the re-interpretation of the supposed round cairn on Barron's Pike (Cumbria) as a Roman signal station (Topping 1987).

Soils and geology are also factors inherent in each location. These have crucial relevance to monuments directly related to the exploitation of natural resources by quarrying or mining, where any failure to gain a secure grasp on such matters can lead both to crass specific error and wider ill-informed interpretation. But that is by no means the limit. Prehistoric field clearance in upland zones will clearly give rise to more marked field remains in areas with naturally heavy 'clitter' or surface stone than in those with less, yet it may be the latter that would have formed the primary targets for early cultivation

42   *Almondbury (West Yorkshire): an Iron Age hillfort with superimposed medieval castle.*
Features around the lower slopes which bear a superficial resemblance to eroded ramparts
are of geological origin.

because of their easier preparation. The 'best archaeology' may therefore not reflect the core or longest lived early exploitation, but more marginal locations.

Fundamental interpretations may depend on the ability to distinguish between artificial and natural features, such as the slumping of clay deposits on a hillside and artificial terraces or lynchets (RCHME 1982, 47, 49), or to recognise that pits visible on the surface over limestone (especially at the junction with a less readily soluble rock) will probably be natural sinks or swallow holes, where the rock has been dissolved by water, as in the Roman camps at Greenlee Lough (Northumberland) and Malham (North Yorkshire) (Welfare and Swan 1995, 104–5, 143–5). Some geologies outcrop in a regular fashion that has led to their erroneous identification as hillfort defences, as at Upper Coscombe (Gloucestershire) (RCHME 1976, xxxi–iv; Wilson 1982, 145); alleged outer defences to the hillfort at Almondbury (West Yorkshire: SE 152 140) are similar geological benching (**fig 42**). Conversely, apparently natural formations may have archaeological implications. At Ribblehead (North Yorkshire: SD 765 785) limestone pavement is crossed by field walls, now fragmentary remains (**fig 43**); as there is little advantage in sub-dividing areas of bare limestone, a possible conclusion is that the walls were built at a time when the rock was turf-covered and that the exposure of the pavement is an ecofact of over-grazing (and see Higham 1996, 58).

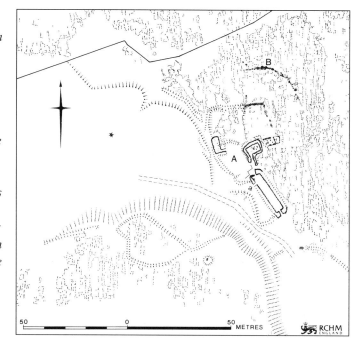

43 Ribblehead (North Yorkshire): extract from field survey drawing, original scale 1:1000. The settlement at 'A' has been dated to the Viking period by excavation. The feature marked 'B' is one of a series of walls crossing limestone pavement. Its appearance has been exaggerated on plan for the sake of clarity — in reality these features are very slight.

Other classes of evidence

Most of the field observations discussed above in themselves give *relative* rather than *absolute* dating. This is usually as far as the field evidence will go. It may do no more than set a framework for the next level of questions or for alternative forms of investigation. It is accepted by those practising non-excavational field archaeology in the British tradition that analytical field survey has limitations as well as strengths. Field survey is, nevertheless, valid in its own right and not a mere preliminary or second-best to excavation.

Other forms of field evidence can and should be brought into play to elaborate understanding, wherever they are available and relevant. The potential range is very great. It includes material finds from the surface of earthworks or partial ploughing. As always, interpretation should seek to avoid oversimplistic conclusions. Roman pottery found in molehills on a moated site does not make that a Roman earthwork; it may more probably be sited over and cut through a buried site of that date. Easily recognised and readily identified material finds can also bias the recorded information about a site. Human skeletal remains are finds of a type especially persistent in local folk memory; in the medieval period at least they are markers of very limited and distinctive categories of site with burial rights and since one of these is monastic sites, report of burials can contribute to the identification of a site of that category (Everson 1989a, 61).

Items of carved architectural stonework, found loose or reused, are similarly distinctive markers. Since they are intrinsically datable, they may offer information about the form of lost buildings; exceptionally in combination with earthwork and other evidence they may allow the recovery in detailed reconstruction of a hitherto completely lost building (Everson *et al* forthcoming; Harding and Lewis 1997, 35–6, 38). Standing buildings can

44 *Haltonchesters (Northumberland): field survey plan, original scale 1:500. At A and B are the earthworks of trenches dug in 1957, while earthworks at C correlate well with an archive trench plan of the unpublished excavations of 1960–61.*

have surprising light thrown on them through their relationship to earthwork sites and landscapes and can contribute in their turn to archaeological site interpretation (see Chapter 10).

Vegetational evidence can be informative even outside the obvious world of parks and gardens, and the datable potential of introduced species within them, like the *Tilia europaea* at Gawsworth (see p150) — sometimes in improbable circumstances. At the former gunpowder manufacturing works at Oare near Faversham, the proof range was lined with wellingtonias (*Sequoiadendron giganteum*), the field evidence for which is the lines of stumps recorded in site survey. Since the species was not introduced to Britain until 1853, this evidence may indicate when the facility for this form of proofing on site was introduced at the Oare factory (Cocroft 1994). Knowledge of their felling date and a tree-ring count could refine that assessment. Less specifically, undated earthworks lying within the boundary of ancient managed woodland and cut into by old coppice stools are certainly likely to be of pre-medieval date.

Even without any of these other forms of field evidence, relative dating does not stand alone. It defines, however generally, a period within which a morphological form can be identified as distinctive. A ditched long mound overlain and ploughed flat by ridge-and-furrow cultivation is possibly a long barrow, whereas if it overlies ridge-and-furrow, it is probably a pillow mound.

Excavation evidence

Depending on their date and scale, information from past excavations may present problems of various sorts. The most direct is their specific location. It may be possible to solve this from the field evidence of the outlines of backfilled trenches identifiable as the most tenuous, and latest, scarps within a site's earthworks. In favourable circumstances, as at Haltonchesters (Northumberland), this evidence can relocate many disparate investigations spread over many years (Blood and Bowden 1990) (**fig 44**). On Stanton Moor (Derbyshire) identification of the location and impact of piecemeal excavations provided the basis for correlation with published accounts and with deposited finds and defined the extent of surviving undisturbed prehistoric deposits (Everson 1989b) (see **fig 38**).

Other problems of integrating excavated evidence lie in their scale (typically small in relation to a whole site), their often narrow focus both physically and conceptually, and their complexity of details which, depending on the excavator, may simply be reported as a heap of uninterpreted information. Terminology for finds and phasing may be different from that now current and they may anyway be misinterpreted, so (like any other documentary source) it is necessary to understand the context and circumstances of production (Barrett 1987). Perhaps the most fundamental obstacle to integration are the preconceptions of the excavators, which may almost inevitably be cast in the framework of thinking of their time (eg Cocroft *et al* 1989).

It is, however, instructive to observe the results of survey tested by excavation; at the medieval hospital of Brough St Giles (North Yorkshire) (Cardwell 1995), a stony bank interpreted as a wall footing during earthwork survey proved on excavation to be upcast from robbing of the wall, and therefore offset from the actual wall line by approximately 1m — a salutary lesson.

Documentary evidence

Historical evidence presents its own problems of use and integration (see above, pp31–7), so much so that it has been said that documents and field evidence run on parallel tracks, never meeting. This underlines the point that historical documentation was rarely created for the uses to which we now attempt to put it. There is therefore a duty of selection and discrimination; a dump of everything that can be drawn together is neither necessary nor helpful. A desirable objective is to set a site and the understanding derived from its field remains in an intelligible context, so that at least its potential will be recognised by interested parties external to the fieldwork process. At Low Ham (Somerset), for instance, the dimensions of a proposed garden from a contemporary letter can be used, the modern earthwork survey again providing the metrically accurate basis and key (**fig 45**) (see p147).

Historical information is extremely variable from one site to another, even of the same category. It may be necessary to delve a little to acquire enough to indicate the context. This is particularly true when the field remains themselves bring forward an interpretation or insight that is unforeseen, novel, problematic or especially worthwhile. Working through the consequences may then be necessary (eg Everson 1988), or finding at least a minimum of documentation, such as a monumental inscription or even a romantic tale, may be just enough to convince (eg Everson *et al* 1991, 63; 184–5) (**fig 46**).

Sensible interpretation may depend on taking a more oblique view of the documentation. The small parish of Wheathill (Shropshire), for example, had been taken, improbably, to contain four or five named deserted villages logged as individual monuments. Changing focus, to view that parish's settlement pattern at large, showed that

45   *Low Ham (Somerset): extract from earthwork survey overlain with the position of garden features, using measurements recorded in a letter of 1690 (Wilson-North 1998).*

46 The site of the bishop's moated palace at Stow (Lincolnshire): this was the setting for Giraldus Cambrensis's tale of St Hugh's pet swan. Giraldus knew the site personally and the flight of the resident flock of swans in the face of the marvellous newcomer of the tale may accurately reflect one function of the 'fishponds' as a swannery.

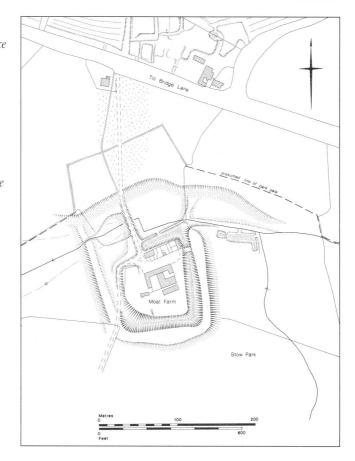

each of these was no more than a single farmstead or small hamlet in a dispersed pattern that was probably as old as the eleventh century (Everson and Wilson-North 1993). At Shenley Brook End (Buckinghamshire), too, a focus on a documented, supposedly lost place-name of Westbury caused the settlement earthworks to be forced into the straight-jacket of categorisation as a DMV, when in reality they were part of a dispersed pattern (Everson 1995a).

Pitfalls and opportunities

Pitfalls in interpretation have already been noted by the various examples of misinterpretation or revised interpretation. This is no surprise or matter for concern in a subject that is inherently dynamic. One of the attractions of field archaeology is precisely the way it affords many opportunities for making interesting new perceptions based on the re-examination of its original evidence in the form of field monuments.

More fundamentally too, archaeology as a subject is continuously shifting and redefining its framework of thought, so that even familiar sites are viewed in different ways and new categories are brought into consideration. This is a natural part of its challenge and interest. The hillfort is one class of monument which is very familiar, but

47   *Cord rig surviving as earthworks in the foreground: Carshope, Upper Coquetdale (Northumberland).*

substantial re-interpretations of the place of hillforts in Iron Age society have been put forward (eg Hill 1995). Cord rig (very narrow late prehistoric ridge-and-furrow, **fig 47**) was an entirely new class of monument, the recognition of which from 1981 has revolutionised the analysis of upland economies (Topping 1989).

As a whole, archaeology does not operate within a framework that believes that it is searching out unique and fixed historical truths. Perceptions of the same place and the same evidence legitimately change (Taylor 1989a) and will continue to do so. This, philosophically, is why an intrinsic activity of the discipline is the creation and curation of records, to standards that allow others — now or in the future — to reinterpret the evidence in different ways.

1   *View along the Whin Sill (Northumberland) (1986): Hadrian's Wall runs along the crest. Milecastle 39 (Castle Nick) can be seen in the middle foreground; the Roman Military Way follows a sinuous course along the dip slope.*

2   *Hanging Lund, Mallerstang (Cumbria): typically, farmhouses in this area occupy terraces low on the valley sides, adjacent to water sources and avoiding north-facing situations. The name of this farm is Scandinavian in origin. Such a site is likely to have been occupied throughout the human occupation of the area.*

3 *Ingleborough (North Yorkshire) from Ribblehead.*

4 *'Celtic' fields overlain by a later enclosure and trackways on Burderop Down (Wiltshire): good light conditions are vital for fieldwork and aerial photography alike.*

5   *Stafford Castle: aerial photograph showing the survey problems presented by the topography and vegetation cover of the site. To ensure that detail points could be placed throughout the site a complex control scheme, comprising a ring traverse and linking closed traverses, was observed with a 'total station' (see Fig 19).*

6   *(opposite, top) Plane-tabling: using a self-reducing alidade to take a primary distance measurement with a surveying staff.*

7   *(opposite, bottom) Plane-tabling: plotting subsidiary measurements from the staff point.*

8   *(above) Plane-tabling: the self-reducing alidade is a flexible instrument which automatically converts slope distance to horizontal distance; it is ideal for surveying sites with severe height differences.*

9   *Cautley (Cumbria): the settlement enclosure can be seen in the middle foreground, while the cairn is just visible on rising ground in the middle distance. The Spout is prominent in the background with Cautley Crag rising to the left.*

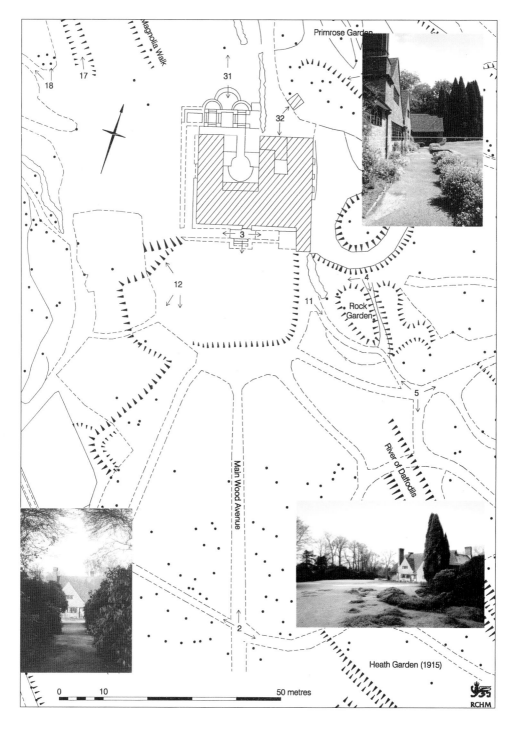

Primrose Garden

Magnolia Walk

18

17

31

32

12

11

3

4

Rock Garden

5

Main Wood Avenue

River of Daffodils

2

Heath Garden (1915)

0   10   50 metres

RCHM

10   *Views of Gertrude Jekyll's house and garden at Munstead Wood (Surrey) related to the survey plan. Taken from positions 2, 3 and 5 on the plan.*

11   HMS Victory *(Portsmouth, Hampshire) photographed with a telephoto lens.*

12   *Long Meg and Her Daughters (Cumbria): infra-red photograph showing the ditched enclosure alongside the stone circle and, unusually for an aerial photograph, proving that the ditch is earlier, as the stones can be seen to be slipping into it (Soffe and Clare 1988).*

13   *Parchmarks at Lockeridge (Wiltshire).*

14   *Rollright Heath Farm (Oxfordshire): 'banjo' enclosure.*

15   *Herberowe Bank, Lower Heyford (Oxfordshire): large prehistoric enclosure.*

16   *Magnetometer in use (by permission of GSB Prospection).*

17   *Brean Down (Somerset): Bronze Age houses in sand cliff deposits.*

18   *Bridgwater Bay (Somerset): intertidal landscape with wooden fish weirs.*

19   *Minehead (Somerset): recording stone fish weirs with GPS.*

20   *Hodgson's High Level, Nenthead lead mines (Cumbria): the lodging shop, where miners lived during the week, away from home and family.*

21   *Pendennis Castle (Cornwall) from the air. The headland is a multi-layered military landscape, with remains of a prehistoric fort, an artillery blockhouse of the 1530s, the large circular Henrician fort, Elizabethan bastion defences, Civil War earthworks and Second World War gun emplacements. Buildings and earthworks clearly form complementary parts of this landscape.*

Holne Moor

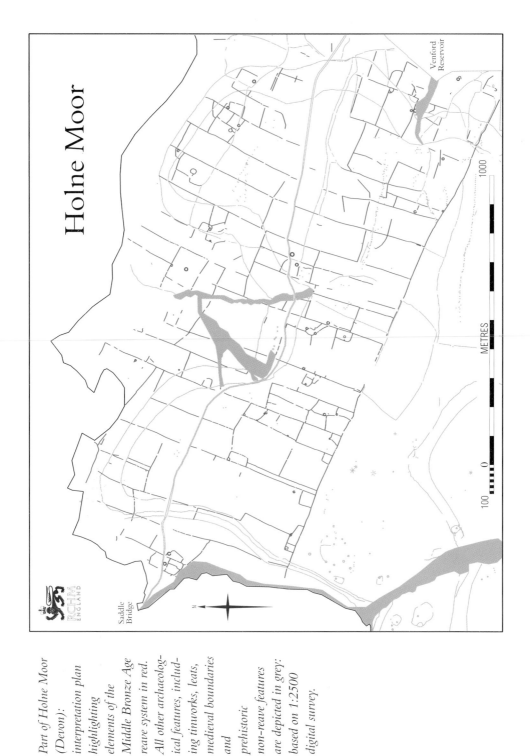

Venford
Reservoir

Saddle
Bridge

100   0   METRES   1000

22   Part of Holne Moor
      (Devon):
      interpretation plan
      highlighting
      elements of the
      Middle Bronze Age
      reave system in red.
      All other archaeolog-
      ical features, includ-
      ing tinworks, leats,
      medieval boundaries
      and
      prehistoric
      non-reave features
      are depicted in grey:
      based on 1:2500
      digital survey.

6 Ground photography

Ground photographs can be taken for a number of purposes in connection with the investigation of archaeological sites and landscapes. They may be taken purely to record specific features such as buildings, architectural details or finds, or to illustrate the broader context of a site, aiding the visualisation of the site in its landscape by a record user (**fig 48**). They can be used to illustrate publications, particularly where their use supplements the interpretation of significant visual aspects of a site; a series of photographs of Bodiam (East Sussex), for instance, lends immediacy to an interpretation of that landscape which emphasises a particular approach route to the castle (Everson 1996b) (**fig 49**). New photography can also reproduce an earlier viewpoint, such as a topographical drawing; this can show how the drawing has emphasised certain elements in the landscape, or how the landscape has changed, for instance (see **fig 11**).

The scope of subject matter in field archaeology offers the photographer a diverse and challenging role in record making, although earthwork sites are notoriously difficult to photograph. For general advice on photography, see Langford (1997a and b) and for the photography of standing historic buildings, see Buchanan (1983).

Equipment

Camera

The choice of camera will depend on the accessibility of the site to be recorded, the budget available and the preferences of the individual photographer.

Large-format cameras will always give the best quality photographs due to the amount of information that can be recorded on the large piece of film used. These cameras also allow for the correction of distortions that may be introduced in the production of the photograph. Large cameras, however, are not suitable for remote areas or confined spaces; they must be used with a tripod and are problematical in high winds. 135mm cameras offer the compact portability required for many sites, but any damage to the negative or transparency produced will be magnified more highly by enlargement. This format also offers an extensive range of different film types and relatively cheap lens options which allow for variable viewpoints. The roll film camera, either 120, 220 or more rarely 70mm, bridges the gap between the large-format camera and the 135mm. The choice of film and lens is also comparable to the smaller format.

Digital cameras do not yet match the quality of the silver image and are very expensive. Electronic images are not archivally stable because of the rapidly changing technology for capture and reproduction, and because of the susceptibility of the storage medium to damage or loss of information.

48   *Slate mines, Honister (Cumbria): landscape photographs complement plans, particularly in areas of dramatic relief.*

Tripod

The necessity of using a tripod for large-format photography can be regarded, to some extent, as an advantage. The process of choosing where to position the tripod forces a more considered approach to choosing a viewpoint. This is a desirable preparation before exposure on any format and, along with the steadiness achieved, will enhance any image produced. Conversely, the spontaneity of use with hand-held cameras will in many instances produce an image which would not be possible using a tripod, such as momentary sunlight on an object or a particular cloud formation.

Film

The choice of film will depend very much on the final product required. Black-and-white film will be suitable for prints. If mechanical reproduction is intended, a monochrome image will reproduce more cheaply than a colour image. The silver particle image of a black-and-white emulsion has proven longevity (given correct processing) which is a primary consideration for archiving.

If the subject matter has subtle and significant changes of colour which would impact on the image produced, then obviously colour film should be used. Colour transparencies are least likely to create distortions in the colour of the image produced due to the production of only one set of dyes in the emulsion, as opposed to two sets in a negative/positive process; they are also the most practical method of illustrating lectures.

49   *Bodiam Castle (East Sussex) from the north-east.*

If display or reproduction of many copies is required, then a colour negative film will allow for a wider choice of options. Modern mechanical processes will allow for either medium, negative or transparency, to be submitted for scanning into a computer.

Modern colour emulsions are said, by their manufacturers, to be stable mediums, but this is not yet proven. To ensure permanency, black-and-white images should be created in addition to any colour records.

Using infra-red emulsions, in either a scientific or creative way, may be considered to enhance the image (see **plate 12**). Infra-red films are available in colour and black-and-white emulsions. The sensitivity of the emulsion to wave lengths of light not visible to the human eye may show additional evidence when reproduced in a visible form; they can also be used to make an unusual and eye-catching image. Exposure of these emulsions is challenging and the results somewhat unpredictable.

When to photograph

Choosing the right time to make your record will be a process of gathering information; this may be done visually whilst at the site, but, in many cases, the gathering of information about the orientation of the site and the subject matter before visiting will produce a greater likelihood of successful photography. In some instances, it may be possible to make a reconnaissance of the site which will allow for a good estimation of the best time for any particular photograph to be taken. Consulting maps or using the knowledge of those familiar with the site is the next best thing.

50   *The Vallum at Cawfields (Northumberland) with Hadrian's Wall emerging from behind Cawfields Quarry on the left and running along the crest of the crags.*

Time of Year

The longer hours of daylight in the summer months may give opportunities for the right direction of light, but often only the clarity and low level of winter sunlight will provide the depth of shadow needed. Other problems, such as vegetation concealing parts of the site, will be the same for surveyors and photographers alike.

Time of Day

The sun is the influencing factor for the majority of photographs; we use its light to give shape by means of highlight and shadow to the objects we record. The position of the light, and the shadows created by the upstanding structures or indentations in the ground, are critical to the success of the photograph.

The most suitable time of day will depend on the orientation of the subject matter and what we want to show or, in some cases, subdue in a scene. A visit can be planned to coincide with the position of the sun in relation to our subject matter. Beware the unwanted shadow from nearby structures, trees or even the photographer, particularly in winter months.

Weather

This is closely connected to timing considerations; it is rarely right. The long calm periods of sunlight on a summer day allow for maximum periods of work time, but a clear blue sky lacks the vigour and interest of fast-moving cloud produced on a windy day (**figs 50, 51**). The choice of lighting available from changeable weather will provide most options on site.

51   *Grimes Graves (Norfolk): low viewpoint and dramatic lighting emphasise the texture of the earthworks.*

Artificial lighting

There are occasions when the optimum choice of time is just not practical and the use of artificial light is the only choice. Artificial light can be used to assist the natural light available by lightening shadows to reveal detail which would otherwise be lost in the photographic process. This 'fill-in' light can only be used where the subject matter is relatively small in size (eg standing stones, rock art), due to the intensity of light required to compete with daylight. Electronic flash is the most practical solution at most sites. The short duration of the flash light will have the most effect upon the shadow areas of a scene and can be controlled by means of the lens aperture, with shutter speed making little or no difference to the flash exposure. The daylight portion of our exposure will be controlled by the shutter speed used in conjunction with the aperture selected for the flash exposure.

At other times, artificial light will be used, exclusively, to light the subject either because natural light is insufficient (**fig 52**) or, alternatively, not suitable for the effect required; for example, an oblique artificial light may be used to provide highlights and shadows to an area to bring out shape and form not visible under a natural flat light.

Enhancing the image

It is possible to enhance an image, usually by increasing the contrast between different parts of a scene using filters.

52   *Medieval carvings and later graffiti in Royston Cave (Cambridgeshire): an example of a photograph taken with exclusively artificial light.*

A greater number of filters can be used in black-and-white photography, where tones are compressed and the emulsion's sensitivity to particular colours produces results unfamiliar to the eye. Blues in particular are prone to reproduce too lightly in black-and-white photographs. A general rule for using a filter is that it will lighten tones of the same colour as the filter and darken tones of an opposite colour. Any coloured filter used with colour film will, of course, affect the colour of the image produced.

A polarising filter does not affect the colour rendition of a scene, but can increase the contrast by eliminating unwanted reflection and is suitable for use on colour and monochrome emulsions.

Some enhancement of the image can take place after exposure. Again, contrast may be altered by adjusting the development time given to the film. This needs to be considered at exposure stage by either increasing exposure and reducing the development time for reducing the contrast, or reducing exposure and increasing development time to enhance contrast. Special developers can be used to control the granularity of the image during development for maximum clarity of the image. Black-and-white images offer more opportunities of manipulation. Colour images do not respond as well to changes in development time because of the way that dyes are produced in the emulsion.

Viewpoint

The viewpoint chosen to photograph will have profound effects on the resultant image (see Buchanan 1983, 37). For record photographs it is important to record a 'truthful' image. This means an image free of distortion introduced in the camera. In general, a

53   *The Devil's Dyke (Cambridgeshire): low viewpoint showing the profile of the ditch against the skyline. The human figures give a good impression of the scale of the earthwork.*

viewpoint farther away from the subject and the use of standard or slightly telephoto lens will produce a more natural or 'truthful' image than one taken close to the subject using a wide-angle lens. The distant viewpoint will show more accurately the relationship between the component parts of a subject. Distances between different objects are more accurately captured using a standard lens. Wide-angle lenses have inherent problems of distortion which are magnified if used carelessly, for example by pointing the camera upwards to include the top of a structure.

When dealing with rectangular structures, a viewpoint from an angle to the subject will record more information than a view straight on to it because, from an angled view, the shape and proportions are evident.

A further consideration must be the height from which the subject is viewed. High viewpoints are helpful in explaining the relationship of a complex of structures, or their remains. The practical difficulties of obtaining a viewpoint high enough to show large sites will frequently require the use of scaffolding, a hydraulic platform or even suspending the camera from a balloon. Many sites may only be recorded in their entirety by aerial photography (see Chapter 7). Low viewpoints can be used to remove a distracting background, to skyline an earthwork (**fig 53**) or to emphasise the height of the subject, if truthful reproduction of scale is not of primary importance.

A static viewpoint can be used to show a subject under different lighting conditions, but it is often important to use relational viewpoints to record a site. By relating photographs with either the viewpoint of previous and or sequential photographs, or by including an object or part of a scene in the whole series of photographs, it is in effect possible to walk around the site and observe features from different directions (**plate 10**).

Depth of field

Another method of separating subject matter from its background is to use a shallow depth of field which will throw surrounding features out of focus; this is most easily achieved by using telephoto lenses and wide apertures.

Scale

It is difficult to interpret from a photograph the dimensions of any particular object, though the comparative sizes of different features will be apparent. We can overcome this problem by introducing into the photograph an object of known scale. This object must be proportional to the size of the object being viewed.

It is necessary to introduce a scale into a scene, then standard objects should be adopted, in metric measurements. With ranging rods a consistency of approach should be adopted, so that rods are placed always on the same side of the scene or that the red end of a rod is always on the left (this latter point easily remembered as political orientation). For large sites, the placing of a human figure will often be the most credible means of adding scale (and interest) (see **fig 53**).

Making notes

The most brilliant photograph is useless without a record of where and what the image is. Making notes of what has been captured on film is vital if the photography is to be of use to future generations. The best time to make this record is at the time of exposure at the site. The information may be written down or recorded electronically. Any caption should record at least:

 (a) The subject matter
 (b) Its location (this may be the site itself or detail within the site)
 (c) Viewpoint (if building or landscape)
 (d) Date of photography.

It must be emphasised that this represents a minimum requirement. Ideally the surveyor should relate the photographs more intimately to the other elements of the record, by making them physically part of 'component sheets' (see Waltham Abbey) or by marking the location and direction-of-view of the photographs on a version of the survey drawing as a key to the photography, as was done in reproducing the viewpoints of Gertrude Jekyll's own photography of her garden at Munstead Wood (Surrey) (**plate 10**).

Storage

Taking the photograph and producing the print or transparency is only part of making the record. Suitable methods of storage need to be adopted if the product is to be a real asset in the future (see Chapter 12).

7 Aerial survey

History and background

The history and development of aerial photography for archaeology go hand-in-hand with the development of the aeroplane and the camera. Before 'heavier than air' aircraft were viable, it was only balloons that allowed photographers to look down and record what they saw below. Stonehenge, photographed by Lieutenant PH Sharpe from a balloon (Capper 1907; Wilson 1982, 11), is one of the earliest of these photographs. The concepts and processes involved in discovering sites from the air were recognised before the First World War by OGS Crawford and JP Williams-Freeman; the latter is reported to have said that 'one ought to be a bird to be a field archaeologist' (Deuel 1969, xi). It was during the War, however, that the means of achieving this new perspective was realised, and immediately afterwards the potential for archaeology of photographing sites and landscapes from the air became a reality in Europe and the Middle East. The most influential of the pioneers was OGS Crawford who developed the practice of using aerial photographs for mapping and archaeological recording (Crawford 1924a and b; 1929; 1954). Crawford pursued a policy of collecting photographs from as many sources as possible, many of which are now in the English NMR. Others took more interest in flying and recording by photography, such as Squadron Leader Insall, the discoverer of Woodhenge (Cunnington 1927).

Between the wars there was a steady growth of aerial photography for archaeology throughout Britain and Europe. It was the British, French and German Empires which produced the opportunities for pioneering work; for examples see Poidebard (1934) in Syria, Baradez (1949) in north Africa, Wiegand (1920) in Sinai and Palestine, and Crawford and Keiller (1928) in England. Detailed accounts of the early history and development are available (Bradford 1957; Deuel 1969).

During the Second World War there was a dramatic and rapid development in aeroplane technology, as well as cameras and films. Coupled with these advances, and although working in a wartime environment, there were a number of trained archaeologists involved in air photo interpretation (Daniel 1986; Nesbit 1996). After the war, therefore, the climate in Britain was right for setting up an aerial photographic unit which included archaeological reconnaissance as one of its major tasks; this unit was founded in 1945 (St Joseph 1966) and it became formally constituted as the Cambridge University Committee for Air Photography (CUCAP) in 1949. Its contribution has been, and continues to be, invaluable in expanding our knowledge of the prehistoric, Roman, medieval, post-medieval and industrial periods (Darvill 1996; Frere and St Joseph 1983; Beresford and St Joseph 1979; Glasscock 1992; Hudson 1984).

Before, during and after the Second World War there was also a small select group of pilots who had a good knowledge of archaeological sites and of the potential of aerial photography. Apart from the work of the Cambridge unit in the 1940s, 1950s and 1960s, the independent (mostly self-funded) airborne archaeologists were recording archaeological sites, mainly those visible as cropmarks (Bradford 1957; Riley 1944). The publication of the RCHME's *A Matter of Time* (1960) helped to raise the awareness of the contribution that aerial photography could make to understanding England's archaeological and historical past, as well as highlighting the massive scale of destruction which had been going on in post-war Britain. For the potential of these disparate collections to be realised, a scheme for a national library of aerial photographs for England was proposed, to include all those photographs taken by (mainly independent) flyers, and based in the NMR (Hampton 1989). This national collection for England has to be seen as complementary to the Cambridge Collection which is also national, in the broader British sense. This collecting policy also spawned another proposal, which was to augment the locally based and therefore individual approach of the independent flyers with a nationally organised reconnaissance programme, which the RCHME began in 1967. Since then the RCHME's collection of aerial photographs has grown from a few thousand to over five million; this is the result of the last 30 years flying and the acquisition of the RAF's historic collection of verticals, taken immediately after the war (1946–8). Similar stimuli prompted national collections and reconnaissance programmes in Scotland and Wales (Bewley 1993). The growth of county and regionally based SMRs also attracted collections of both oblique and vertical aerial photographs.

Ten years after the creation of the RCHME's library the dry summers of 1975 and 1976 increased the need for national co-ordination of aerial reconnaissance. The drought conditions provoked a number of exceptional discoveries and the realisation that the current organisation and funding of aerial photography was not adequate. A group of interested parties, under the umbrella of the CBA, formed an Aerial Archaeology Committee which successfully lobbied the Department of the Environment to fund more independent, regionally-based flyers. This system continued under the DoE and subsequently English Heritage until 1986/7, when the responsibility was transferred to the RCHME (Bewley 1993), which now co-ordinates a national programme of reconnaissance using its own staff and the 'regional flyers' (as they have become known). Similar arrangements are in place for Scotland and Wales.

Although aerial survey (which includes reconnaissance and mapping) is a very cost-effective and relatively rapid method of discovering archaeological sites, it has limitations if used in isolation. These limitations include adverse weather, the difficulty of classifying and dating sites which have had no fieldwork, and the fact that many landscape types (eg woodland, marsh) are not amenable to aerial survey. Its potential, however, as one of the first stages in the survey of an area, to be enhanced by linkage with other survey techniques, is enormous.

In the face of huge changes to the present landscape (woodland planting, gravel extraction, intensive arable cultivation, suburban development), all of which have a destructive effect on archaeological sites and landscapes, aerial survey can provide the first level of information on which future requirements for survey, interpretation, management and protection can be built.

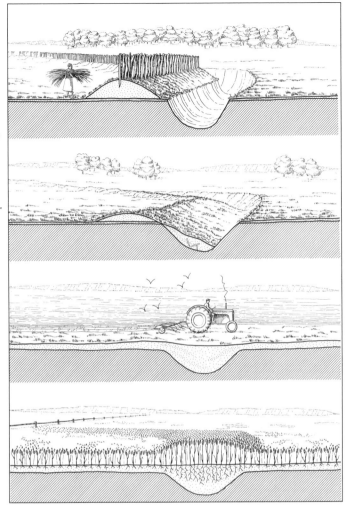

54　Diagram illustrating the formation of cropmarks over a levelled ditch. Conversely, a buried wall would result in stunting, rather than enhancement, of crop growth (illustration by Angela Grove © West Yorkshire Archaeology Service).

AERIAL RECONNAISSANCE

Archaeological sites visible as cropmarks (**fig 54**), soilmarks or earthworks can be photographed most effectively from the air (Riley 1987; 1996). The photographs are the first and most direct product of a flight, but aerial reconnaissance is a form of archaeological survey and the airborne perspective gives an extra dimension for assessing the archaeological potential of an area. By combining the results of many flights and photographs, a picture of past human landuse can be built up through consideration of the location, distribution and form of the sites and landscapes recorded.

Reconnaissance, as part of archaeological survey, uses an aircraft to cover the ground, rather than a vehicle or feet, and relies on the 'surveyor' to identify and record the archaeological sites and any other features seen. The methods for recording the survey include photography, written notes, annotated maps, a flight record form and more recently the use of GPS. GPS has enabled automatic recording of the route of the flight

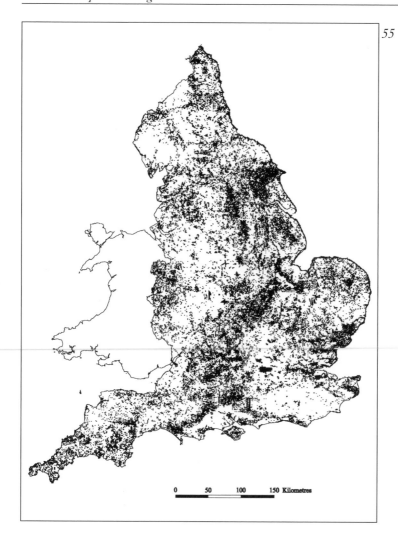

55   Distribution map of specialist oblique aerial photographs held by the RCHME, summer 1998.

0   50   100   150 Kilometres

and the points at which any photograph was taken (but see p110). One of the advantages of recording with GPS is that it provides a context for all the distribution plots of the photographs taken for any given area, or for surveys over a number of years.

In England, archaeological aerial photography has been going on for over 70 years and the distribution maps of photographs held by the RCHME reveal not only how much has been done, but also how much more there is to do (**fig 55**). With the information from the distribution maps, it is possible to see which areas have been surveyed from the air and how many times. This is analogous to fieldwalking, where it is important to record which ploughed fields have been 'walked', even if nothing has been found; so with aerial reconnaissance the area covered is as important as the photographs of new sites, and a lack of finds does not mean that sites do not exist. Aerial reconnaissance is perhaps the most cost-effective means of discovering new sites, as well as rapidly recording sites which have been known for many years.

Methodology

It is essential to be able to respond flexibly to the prevailing soil and weather conditions in any year. Therefore, despite the need for professional expertise in aerial photography, it is a technique which can be used flexibly and extensively by anyone wishing to learn more about their local archaeological and historical landscape. Convincing an interested local pilot to take you on a flight, in suitable conditions, to survey and photograph your study area is a good way to learn; it will also be exciting and stimulating and will give a different perspective.

For aerial reconnaissance to be carried out successfully there are a number of requirements:

1. A suitable aircraft, usually a high wing two- or four-seater (Cessna 150/152 or 172). Helicopters also provide a reasonable platform, but their availability and cost can be prohibitive.

2. A sympathetic pilot: someone who understands the speeds and angles required and is willing to stay in orbits all day, over a variety of sites.

3. The appropriate equipment for in-flight recording:

i) Cameras: 35mm cameras with automatic metering should have a 'shutter priority' facility (so that whatever the light level the shutter stays at least at 1/500th second, as the aperture varies). The lens should be the best possible, depending on the budget available; a 50mm 1.4f lens will usually be sufficient, but other zoom and telephoto lenses do provide for greater flexibility (**plate 11**). Medium format cameras, which take 120, 220 and 70mm film (the latter requires special handling) are also recommended, but they more than double the purchase price. The results may justify the extra investment, depending on the nature of the reconnaissance programme. Ideally, you should have at least three cameras in the air; one for colour, one for black-and-white and one spare.

ii) Films. For 35mm general purpose black-and-white films such as Ilford FP4, Delta, etc, and Kodak Tri-X and Technopan are very suitable. Kodak's Technopan is sometimes chosen for its high contrast and, although it requires particular development times (Palmer 1995), the results are very good for photographing cropmark sites. For colour slides Fuji and Kodak ranges produce very good results. Colour print films also produce very good results and have recently been evaluated by Crawshaw (1995). In deciding which film to use the archival stability has to be a factor (see Chapter 12). Infra-red films, although they produce stunning results (**plate 12**), are much harder to handle and are considerably more expensive.

iii) Maps: it is essential to have maps of the areas being surveyed — OS 1:50,000 maps are excellent for this purpose. These maps should be marked up with information about sites which have been recorded previously and with the targets to be photographed. It is also essential to make notes and descriptions of the route of the flight and record which sites have been photographed. Matching the film and frame number to a location (usually a six- or eight-figure grid reference) often takes place weeks after the flight (though it should be done as soon as possible) and means that proper records must be kept. (It is possible to use hand-held tape recorders, but they can malfunction and are not as reliable as pen and paper.) For many professional aerial surveyors the use of GPS is now becoming standard practice but should not yet totally replace manual note taking and map annotation: the output from the GPS can speed up the post-reconnaissance cataloguing, but a power failure or satellite failures could result in the loss of records from any flight.

4. The weather: planning your flights requires careful attention to the weather and a basic understanding of meteorology is an advantage. Surveys for sites revealed by cropmarks require different conditions to a flight for recording earthwork sites or buildings. If surveying for cropmarks, the conditions over the preceding weeks and months will determine the extent to which the cropmarks have formed. In Britain, the Meteorological Office publishes figures on rainfall, temperature and transpiration rates, which give a good indication of the level of drought. These are measuring the Soil Moisture Deficit (SMD) of the topsoil. Usually the best days for photography are those with still, clear air and little haze; often less-than-suitable conditions are all that are available, especially in the dry summers when cropmark formation is good but the weather does not always produce the best photographic conditions. For illustrative photography, especially for publication material, the choice of the day is critical; for archaeological surveying the weather is less critical, but it still requires visibility of more than 5 nautical miles. Photography of each type of site or target requires particular conditions, so it is important to have a clear plan of the purpose(s) of each flight; being able to take opportunities at short notice (eg when there has been a recent snowfall — see **plate 1**) is also important.

5. Apart from the pilot, the most important person in the air is the 'surveyor photographer'. In some cases this will be one person; the advantage of only two people in the air is not only cost, but also good communication and teamwork. Adding an extra pair of (archaeological) eyes has the advantage of doubling the chance of seeing sites and can be very useful in years when there is a high number of sites revealed as cropmarks in a small area; training the pilot in what there is to see is one way of achieving this. (Some pilots perform all three functions, pilot, surveyor and photographer, but this is the exception and is not recommended in areas of intense aircraft activity.) To operate efficiently a number of specific plans for each flight are essential. Invariably Plan A will be compromised, so Plans B, C, and D have to be activated. In aviation the weather, air traffic control or other air traffic restrictions can enforce a change of plans at any point. A strong stomach is also an advantage.

6. Knowledge: another requirement is the knowledge and experience of what is being surveyed and recorded. Aerial reconnaissance is the first level of

56   *Cherwell valley,
north
Oxfordshire: map
showing numbers
of cropmark sites
discovered per
decade, from
before 1967 until
1995,
highlighting the
increase in sites
recorded since
1987. The broken
lines represent the
locations of current
and former civil
and military
airfields.*

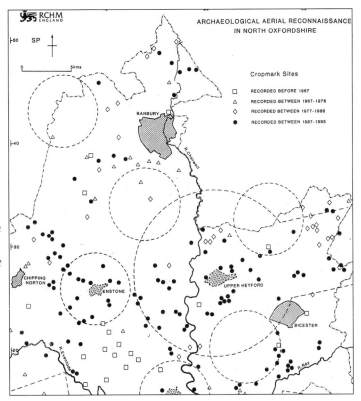

archaeological interpretation and a basic understanding of the formation processes (see **fig 54**), types and forms of sites is necessary and the ways in which different soils on a variety of geological bedrocks produce differential responses to drought (**plate 13**). These topics can only be learnt with experience, but there are a few basic text books, such as Wilson (1982), Riley (1987; 1996) and Bradford (1957). It is important to produce photographs which are appropriate for their use, such as near vertical photographs, including at least five control points, for the mapping stage. The control points (field boundary junctions, buildings, etc) allow features on the photograph to be matched to the same features on the map. Photographs of buildings have different requirements and a more oblique view might capture the building and its setting to the best effect (see **figs 79, 82**).

Immediate post-reconnaissance tasks

The cataloguing and storing of all the photographs is an essential part of the process. For any flight all the photographs need to be collated (slides and prints) and then catalogued, so that film and frame numbers are cross-referenced to the National Grid reference system and are given a preliminary classification. In the RCHME, all the specialist oblique aerial photographs are catalogued and stored by kilometre square; the advantage of this method is that most requests for examining the photography are by geographical region.

Other libraries, however, organise their catalogue by subject index and keep the prints in film order, and have the subject catalogue cross-referenced geographically. Thus a request to examine all the hillforts in Wessex, for instance, could be easily obtained.

Aerial survey does not end when the plane lands; one hour's flight generates at least one day's cataloguing work. Cataloguing is vital because photographs have to be easily retrievable and accessible. Accessibility is essential for the next step, which is to produce a brief description of the features seen on the photographs. This is no small task even for one season's photography.

After 75 years of aerial photography for archaeology, it is reasonable to ask if new sites are still being discovered. Fortunately this is very much the case (Griffith 1990; Featherstone 1994; Featherstone *et al* 1995; Bewley *et al* 1996); in each good year the new sites can be numbered in their hundreds, revealed as cropmark and earthwork sites.

A brief example emphasises the need for a continued programme of reconnaissance. It is centred around the Cherwell Valley in north Oxfordshire; **figure 56** charts the increase in new sites discovered as a result of the closure of Upper Heyford USAAF air base (hence making the airspace available) and the use of Kidlington airfield, near Oxford, as a base for archaeological flying, since 1990. This distribution map also reflects the exceptionally good conditions for cropmark formation in the years 1995 and 1996. **Plates 14** and **15** are two examples of the types of sites which have been discovered.

INTERPRETATION AND MAPPING

Aerial photography for archaeological mapping has been developing for over 70 years. The beginning can be seen in Crawford (1924b), where his purpose was to make maps from the photographs and, although he intended to show possibilities rather than to establish conclusions (*ibid*, 3), the rest of his text is an explanation and interpretation of what has been mapped. Although Crawford himself also saw the possibilities of using aerial photographs for other purposes, his major contribution was in establishing the principle of transferring the archaeological information from photographs to maps. This tradition has continued since the 1920s through, for instance, the works of Riley (1944), Bradford (1957), the RCHME (1960), Benson and Miles (1974), Palmer (1984), Whimster (1989) and Bewley (1994). The principles of interpreting archaeological remains on aerial photographs have been expounded by Wilson (1982).

For any mapping and interpretation exercise, it is important to consult all available photographs. To be able to undertake interpretation and mapping projects, the required skills and knowledge are in understanding aerial photographs (especially the differences between verticals and obliques) and in interpreting the information contained on the aerial photographs. The basics of photographic interpretation can be taught, but, like any other form of survey, it is a constant learning process: a knowledge of sites of all types and periods should be built up.

The interpretative process can only be done with human (as opposed to computer) skill; it is a subjective process, though computers can assist in the technical recording and representation of the interpretation. For the majority of sites which have been recorded, it has not yet been possible to assign a date or function; this is not a reflection of air photograph interpreters' level of skill, but of the current state of knowledge. More fieldwork and excavation are required to advance our knowledge. This is a recognised limitation of aerial survey which, as noted above, emphasises the need for integration with other forms of survey.

To be well informed, interpretations require the input of highly developed knowledge, and are, to that extent, therefore subjective. The plan or map is a personal (or team) effort and is a representation of the archaeological (and, where appropriate, geological) features. Any accompanying reports and records are also subjective, but should be well informed.

Mapping on its own, however, is not enough and there needs to be a classification of the sites which have been interpreted and mapped. Classification of sites visible on aerial photographs is relatively new and some sites (eg Roman forts and camps, long barrows and cursus monuments) can be classified more easily than others (eg enclosures of various shapes and sizes). An early attempt at examining a landscape and classifying the sites was that by Palmer (1984) around the hillfort at Danebury (Hampshire). The area was mapped and many of the sites (which were visible as cropmarks) were classified according to their size and shape. Subsequent fieldwalking, geophysical survey (which should always be done if possible) and excavation have tested the classifications with interesting results (eg Cunliffe 1994). During the 1980s, the discussion and results on classification of archaeological sites discovered through aerial survey and mapping were developed and published (Whimster 1983; Edis *et al* 1989; Bewley 1994). The basis of the recording system is geometric shape, with an emphasis on simplicity and the need for the descriptions to be systematic and repeatable. The assumption for any morphological classification is that sites of a similar size and shape may be of a similar date and function. For certain well-known site types (eg Roman camps) this is generally accepted, but for the multitude of (undated) enclosures which have been photographed, mapped and recorded, it is necessary to group the sites into classes (eg square enclosures with a single ditch and area of less than 2500 sq m) (see Bewley 1994). This classification is only a first step on the road to a secure interpretation. To allow for the creation of such groupings, a systematic and consistent approach to describing sites is required (Edis *et al* 1989; Bewley 1994). If a site is described as a square enclosure of a certain size and shape, then all other similar sites can be grouped and new classes of monument might emerge. Each site in the National Mapping Programme for England is described in this way and also given an interpretation according to the rules defined in the *Thesaurus* (RCHME/EH 1998).

How then is the interpretation, mapping and recording process carried out? There are a number of basic stages for all air photo interpretation projects:

i) Collection and collation of all the information relating to the area to be surveyed; this may be a large or small area, but information from the NMR, SMRs, maps and documents as well as the available aerial photographs should be collected. There will always be some photographs which are not accessible and these should be mentioned in the specification of the project; it is important to record the sources of photographs used.

ii) Having collated the photographs (verticals and obliques), these are then examined (or 'read through'), so that an idea of the sorts of archaeological features and sites (ie distribution, number, form and range) and the nature of the area can be gained. This helps to plan the interpretation stage.

iii) The project specification will define the scale and intensity of interpretation required for any plan. For a 1:10,000 manual transcription an accuracy of ± 2m should be readily achievable with care. The aim at this stage is to convert or transform the oblique view (not all vertical photographs are truly vertical) to a plan view. The essential requirement for an accurate plan from a photograph is that at least four control points, eg field boundary angles, corners of buildings, roads, intersections of a number of features, are shown (see **plate 14**), which can then be matched to those on the map. These control points provide a framework, in which the archaeological features to be mapped can be fitted. The transformation can be done manually, using a variety of techniques (see Riley 1987), or by computer using a range of programs (Haigh 1991). A final drawing is produced either manually or by computer (see Boutwood 1996).

iv) The nature of the final drawing will depend on the requirement; different products are produced depending on the specification of the project. All transcriptions require a report on what was done and by whom.

v) Archaeological records describing and interpreting the site should also be created for use in the appropriate database (the NMR, the SMR, or both).

Photogrammetry

Detailed photogrammetric mapping can be undertaken in advance of field survey, particularly Landscape survey (see Chapter 5). At a professional level, it is possible to produce very accurate photogrammetric transcriptions with a digital stereo photogrammetric plotter. It requires the use of pairs of stereo photographs in the form of film diapositives (a positive image on a film, not paper, base) and a suite of software programs.

The accuracy of the plots depends on a number of factors, most importantly the scale of the photography being used and the nature and accuracy of the mapped control. The results allow for the production of very accurate plans (with errors of less than 1m) at scales up to 1:2500, which can be used in the field to accelerate the process of analytical field survey. This approach can double the speed of a survey and the results can be used for detailed management and interpretation plans of complex sites and landscapes. Recent examples of such work include large areas of upland with dispersed settlement and field systems, such as the Cheviots (see **fig 8**), Exmoor and Salisbury Plain, and industrial complexes such as the Cumbrian mines at Greenside (lead), Coniston (copper) and Honister (slate). In another example at Wimpole Hall (Cambridgeshire), photogrammetry was used to plot not only the archaeology of formal gardens and cultivation, but the positions of existing and former trees, for the National Trust's management purposes.

SUMMARY

Aerial survey can therefore be seen as an end in itself, as a means of discovering and recording sites, landscapes and buildings, but it is also valuable as an element of preparation for ground-based survey. Collections of specialist photographs built up from decades of reconnaissance then form an invaluable resource in preparation for local fieldwork or for thematic studies. The creation of maps by transcription, using vertical air photographs supplemented by specialist oblique photography, is a valid survey technique in its own right, but also, in combination with ground survey, forms part of a very powerful suite of survey techniques.

MULTIPLYING TECHNIQUES
YARNBURY (WILTSHIRE)

A survey programme at Yarnbury hillfort and its immediate environs demonstrates what can be achieved by a multi-disciplinary approach.

The 11 ha hillfort was described, planned and partly excavated by Colt Hoare (1812, 89–90). Further interest in the site was stimulated by the publication of an aerial photograph (Crawford and Keiller 1928, pl VI), showing an inner enclosure: this had been planned by Colt Hoare, but subsequently forgotten. The inner enclosure was excavated in 1932 and shown to be of early Iron Age date (Cunnington 1933).

Close examination of the earthworks reveals a number of interesting features; for instance, marked hollows in the ditch bottoms are often mirrored by dumps on the rampart crests, possibly reflecting gangwork construction or refurbishment, as may the straight lengths of which the entire circuit is constructed. Of seven breaches in the ramparts, only one on the east appears to be an original entrance; cartographic evidence (Andrews and Dury's Map of Wiltshire (1773)) suggests that the remainder are associated with downland tracks which converged on the site in the post-medieval period. The density of occupation within the fort is graphically demonstrated by the earthwork remains of over 130 possible structures. Many of these clearly post-date the inner enclosure, and there is further evidence of chronological depth within the earthwork remains (see **fig 87**). Within the south-east quadrant of the fort are the remains of the Winterbourne Stoke sheep fair — an event of unknown antiquity held twice yearly until 1916 — consisting of boundary stones and the earthworks of the sheep pens and ancillary structures dug into the inner rampart of the fort. These earthworks probably date from the nineteenth century, as they are not shown on Colt Hoare's plan and the south-west corner overlies a track shown on the Andrews and Dury Map.

Earthwork survey was supplemented by geophysical survey which established the entire course of the inner enclosure and identified further entrances. Numerous anomalies indicate a dense distribution of pits and further compounds and structures, some in areas without surface remains. Geophysical survey also confirmed the presence of a suspected rectangular masonry structure.

The systematic collection of artefacts (see **fig 62**) brought to the surface by moles within the fort suggests intensive occupation from the sixth century BC until the late fourth century AD. Iron Age pottery was recovered from the entire area with some concentrations within the inner, earlier enclosure. Romano-British pottery was similarly well distributed. Later material, perhaps associated with the sheep fair, was concentrated in the south-eastern quadrant.

Aerial photography has allowed the construction of a detailed picture of settlement and land use in the environs of the hillfort in an area of 70km². Round barrows, extensive field systems and eighteen enclosures, probably settlements, have been identified; only one of these enclosures survives as an earthwork and only one has produced datable (mid–late Iron Age) material, but all may be considered, on morphological grounds, as broadly contemporary. The hillfort itself lies within an area largely devoid of field systems, defined by four linear ditches. The linear ditches are demonstrably later than the fields, however.

Extract from RCHME earthwork plan; original scale 1:1000.

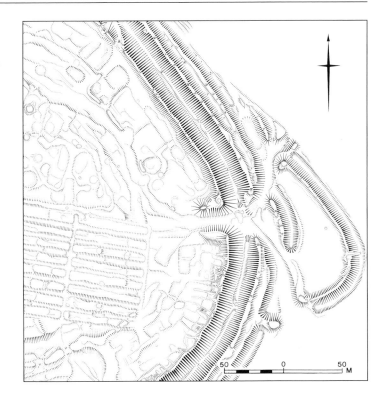

Extract from geophysical survey by GSB Prospection, showing the same area.

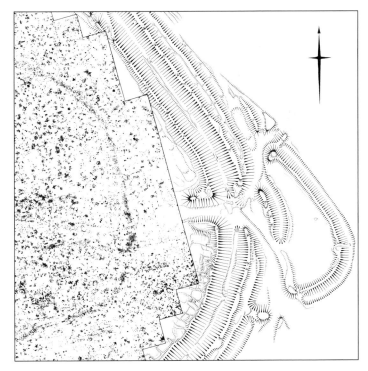

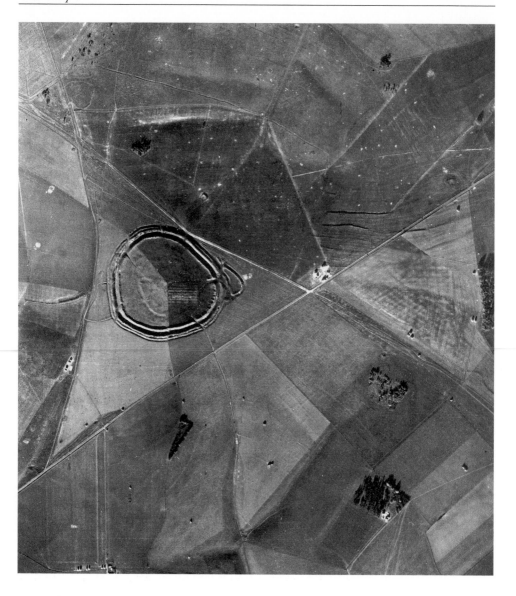

Vertical aerial photograph of Yarnbury (RAF photograph).

8 Other survey techniques

There are now many techniques, often science-based, which are available to the investigator of landscape archaeology. These include probing, bosing, metal detecting, radioactivity and neutron scattering, thermal prospection, vegetation mapping and geochemical analysis (Renfrew and Bahn 1996, 85–97), but the most widely used and generally applicable are geophysical techniques and surface artefact collection or 'fieldwalking'.

A number of projects which have combined such techniques with considerable success form exemplars. These include Yarnbury (see Case Study 4), Wroxeter (*Current Archaeology* 157 (14 part 1) 1998, 8–14) and the Fenland Project (Coles and Hall 1997).

GEOPHYSICAL SURVEY

Geophysical survey (geophysics) is the search for sub-surface features by means of electric resistivity measurement, magnetometery, seismics, ground penetrating radar and similar techniques (**plate 16**).

Geophysics were first recognised as having a potential application in archaeology in 1946, when Richard Atkinson used an early development of the resistivity meter to locate a series of prehistoric features at Dorchester-on-Thames (Oxfordshire) (Clark 1990, 11–12). This early equipment was rather cumbersome and slow, but clearly demonstrated the potential for archaeological prospection. Development and experimentation continued throughout the 1950s and in 1956 A J Clark and J Martin developed the first resistivity meter specifically for archaeological applications. This equipment was field tested at the Roman town site of Mildenhall (Wiltshire) and soon demonstrated its value in the field, locating a substantial Roman wall with associated bastions (Clark 1957). By the late 1950s, the value of magnetometery was also being realised in archaeological applications with the successful location of a number of Roman pottery kilns at Water Newton, near Peterborough (Clark 1990, 16–17). Thus, by the early 1960s, the two main geophysical methods used in archaeology, resistivity and magnetometery, had been established. Official recognition of the worth of archaeological geophysics came in 1967 with the establishment of a geophysics section in the Ancient Monuments Laboratory (now part of English Heritage). The widespread application of geophysics in modern archaeology has been aided and developed by the establishment of a number of commercial companies and continuing research at universities. The last two decades have seen many further refinements to the sphere of geophysical investigation and a wide range of techniques is now available.

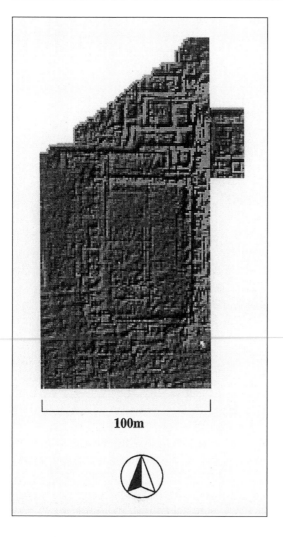

57   Witham (Somerset), Carthusian monastery and later country house: electrical resistivity survey results (survey by GSB Prospection).

100m

Geophysical methods commonly applied in archaeological survey

For a comprehensive account of the full range of geophysical methods available, the reader is referred to Clark (1990), David (1995), Gaffney *et al* (1991) and Scollar *et al* (1990). Spoerry (1992) provides a number of case studies.

Electrical Resistivity Survey

This method involves the passing of an electrical current between probes set in the ground. The resistance to the passage of the current is measured in ohms and, based on the nature of the materials restricting the current flow, an interpretation of the buried archaeology made. The depth of ground penetration by the current is dependent upon the spacing between the probes. For example a spacing of 0.5m will give a penetration of approximately 0.75m. Features such as buried walls and metalled surfaces will give a fairly high resistivity reading, whilst infilled ditches or pits which retain moisture will give a

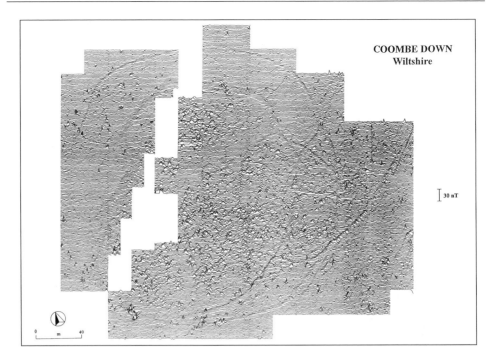

COOMBE DOWN
Wiltshire

30 nT

0   m   40

58   *Coombe Down, Salisbury Plain (Wiltshire): magnetometry results (survey by GSB Prospection).*

lower response. The method is especially well suited to the investigation of stone structures and has been used with considerable success, for example in the investigation of Roman villas and medieval monastic remains (**fig 57**). The success of a survey, however, may be affected by weather conditions and by geology. Excessively dry or wet conditions can adversely affect the quality of the results, as they will affect the efficiency of the current flow.

Magnetic Methods

Magnetometery

Magnetic survey is based upon the presence of weakly magnetised iron oxides in the soil. Past human activity can alter and redistribute these, creating stronger or weaker responses to measurement which can be detected as magnetic anomalies. These anomalies can be recorded with a Fluxgate Magnetometer or Gradiometer. Such instruments are highly portable and have been developed in Britain for rapid archaeological survey. The method can produce quite remarkable and detailed results (**fig 58**), being especially well suited to identifying buried ditches, pits, ovens, hearths, kilns, brick and tile. Subsoil types can influence the quality of results, the most responsive being chalk, limestones and ironstones. Areas covered by deeper deposits of alluvium and colluvium may be difficult to penetrate and the results on clay can be erratic. Areas of igneous subsoils are the most difficult to investigate with this technique, as the high natural magnetic background will frequently mask subtle archaeological anomalies.

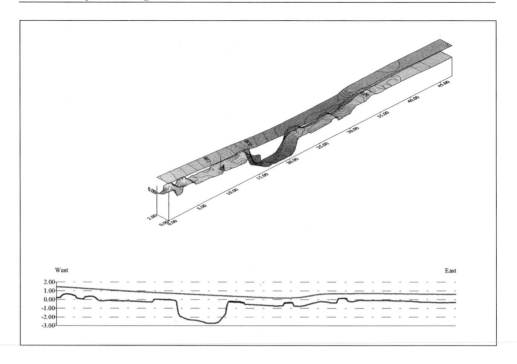

West   East

59   *Harbottle Castle (Northumberland): GPR results showing the profile of the ditch*
          underlying the causeway at the eastern entrance to the bailey (survey by Northumbrian
          Surveys for the Northumberland National Park Authority).

Magnetic Susceptibility

By recording the areas of enhanced magnetic activity in the topsoil, it is possible to predict areas of human activity. Working on the same principles as magnetometery, this method can be more time consuming, requiring the placing of an instrument directly onto the ground surface. This method has been used, for instance, in conjunction with resistance and magnetometer surveys to produce a detailed assessment of archaeological activity over a Roman villa site in Wiltshire (Corney *et al* 1995). The reduced levels of magnetic susceptibility were found to coincide with ring ditches noted on air photographs and have been interpreted as evidence for the survival of earlier barrow mounds in the Romano-British landscape.

Other Methods

Seismic Refraction

A series of soundings (generated by a 9lb sledgehammer) are taken across a known archaeological feature. The velocity of the shock wave is altered by interfaces encountered in the penetration of the subsoil. These variations are recorded and it is possible to produce a 'pseudo section' through the archaeological strata. The technique is in its infancy but, given the right conditions (eg a buried rock-cut ditch), the results are clear and worthwhile (Goulty *et al* 1990; Goulty and Hudson 1994; Ovenden 1994).

60   *New Farm: geophysical results presented as a greyscale plot (survey by GSB Prospection).*

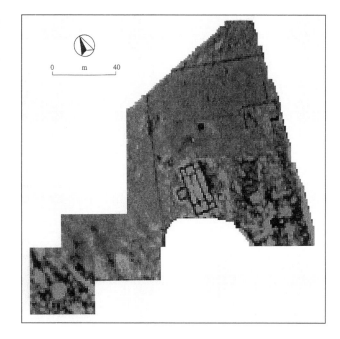

Ground penetrating radar

Ground penetrating radar gives a geo-electric depth section and, when more than one section is generated, a series of three-dimensional representations (known as 'time slices') of the site may be built up. At present this technique is still experimental and relatively expensive in comparison to other geophysical methods, and the results obtained in the UK have been of variable quality. However, the potential for this technique has been demonstrated; at Harbottle Castle (Northumberland) it is not certain from surface inspection whether the eastern entrance to the bailey is a causeway of bedrock or a built feature across a previously continuous ditch, but radar survey (Northumbrian Surveys 1997) indicates that the latter is the case (**fig 59**).

Location

Whatever technique is used, it is, of course, essential that the precise location of the prospection area is recorded. It should therefore have its own survey control scheme (see Chapter 4), if conducted as an independent exercise, or be located by reference to the control scheme of a wider project of which it forms part.

The display and presentation of results

The display of results can be made in a variety of ways. The two most widely used methods are by linear plot showing the recorded data on an X – Y plot, where the more significant readings appear as a series of peaks and troughs (see **fig 58**), or by presenting the filtered and enhanced data as a greyscale plot (**fig 60**). To aid easy understanding for the non-specialist user, an interpretative plan of the survey is usually provided for easy visual reference (**fig 61**).

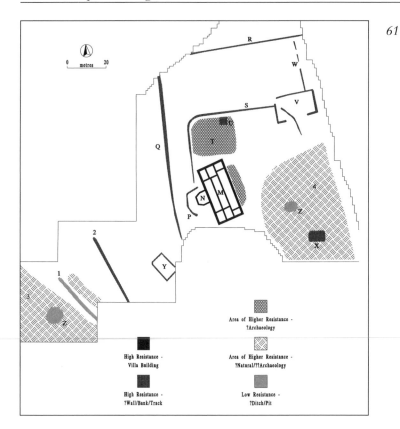

61 *New Farm: interpretative plan of geophysical results (survey by GSB Prospection).*

Legend:

High Resistance - Villa Building

High Resistance - ?Wall/Bank/Track

Area of Higher Resistance - ?Archaeology

Area of Higher Resistance - ?Natural/??Archaeology

Low Resistance - ?Ditch/Pit

Access to geophysics

For individuals and archaeology groups, access to geophysical survey may be possible through a college or university department which has the equipment and is looking for student projects. Alternatively, the acquisition of an instrument such as a fluxgate gradiometer, which is neither expensive nor difficult to use, would be within the grasp of most.

Use of geophysics with other survey techniques

The benefits of integrating geophysics with other established survey methodologies are considerable. Over the last decade selective geophysical surveys have been increasingly used to answer specific questions raised by topographic and aerial investigations. Non-destructive archaeological survey is increasingly reliant upon specialist skills and it is of the utmost importance that an integrated approach is adopted to harness the full range of techniques available.

Recent use of geophysical survey has radically altered our understanding of past settlement patterns in many areas. A major survey of Salisbury Plain (McOmish *et al* forthcoming) has used geophysical survey to locate a number of villas which must have played a key role in the exploitation of the region during the Roman period. Investigation of the Iron Age hillfort at Ham Hill (Somerset: ST 482 670) has revealed a hitherto unsuspected density of features, and a geophysical study of Carthusian monastic sites has added further layers of detail to the monuments investigated (eg Wilson-North and Porter 1997, 84).

Fully integrated non-intrusive survey can provide a surprisingly high level of quality data. The application of earthwork survey, air photography, geophysics and surface collection at Yarnbury hillfort (Wiltshire) (see Case Study 4) has demonstrated the degree of detailed information which can be gained from a site and its environs without resort to destruction through excavation.

SURFACE ARTEFACT COLLECTION ('FIELDWALKING')

The origins of collecting artefacts from the surface of ploughed fields, as an archaeological technique, lie in the nineteenth century with the 'flint hunting' described by Pitt Rivers (Bowden 1991, 75–6 *et passim*), but it was first undertaken in a systematic manner in Europe and the Americas from the 1940s onwards. The great boom in fieldwalking in Britain during the late 1970s and 1980s led to a number of publications on the theory and methodology of the technique (eg Woodward 1978; Haselgrove *et al* 1985; Macready and Thompson 1985; Brown 1987, chapter 2; Schofield 1991). Many of these large fieldwalking projects have now been published (eg Gaffney and Tingle 1989; Richards 1990; Davies and Astill 1994) and form a corpus of case studies and exemplars. However, there are still no national (or international) standards of methodology, recording and dissemination which would enable direct comparison of results between projects in different regions.

Whereas the purpose of 'flint hunting' was the acquisition of a large number of ancient artefacts for museum collections, or for building typologies, the objective of fieldwalking is the location and characterisation of past human activity in the landscape. The aim of fieldwalking is not, therefore, to recover *every* artefact from the surface of a field but to collect a representative sample in a consistent manner, in order to map patterns which may reflect past activity.

Fieldwalking is an activity that is widely practised, largely because it can be done by any number of people, from an individual to a large group, of any level of expertise, and with a minimum of equipment.

Recovery factors

The season and the prevailing weather are the principal factors affecting recovery rates. Most fieldwalking is done during the winter months, when fields have been ploughed; consequently shadows are long and walking towards or away from the sun will produce different recovery patterns. One way of countering this is to walk the field in two directions, but a better one is to undertake fieldwalking on dull days. The soil type is another important factor; clean sandy soils allow artefacts to be observed clearly, whereas on clay-with-flints it is difficult to distinguish artefacts from the background of naturally fractured flint. The soil condition is also crucial, a field that has been harrowed and washed by rain giving much greater visibility than one which is freshly ploughed.

A further set of variables is introduced by the individuals undertaking the survey. Levels of expertise and ability to see artefacts will clearly differ, but fatigue and lapses in concentration lead to declining recovery rates as the day wears on.

Finally, the research design is a governing factor; artefact collection *may* be done at random or be conducted like a treasure hunt, but it *should* be undertaken to a design which specifies 'intensive' or 'extensive' collection according to a regular grid. 'Intensive' collection involves the search of the entire ground surface, usually over a very restricted area, 'extensive' collection involves sampling, usually in a series of regularly spaced transects, to cover much larger areas.

Standardisation

Some of these variables will always be present. Others should be reduced as far as possible so that results are meaningful and comparable.

The principal starting point for fieldwalking projects in Britain is the OS map and National Grid. On the ground the grid can easily be found to an acceptable level of accuracy by scaling distances along field boundaries from the map and then taping them out and marking intersections with ranging rods or bamboo canes. This gives a consistent grid throughout a project and, importantly, between different projects, and is therefore preferable to the 'lazy' option of using a long field boundary as a baseline from which to offset transects. The relatively time-consuming task of laying out the grid can be left to one or two individuals, working slightly in advance of the fieldwalkers.

Walking always north and south along grid lines also addresses the problem of the light source, the low winter sun. However, fieldwalking on dull days will always produce better results.

Fieldwalking should be left as late in the agricultural cycle as possible. The more rain and weathering the fields have had the better. Ideally, therefore, fieldwalking should take place even after the crops have begun to show, and on light soils this should not be a problem as no damage will be done; on heavier soils, however, seedlings may be disturbed and the farmer may not readily give permission for work to take place at this stage.

Individual bias cannot be eliminated, but some standardisation can be achieved by setting a time for walking a set distance, thus slowing down those who are prone to skimp the work and speeding up those who are over-meticulous. Working periods should be kept short to reduce fatigue.

Methodology

The 'extensive' method involves walking fields in a series of lines at set intervals. In order to control collection across different types of topography, these are laid out on a north–south alignment. An interval of 25m has usually been adopted. This allows relatively rapid reconnaissance over large areas, while giving a realistic chance of finding most artefact scatters. However, on some soils, such as the greensands of south-east

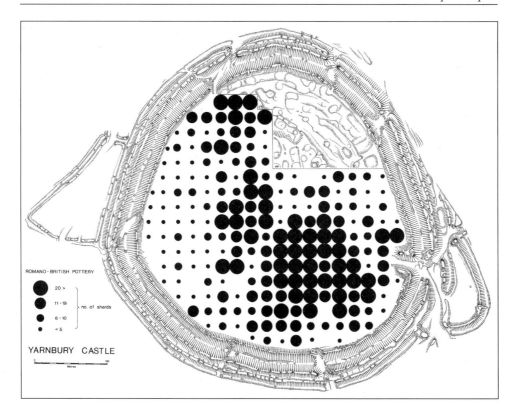

62   *Yarnbury (Wiltshire): Romano-British pottery distribution depicted by proportional circle.*

England, artefact scatters are very small and a narrower interval needs to be adopted.

The 'intensive' method involves laying out grid squares, based on the National Grid again to promote comparability of results. The scale of the project will dictate the size of the squares, but once again comparability demands a small grid size; the results from many small squares can be combined if necessary, but the result from one large square cannot be subsequently subdivided. Squares of 25m sides (625 sq m) are often used for general reconnaissance, but squares of 5m sides (25 sq m) were adopted by most of the cited projects and allow for the elucidation of different activity areas by plotting the spread of different classes of artefact, especially when combined with other techniques including excavation (eg Bowden *et al* 1994).

Interpretation

The interpretation of fieldwalking results generated much discussion in the 1970s and 80s and was deeply involved in the development of an 'off-site' or landscape approach to archaeology. This was focused on the realisation that human activity in the past took place throughout the landscape and not just at discrete 'sites'. The act of manuring from farmyard middens was quickly recognised as one activity which led to the scattering of discarded artefacts across cultivated ground (eg Gaffney and Tingle 1989, chapter 14). It soon became clear from sample excavations that artefact scatters did not necessarily correlate directly with sub-surface features (eg Bowden *et al* 1994), leading to further consideration of discard patterns and abandonment practices (see Schofield 1991), and more sophisticated models for the behaviour of artefacts in ploughsoil were sought (eg Yorston *et al* 1990; Boismier 1997).

It is clear from all this that the interpretation of artefact scatters on their own is a hazardous business and that, though fieldwalking is a powerful tool, its results need to be integrated with the results of other survey techniques, and excavation, to realise their full potential.

Presentation of results

Results should be presented as a series of plans or diagrams using proportional circles (**fig 62**), shaded squares or 'contours' to illustrate differing densities of artefacts. Whatever method is adopted, it should be designed so that the plan can be read at a glance. Proportional circles ensure that this is the case, whereas shading has to be carefully thought out, so that the gradations of darkness accurately match the numbers represented; failure to do this results in a meaningless plan (eg Brown 1987, 30).

Archiving considerations

One important result of using the National Grid as the basis of survey is that the results are compatible with the NMR and SMR databases. However, the sheer bulk of finds generated by fieldwalking projects is another problem, as museum stores are beginning to creak under the weight of material found in recent times; the extensive surface collection phase of the Stonehenge Environs Project alone amounted to over 100,000 pieces of worked flint (Richards 1990, 15).

9 Special landscapes

All landscapes are 'special' in the sense that they are unique, but some types of landscape pose particular challenges for the investigative archaeologist. These include: maritime landscapes, subterranean 'landscapes' (both natural (caves) and artificial (mines) **(fig 63)**), urban landscapes, buried landscapes in wetlands and river valleys, and landscapes of leisure. In this chapter, we discuss four landscape types with a variety of natural and artificial elements.

THE INTERTIDAL AREA

The intertidal area is the zone between high and low tide and needs to be studied with the coastal strip which backs the foreshore. The survey and recording of archaeological and palaeoenvironmental sites in this area has only recently become standard practice, though the importance of the intertidal area was recognised by antiquaries as early as the eighteenth century. William Borlase, writing in 1756, observed that, between the Scillonian islands of Samson and Tresco, '...Hedges and Ruins are frequently discovered upon the shifting of the Sands, and upon which at full sea there are ten and twelve feet of water' (quoted in Ashbee 1974, 19). During the nineteenth century, many remote coastal areas were opened up by the railways and seaside holidays became popular. At the same time, the natural sciences, particularly geology, were developing. This interest was particularly keen in the West Country and submerged forests were discovered at Torbay, Mounts Bay, Westward Ho! and Porlock (Bell 1995). The nineteenth century also saw expansion of most of the major British ports and harbours, themselves now a subject of study (eg Milne and Hobley 1981; Good et al 1991).

During the 1970s and 1980s an increased awareness of the potential and importance of wetland archaeological sites was driven by projects in the Somerset Levels (Coles and Coles 1986) and the Fens (Pryor 1991; Coles and Hall 1997). The expertise gained in this field has proved invaluable when tackling complex intertidal sites, such as the Iron Age structures at Goldcliff (Gwent) (Bell 1993).

Since the late 1980s intertidal archaeology has emerged as a discipline in its own right (Coles and Goodburn 1991; EH/RCHME 1996; Fulford et al 1997). Intertidal archaeology is now regularly considered in the planning process (DOE 1990; 1992) and so forms part of evaluations before coastal development.

63 *Subterranean
'landscape': the
Kimberley
internal incline,
Honister slate
mines.*

Sea-level change

The intertidal area contains archaeological sites which were once on dry land, showing that sea-level has risen since these sites were occupied. The chronology and magnitude of this change is complicated by a number of factors. Sea-level change is the result of the dynamics of the solid earth (tectonic movement), the world ocean (eustatic movement) and the atmosphere. Tidal oscillations also exert an influence on global sea-level changes (Everard 1980). There has been a considerable diversity in the rate of sea-level change in Britain in the post-glacial period. This is mainly caused by differential crustal movements, a result of the effects of the last glaciation. For much of this period, Scotland and most of northern England have undergone crustal uplift, while southern England experienced crustal subsidence. The results of recent work on sea-level change around the English coastline have been synthesised by Long and Roberts (1997).

Archaeology in the intertidal area

The range of archaeological sites encountered within the intertidal area is as diverse as those on dry land (see, eg, McDonnell 1995, 22). Palaeoenvironmental sites, such as submerged forests, peat deposits and buried channel fills must be considered as part of the archaeological resource in the intertidal area, as should the coastal strip behind the foreshore which should also be integrated into an intertidal survey project (Riley 1995).

Coastal finds of the earliest prehistoric periods comprise chance finds of artefacts, together with occupation sites which are now on the coast, such as the Upper Palaeolithic occupation site at Hengistbury Head (Dorset) (Campbell 1977). In the earlier part of the post-glacial period, the coastline of the British Isles was approaching its present configuration (Evans 1975). Mesolithic flint assemblages have been found on cliff-tops and in deposits associated with submerged forests. A good example of the latter is near Hartlepool (Cleveland), where submerged forests are associated with Mesolithic artefacts and palaeoenvironmental evidence (Trenchmann 1936).

Later prehistoric sites have been discovered eroding from cliffs or sand dunes. Bronze Age settlement sites were excavated at Brean Down (Somerset) and Gwithian (Cornwall) (Bell 1990; Thomas 1958; Megaw *et al* 1961) (**plate 17**). At Harlyn Bay (Cornwall) an Iron Age cemetery was discovered (Bullen 1930). Other prehistoric finds may be directly connected with coastal or maritime activities, such as the Bronze Age boats found at North Ferriby (East Yorkshire) and Dover (Kent) (Wright 1990; Parfitt and Fenwick 1993), and the Iron Age buildings and trackways at Goldcliff (Gwent), which may have been for fishing, wildfowling or pasturing (Bell 1993). Coastal salt production occurred in later prehistory, with evidence in the form of briquetage from excavated sites (Morris 1985; 1994) and, more rarely, as field monuments (Fawn *et al* 1990). The foreshore can also preserve prehistoric land surfaces, such as the Neolithic palaeosol discovered at the Stumble (Essex) (Wilkinson and Murphy 1986). As well as plant macrofossils and pollen grains, such surfaces may preserve human and animal footprints, as at Uskmouth and Goldcliff (Gwent) and Formby Point (Merseyside) (Aldhouse-Green *et al* 1993; Bell 1993; Roberts *et al* 1996).

Roman artefacts have been found on the foreshore. Field monuments from this period also occur on the coast, giving evidence for the chronology of coastal change. For example, the positions of the Saxon Shore forts on the south-east coast (Johnson 1979; Johnston 1977) show that coastal change has occurred and the reconstruction of the Roman coastline may be attempted.

For the medieval and post-medieval periods, archaeological evidence becomes more abundant. Sites include stone or wooden fish weirs, designed to function in the intertidal area (Aston 1988) (**plates 18, 19**); there are radiocarbon dates for wooden fish weirs in the Severn Estuary as early as the ninth century AD (Godbold and Turner 1994). The built environment often occupies the very edge of the intertidal zone and includes sea-walls, quays and military sites. Artefacts found in the intertidal area may indicate the location of an eroding site or deposit, or objects from a shipwreck. The remains of extractive or processing industries also occur on the coast: there is documentary evidence for salt production around most of the English coast, but the best-preserved field monuments are now stranded inland, for example at Wainfleet St Mary (Lincolnshire) (McAvoy 1994); cliffs provided a source of stone, as on the Isle of Portland (Dorset), and the intertidal area was often used as a source of gravel for ballast, well-documented at Great Yarmouth (Norfolk) (Tooke 1984); coal, iron, jet and alum were mined from the cliffs of north-east England from prehistoric times onwards (eg Pybus 1983).

Survey methods

Desk-top survey

The county SMRs and the NMR do not generally contain an exhaustive list of intertidal sites for any given area, though the NMR does contain maritime records — the Maritime Inventory (RCHME 1996a) — some of which lie within the intertidal area. County Record Offices may hold relevant documents, and nautical surveys and charts can be consulted at the Hydrographic Department of the MOD, Taunton. Local knowledge is an important source.

Aerial survey

Existing aerial photographs of the survey area should be consulted before ground survey commences, both to assess the archaeological potential and to note obvious hazards and access problems. Wrecks, fish traps, salterns, oyster beds, sea defences and land reclamation, military remains and submerged field systems can all be identified on aerial photographs. There are, however, several limitations to their use. Collections rarely have the state of the tide marked on them so the parallel use of a chart or large-scale map is essential. Sediment cover can hinder interpretation. Accurate transcription of features is often hampered by the small scale of photographs and a lack of control in the intertidal area. A survey of existing aerial photography in the intertidal area highlighted the potential of the collections at the Hydrographic Department, the Environment Agency and the National Environmental Research Council (Crutchley 1994).

Targeted aerial reconnaissance can prove very useful. In Essex, mainly around the Blackwater Estuary, a few flights in 1992–3 doubled the number of known sites in the intertidal area of that county (Crump and Wallis 1992). Good photographs taken under ideal ground conditions (low tide, good light, no sediment), possibly integrated with GPS control work, can form the basis for terrestrial survey work, as at Langstone Harbour, Hampshire (Allen *et al* 1994; Adam *et al* 1995).

Ground survey

There is no difference between intertidal survey and terrestrial survey in that all of the methods already outlined can be used. The tidal window for the area in question must be established, usually from local tide-tables which give the time of mean high water: check for BST/GMT. Consideration must be given to the time taken to walk out to a particular site and to local weather conditions. The expense of hiring a boat may be justified by the time saved to get to an inaccessible area, but the walk out to a site can be a valuable way of 'fieldwalking' the area. Fieldwalking is a good way of covering the ground and was used successfully at Bridgwater Bay (McDonnell 1995) and on the Lincolnshire coast (Brookes *et al* 1990).

Sites may be located by any practical method. A preliminary assessment survey may rely on prismatic compass fixes (McDonnell 1995), although visibility and configuration of suitable objects may be a problem. Conventional EDM survey can also be used successfully, where local control, such as a stretch of sea-wall, is available. Where the area in question is remote and the local map base is inadequate, GPS may be the most cost-effective survey method, particularly if the tidal window is small. GPS may be used to establish control points or to survey the features themselves (**plate 19**).

Heighting information is important for intertidal survey work, particularly for palaeoenvironmental deposits. For archaeological intertidal work, the survey data is usually related to an OS map base, so that the archaeological or palaeoenvironmental features are tied to the OS levelling network (Everard 1980). This can be achieved by levelling or appropriate transformations of GPS data. Chart datum is not a fixed value in relation to OD (McDonnell 1995, 6).

Monitoring

Accurate ground survey of features in the intertidal area is crucial to monitor threat from erosion. If no other equipment is available, then a prismatic compass fix, a sketch plan, description and photographs are perfectly adequate. The site may not be uncovered again for months; equally it may be eroded away.

Other techniques

Augering can be used to indicate the presence and extent of buried archaeological or palaeoenvironmental deposits in the intertidal zone. It has been used, for instance, to prospect for intertidal and sub-tidal sites at Langstone Harbour (Allen *et al* 1994) and to plot the buried land surface and sub-surface topography in the Hullbridge survey project (Wilkinson and Murphy 1995).

Little work has been done with conventional geophysical survey techniques in the intertidal area, though such techniques were used at Porth Killier, St Agnes, to investigate the extent of an eroding cliff edge site (Ratcliffe and Parks 1989). Acoustic and seismic survey methods, such as side-scan sonar, developed for commercial hydrographic survey, can be used for archaeological prospection in the sub-tidal environment. Off the coast of the Isle of Wight sub-bottom profiling, a technique designed to resolve sub-surface features, has recorded palaeochannels on the seabed (Tomalin 1994). Ultimately, excavation may be the only way to understand and record a feature, particularly if it is under threat from erosion.

Vessel recording

The work at Whitewall Creek on the Medway (Kent), where a group of vernacular craft were recorded in advance of development, pioneered vessel recording on the foreshore. The scheme developed there (Milne *et al* 1998) was successfully used during the Bridgwater Bay project (McDonnell 1995).

Health and Safety

The intertidal area is a dangerous environment. Workers must never be alone on the foreshore and must always carry watches and consult tide-tables. The coastguard and/or harbour master must be informed what work is being undertaken, where and how many people are involved. A safety margin must always be allowed, work finished and the walk back to shore begun about an hour before the tide turns. Appropriate weather forecasts should be noted, and an eye kept out for incoming squalls. All workers must be adequately equipped with warm and brightly coloured waterproof clothes and wellingtons, which are easy to kick off, not waders. Beware of mud and quicksand. Local information should be sought about conditions before going out: someone with local knowledge could be asked to accompany the team on an initial trip to an unfamiliar area. A shore contact who is aware of your location and time of return must be arranged. A mobile phone or two-way radio (leaving the other one with the shore contact), compass, whistle and distress flares must be carried. Check any insurance requirements, particularly if you are using a boat. Detailed advice on health and safety is given in McDonnell (1995).

WOODLAND

Woodland, both broad-leaved and coniferous, is a prominent part of the British landscape, its distribution reflecting much of the agricultural and social history of the past six or seven centuries. Before the advent of iron, steel and concrete, timber was a universally important construction material and was also widely used, of course, for a variety of portable artefacts; likewise, before coke and coal came into general use, wood and charcoal were the chief fuels. Today, the focus of the commercial forestry sector is on fast-growing conifers, mostly for pulp and construction.

Excellent accounts of the history of woodland development exist (eg Rackham 1976; 1980), but it is important to highlight the longstanding nature of the human relationship with the woodland environment. The effects of human activity on woodland in England are first detected in the pollen record during the Mesolithic, between approximately 10,000 and 5,500 years ago (Simmons and Innes 1981; 1988; Jacobi *et al* 1976). Archaeological evidence for Neolithic woodland management has been provided by the discovery of the coppiced hazel foundations of the 'Sweet Track' (Somerset) (Coles and Coles 1986).

The woodland flora and fauna itself may provide some information about the history of the site. There is growing biological evidence that certain species, generally termed 'ancient woodland indicators', appear to be characteristic of long-established woodland. These species, usually vascular plants, lichens, bryophytes and distinctive communities of deadwood-inhabiting insects ('saproxylic fauna') are characteristically slow to colonise new sites and are absent from known secondary woodland. Thus, if such a range is present, it may suggest that the woodland is at least a few centuries old (Marren 1990, 112–29).

Alternatively, a documentary approach can be taken: woodlands which can be demonstrated to have existed since at least AD 1600 are defined as 'ancient' woodland (Kirby 1984) on the assumption that such woodlands are likely to contain elements which have been continuously wooded since prehistoric times. Traditional methods of woodland management used in such woods include coppicing and pollarding, practices which cause little ground disturbance, thus facilitating the good survival of archaeological earthworks. In contrast, modern silvicultural techniques of ground preparation prior to planting, clear felling and the construction of forestry tracks may be extremely destructive; in recognition of this, commercial operators usually now seek to avoid archaeologically sensitive areas when planting (Forestry Commission 1995). This is not to say that earthworks do not survive in afforested land; in some areas the periodic cropping of timber has not been as comprehensively destructive as annual cereal cropping (Lee 1995, 98). Some earthworks, such as those on Stanton Moor (Derbyshire), owe both their preservation and their degraded state to short-term episodes of woodland growth.

Woodland archaeology

Although not a conventional archaeological 'monument', a wood may be regarded as a distinct archaeological entity. Woods may be part of a specific historic design, have early origins or a historical association within the landscape, and the trees themselves (coppice stools, pollards and standards) are crucial evidence of past management. Indeed, it can be said that the most informative 'archaeological' features of ancient woodland that survive are the managed trees (see Rackham (1975 and 1989) for two eye-opening case studies). Specialist ecological input is therefore typically necessary to the archaeological study of woodland, making for an ideal interdisciplinary co-operative task. In addition, many different types of archaeological monument occur within a woodland context, including many specific to woodland itself. The types of remains present will largely depend on how the wood has been managed, whether for timber, other wood products, as a habitat for animals, as an opportune area to exploit other natural materials, or a combination of these through time. Woodland earthworks fall into three broad categories: those features associated with managing the woodland resource, those related to woodland-based industries and archaeology not specific to woodland.

Woodland management

Features relating to past woodland management typically include banks, ditches and enclosures (eg Smith in prep). Woodland boundaries, especially significant and quite distinctive, are usually marked by a bank and external ditch. Early wood-margins tend to be broad and sinuous — many lay at manorial boundaries and became parish boundaries — or have zig-zag shapes with abrupt changes of direction — this unevenness being the result of small intakes, or assarts, of farmland from woodland.

Post-medieval wood boundaries tend to be straight or regularly curved in plan and the woodbanks are less massive. Profiles vary considerably, earlier examples being rounded, while those formed in later periods are more angular in profile. Wood boundaries continued to be created well into the nineteenth century, by which date wood margins are typically very straight.

A wood with a complex history may contain many kinds of earthwork recording its changes; for example, when a wood is enlarged, a wood bank may be left behind demarcating its former extent or, when a wood is truncated, the ghost of the old perimeter sometimes remains as a hedge or soil mark. Former woods and wood pastures (woodland which was also grazed) may be identified in the landscape by a high incidence of old oaks, pollarded trees and thick hedges rich in species (see, eg, Fleming 1997).

Apart from boundary banks and ditches, the commonest earthworks specific to

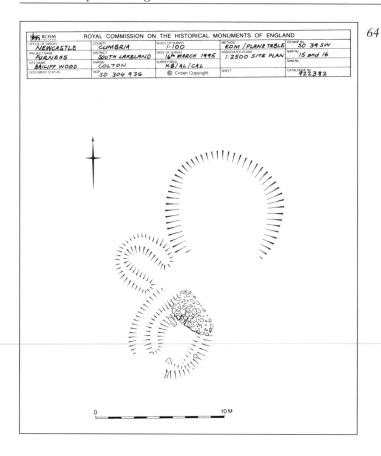

RCHM ENGLAND	ROYAL COMMISSION ON THE HISTORICAL MONUMENTS OF ENGLAND				
OFFICE OF ORIGIN NEWCASTLE	COUNTY CUMBRIA	SCALE OF SURVEY 1:100	METHOD EDM /PLANE TABLE	OS MAP No. SD 39 SW	
PROJECT NAME FURNESS	DISTRICT SOUTH LAKELAND	DATE OF SURVEY 16th MARCH 1995	ASSOCIATED PLANS 1:2500 SITE PLAN	NAR No. 15 and 16	
SITE NAME BAILIFF WOOD	PARISH COLTON	SURVEYOR(S) KB/AL/CAL		SAM No.	
DOCUMENT STATUS	NGR SD 304 936	© Crown Copyright	SHEET	CATALOGUE No. 922382	

0   10 M

64   *Bailiff Wood (Cumbria): field survey archive drawing, original scale 1:100. A pitstead and bark peelers' hut (with collapsed stone chimney). They are in close proximity, but are not directly associated with one another — the hut has its back to the pitstead. The horseshoe-shaped bank possibly represents the site of the charcoal burners' hut.*

woodland are drainage channels, usually found in woods on flat ground with very little natural drainage and usually of post-medieval date. These systems may take a straight course along rides or meander among the trees. Often there is a branching system of very small channels, without banks, laid out to follow the lie of the land, often incorporating streams and using pre-existing ponds.

Other features occur. In the New Forest, for example, in woodland which also had the legal status of a hunting preserve several small rectilinear enclosures have been shown by a combination of archaeological and documentary evidence to be the sites of twelfth-century hunting lodges (Smith in prep).

Woodland industries

Woodlands provided the raw materials and fuel for numerous industries and crafts. Sawpits, trackways, logging paths and relict trees are all evidence of past forestry operations (Hendry *et al* 1984; Sparkes 1977, 4–7; Tolan-Smith 1997, 45). Charcoal burning platforms and bowl-shaped wood-drying kilns produced fuel for a variety of industries (Kelley 1986; Hart 1993, 58–60). Often the industry was brought to the fuel source which explains the presence of iron working sites, for instance, within woodlands (Crossley 1994, 246). Likewise kilns for pottery (Swan 1984, 108–9), brick and tile (eg Bailey's Hard — SU 396 014) of various dates are found in the New Forest, and early glass

65 *'Banjo'*
enclosure in
Micheldever
Wood
(Hampshire):
field survey
drawing,
original scale
1:1000.

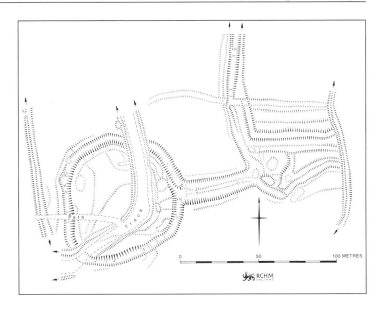

making sites in the woodlands of Staffordshire and Worcestershire. Gunpowder manufacturing was also often located in woodland, both because of the need for coppice poles for charcoal production and because trees were used for blast protection (eg Cocroft 1994). Oak bark was harvested for the tanning industry, while bracken and other vegetation was burnt in simple kilns to produce potash (Jones 1993, 50–4; Marshall and Davies-Shiel 1977, 93–4). Much of this work was seasonal and often cyclical too, so woodlanders sometimes lived in semi-permanent cabins which can be identified by their stone chimneys, or stone or turf footings (Armstrong 1978) (**fig 64**).

Archaeological features not specific to woodland

Many archaeological sites found in woodland contexts were originally located in open country or large clearings in primary woodland which was subsequently recolonised. Earthworks of all types and periods have been recorded. Often the earthwork is the reason for the existence of the wood, because it was uncultivatable ground on which woodland developed. When such earthworks do occur in a wood, they prove that this is secondary woodland and set a limit to its possible age (**fig 65**).

Industrial sites such as quarries and lime kilns are often found in woodland; trees may be allowed to colonise land that has become non-productive because of former industry or alternatively these types of industry may be sited on less intensively used land.

Documentary, cartographic and other sources

It is often possible to establish the existence of woodland in the medieval and post-medieval periods using textual and cartographic sources. Surveys, accounts, charters, deeds, leases, wills, manorial court proceedings and maps of various kinds can provide detailed information about acreages, sites and shapes, coppice cycles, compartmentation, composition and structure and markets for timber and underwood. A well-known example is Hayley Wood (Cambridgeshire) (Rackham 1975). The earliest record of woods in precisely identifiable places are provided by the Anglo-Saxon charters of the ninth to eleventh centuries which describe woodland features in detail. Individual hedgerows and free-standing trees are recorded, often by species.

Domesday Book, analysed by Darby (eg 1971), provides a partial survey of woodland in England in 1086. Although it is clear that large areas were wooded and managed in some way, for instance as wood pasture or coppice, the survey is useful only on a broad scale rather than for the history of particular woods.

From the mid-thirteenth century, there is a wealth of documentation providing information on woods in surveys, estate accounts and court rolls. Because woodland is such a prominent landscape feature, it has often been portrayed on maps. From the late sixteenth century, some estate maps show hedges and hedgerow trees and wood boundaries in great detail; however, particularly where it is not the main purpose of the map, such information may be stylised. Large-scale county maps attempted to record woodland, but are not especially reliable (Watkins 1990, 29).

In OS mapping, since the nineteenth century on the 1:2500 County Series, the relative density of woodland cover has been shown. With the post-1830 maps the portrayal of woodland detail reached its apogee. For example, separate symbols were used for birchwood and underwood; single trees and hedgerow timber were also depicted (Harley 1979, 37–39). After 1880, however, changes in OS specification resulted in the simplification of woodland detail and other land-use categories on large-scale maps. Between 1855 and 1888 the OS 1:2500 series maps were accompanied by a Parish Area Book (or Book of Reference) which gave acreage and, before 1884, land-use of each parcel. Books of Reference provide a useful supplementary record which can be deployed in conjunction with other contemporary sources such as tithe documents or, after 1866, with the official agricultural statistics compiled annually on a parish basis.

Archaeological features may show up on aerial photographs in open or scattered woodland particularly in winter when trees are bare. Generally, however, air photographs are of limited value when it comes to locating archaeological activity within wooded areas (something which should be borne in mind when evaluating transcribed material over a wide area). Aerial photography may, however, provide evidence for the former presence of woods, the shapes of which are fairly distinctive, especially when the interior is dappled with cropmarks of holes where stumps have been dug out (Wilson 1982, 165–7).

Survey

Thorough, but quick archaeological survey is dependent on a combination of good visibility across the site and clear visibility of the ground surface. In woodland both these factors tend to be unfavourable, with the result that survey may take up to four times longer than in open ground.

Shrubs and coppiced trees cause problems because the foliage is at eye level, whereas mature, widely spaced standards are relatively easy to work around. Unchecked by grazing animals, dense undergrowth may cause more fundamental difficulties, since it obscures the archaeology and hinders survey. Exceptions include beech woodland where the dense tree canopy prohibits undergrowth. These problems are minimised by surveying during the winter months when trees have shed their leaves and undergrowth has died away.

Conifer plantations have their own unique challenges, their dense foliage surviving year long. However, one advantage of the rigid planting regimes commonplace in plantations is that in many circumstances long sightlines may still be achieved between the rows of trees and along rides and firebreaks. Where possible, survey prior to felling is desirable since the felling process, which may be destructive itself, often leaves large amounts of brash behind, masking any earthworks.

Archaeological features may be relatively difficult to identify in woodland because of the large amount of 'background noise'. Root systems, holes left by uprooted trees and the inability to stand back and get an overall view may all confuse the eye. Furthermore, woods may be very disorientating with few points of reference to work from: maps rarely show all paths, walls or topographical features. All these factors make the recce stage doubly important in order to check that all ground has been covered thoroughly and to allow sufficient planning for the main survey.

The establishment of survey control is often time consuming, not only because of the short sight lines and the lack of hard detail, but also because of the nature of woodland archaeology, which can often be linear or dispersed; boundary banks or scattered charcoal burning platforms, for example, may cover long distances or large areas. All sites need to be related to map detail, using whatever technology is available. Control may have to be brought in from the margin of the woodland, if there are no suitable fixed points within the wood, or permanent survey markers can be established around the site. GPS technology may provide a solution to this problem: it works well in rides and clearings but not, at present, under canopy, though the equipment manufacturers are trying to overcome this limitation.

Carrying out the detail survey should not present many exceptional problems, if an adequate control network has been laid out with a generous number of control points, although it is wise to be flexible about techniques. For example, in dense woodland the close conditions make orienting a plane-table and reading the staff with an optical alidade more difficult than normal, but it does have the advantage of taking the measurements above the level of undergrowth, where taped measurements may be distorted.

INDUSTRIAL LANDSCAPES

The techniques of industrial archaeology do not differ from those of the archaeologist studying earlier periods. For discussions of the study of industrial archaeology, see Buchanan (1972), Clark (1987), Crossley (1990; 1994) and Palmer (1990). Excavation was quickly embraced by industrial archaeologists: once characterised by rudimentary clearance, it has now reached high professional standards (Cranstone 1990, 231–33). However, the study of industrial landscapes using the techniques of the landscape archaeologist is a relatively recent phenomenon. The wider post-war desire to sweep away the remains of Britain's nineteenth-century industry and a nostalgia for a lost rural past led to an antipathy towards derelict industrial landscapes (eg Hoskins 1955, 166–77).

66   St Austell (Cornwall): waste heaps of the china clay works (Steve Hartgroves/ Cornwall Archaeological Unit).

Meanwhile, many contemporary industrial archaeologists narrowly focused their interests on an individual engine or building, often with a view to preservation, and have not always fully understood or recorded its context.

Industrial landscapes can be some of the most challenging and rewarding to unravel. Six main themes of analysis have been identified for industrial archaeology: the source of raw materials, process plant, power, secondary industry, accommodation and transport (Palmer and Neaverson 1994, 14–17). To this we may add industrial waste. Waste tips are often the most visible features of the impact of industry on its local environment and landscape (**fig 66**) and are a source of information about manufacturing processes and products.

The consideration of techniques and Levels of survey are identical to those discussed elsewhere in this book. In many instances, industrial archaeologists are able to rely on readily available large-scale modern or historic OS maps to provide the control for more detailed survey. Archaeologists working on upland sites are not so fortunate, as in many areas the largest scale modern maps are at 1:10,000. One solution is to plot the information from aerial photographs before proceeding into the field to check the evidence on the ground, though this option is beyond the resources of many people (White 1995, 61–6). A large-scale diagram, if available, should be checked in the field against the surviving remains, and features not shown surveyed onto the diagram and losses noted. A plan is both essential to aid the understanding of the developing morphology of a site and as an index for more detailed records. Very rarely are the functions of all the buildings within a complex named by the OS. One of the first tasks is to identify the buildings and structures, while accepting that many will be unidentifiable by field evidence alone. Lack of detailed knowledge of architectural styles should not inhibit an industrial archaeologist considering the buildings, as often an understanding of the production processes will be a better guide to their former function.

In studying industrial monuments, it is not sufficient to record the most outwardly appealing structure or surviving piece of plant. This must be given a context whether in a

67   *Newland (Cumbria): workers' housing forms a community around the blast furnace and ancillary industrial buildings.*

factory or a wider landscape. By analysing the physical relationships between features, it should be possible to distinguish functional areas and begin to annotate production flowlines. It may also be possible to colour the diagram to represent the constructional phases. In analysing a factory plan, it is necessary to consider the articulation between buildings and how these linkages have changed through time. Relationships between buildings might be defined in terms of production flow, power supply or transport networks. Beyond the confines of the workplace there may be evidence of the type of society a particular industry supported. In remote rural areas, industry might result in the workers being housed in barracks (**plate 20**) away from their families, or it might form an integrated part of the rural settlement pattern (**fig 67**). The affiliation of local churches and chapels built to serve these settlements might allow us to say something about the spiritual aspirations of these communities.

The compilation of a supporting photographic record will be of greater importance where more than earthwork remains survive. It is particularly effective for the recording of surviving buildings and machinery. Aerial photography is also invaluable in illustrating the relationships between buildings and between a site and its landscape (**fig 68**).

The recording of any industrial site will be aided by breaking it down into its component pieces (see Waltham Abbey, Case Study 5; Cocroft 1994; 1996). Such a system allows all the collected cartographic, documentary and photographic material to be indexed against the field description of a monument. At an initial stage, it may also form a checklist against the suite of components which might be expected on a given site type. Its use removes the need for lengthy building and machinery descriptions in the analytical description of the monument, as readers may simply be referred to the supporting documentation. In the more detailed analysis of the monument, the forms may be used to

68   Beckton gasworks (Greater London).

phase a site's development sequence and thus to understand changing relationships between components.

This form of record is also preferred by many higher level records such as the NMR or SMRs. In the NMR system the site as a whole is indexed as a 'parent' record, while the components are indexed against it as its 'children'. The Index of Record for Industrial Sites (IRIS) devised by the Association for Industrial Archaeology (AIA 1993) uses an analogous system, listing the components of a site on its recording forms. A similar system is used by EH in the Monuments Protection Programme to assess the relative completeness of sites. The Nuffield survey of the Ironbridge Gorge took individual plots of land shown on the 1902 OS map as its basic unit of record, individual features within each unit being assigned unique numbers. This information could then be presented in a stratigraphic manner to unravel the chronological sequence and phasing of the more complex sites (Alfrey and Clark 1993, 5–6).

Finding information

The potential for more detailed analysis of a site or landscape will often depend on the survival of supporting documentation. Apart from the information held by various heritage bodies (see Chapter 3), the reports on English industries produced for EH's Monuments Protection Programme (available in the NMR) will — as they increase in number — form a useful summary of research to date, and of the surviving features of an industry, and will provide a guide to the principal sources. Another series of reports has been produced under the Department of the Environment's contaminated land research

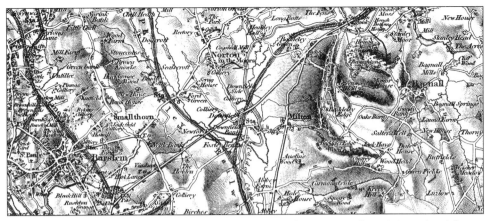

69   *Stoke-on-Trent (Staffordshire): OS 1-inch map of 1836, revised 1879 (reproduced from the 1879 Ordnance Survey map).*

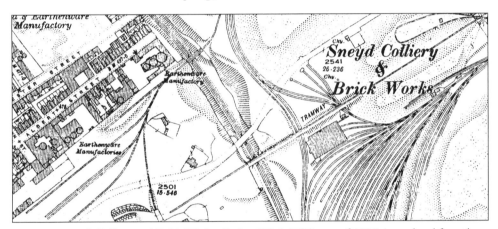

70   *Sneyd Colliery and Brick Works, Stoke: OS 1:2500 map of 1925 (reproduced from the 1925 Ordnance Survey map).*

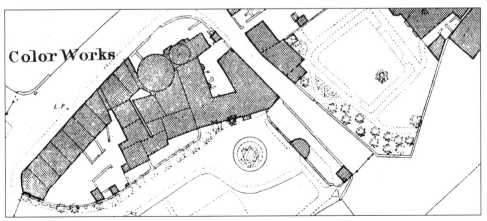

71   *Hamil Color Works, Stoke: OS 1:500 map of 1879 (reproduced from the 1879 Ordnance Survey map).*

programme. A good starting point is *Documentary Research on Industrial Sites* (DoE 1994) and the more specialised DoE *Industry Profiles* which contain summaries of individual industries. Other national institutions, such as the Science Museum and the Public Record Office, contain collections of primary source material.

As we approach the present day, there is an embarrassingly large range of material which might shed light on the history and development of a particular industry. Selectivity is required, if this material is not to become an impenetrable mass. On the larger sites the amount of documentary material available will only be constrained by the Level of the survey (see Appendix I) and the ingenuity of the researcher. To begin with the interpretation of a site's physical remains, all available historic maps should be consulted. From these it should be possible to construct outline chronologies of a site's development (see **fig 12**) with perhaps some building functions annotated on the diagrams. Sequences of aerial photographs may be used in a similar manner for more recent sites. Many of the conventional cartographic sources described elsewhere are valuable sources for the industrial archaeologist. To this list we can also add design plans for railways and canals, which may also contain incidental information on adjacent industries; these should be used with caution, however, as projected designs are not always executed. Most larger companies also had specially commissioned surveys of their sites. The survival of company records is, however, very patchy. More dependable sources are historic OS maps. The small-scale maps will often only identify a site by name, whereas the largest scale maps at 1:528 and later at 1:500 even show items of street furniture (**figs 69–71**). Archaeologists concerned with mining history should also consult the records of the BGS. The principal records of interest are the 6-inch record maps showing the position of mines and quarries, and their collection of historic mine plans, held at the BGS Library, Keyworth, Nottingham.

The most obvious source of documentary material for any site is the present owner. Failing this, the County Records Office is the most likely repository for information on local firms. These may include trade pamphlets issued for advertising purposes which often show views of the factory at work. Large city libraries will often hold runs of contemporary trade and technical journals, including *Engineering* and *The Engineer* which describe many of the innovative factories and plant types. Other contemporary information on working practices in various industries is contained in manuals and encyclopedias, many of which are illustrated with engraved plates. Literary accounts by travellers, such as Celia Fiennes, Defoe and Cobbett, often contain asides on local industries. Company histories may be reconstructed from local trade directories. Local guides to genealogy may reveal family links between industrial activities and suggest further lines of enquiry. Census returns are useful sources for the social background of the workforce. The legislation pertaining to industry should not be ignored, as regulation increasingly influenced the form and conditions of the workplace. The reports of various inspectorates set up to regulate industry from the nineteenth century also contain valuable information on contemporary conditions. Accounts of accidents in these reports or journals and newspapers can often disclose information about working practices. Topographic drawings are another source of information which should not be overlooked. Where historic photographs are available, they are a more reliable source, as they do not suffer from the additions, omissions and re-arranging that artistic licence grants to the landscape painter.

Industrial archaeology of the twentieth century

The industrial archaeologist should not neglect the legacy of the twentieth century. Many assume that this century is so well documented that archaeology has no role to play in interpreting the recent past. Closure, bankruptcy, takeovers, or the view that the material is too recent to be of any interest, have resulted in the destruction or dispersal of many company records (see Atterbury 1995). Photographic recording is invaluable. With recently closed industries, oral history will provide insights into processes and working practices which may be unrecoverable from the physical evidence alone.

In attempting to understand the development of many large factory types such as chemical or steel works, it is the investigative skills of the landscape archaeologist which are best placed to interpret these complex monuments. The techniques of looking at plan form and its development through time are also essential for understanding the functioning of large defence sites. These often comprise hundreds of individual structures and can cover hundreds of hectares. Military activities on these sites, underpinned by a technological industrial society, may also be characterised as semi-industrial. Large sections of airfields, naval dockyards and army depots are taken up with maintenance activities and the supply of the services. To maintain these activities is an industrial undertaking, in the feeding and housing of thousands of personnel often supported by internally generated power, transport and sewage systems. Many of these sites have gone on to have a civilian afterlife, often longer than their service life, providing accommodation to many unattractive and peripheral industrial activities. An illustrated handbook produced in support of the Defence of Britain Project (Lowry 1995) is a useful guide to identifying modern military buildings.

PARKS AND GARDENS

The archaeological field study of early gardens is a recent and rapidly developing topic (Taylor 1983; Brown 1991; Pattison 1998). It has sprung from the recognition, as earthworks, of the layouts of formal gardens of the sixteenth to eighteenth centuries. These earthworks show: massive earthmoving for mounts, terraces and water features, a geometrical basis and clarity and elegance of form of individual elements and of combinations making up an overall layout (Brown and Taylor 1973; Whittle and Taylor 1994). Such neatness and evidence of purposeful design is commonly present in the field evidence across a very wide range of size; compare, for example, Chipping Campden (Gloucestershire) (Everson 1989c) with Croxby (Lincolnshire) (Everson *et al* 1991, 198–200) (**figs 72, 73**). With many early garden sites wrongly categorised as mottes, moats or villages, this can be the distinctive factor that allows a confident re-interpretation.

Historical research into gardens is also advancing rapidly. Particularly good advice about sources for investigating parks and gardens is available in Lambert *et al* (1995).

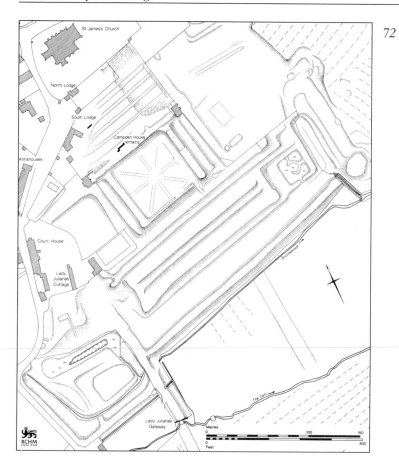

72 *Chipping Campden (Gloucester-shire): field survey plan of house, gardens and environs; original scale 1:1000.*

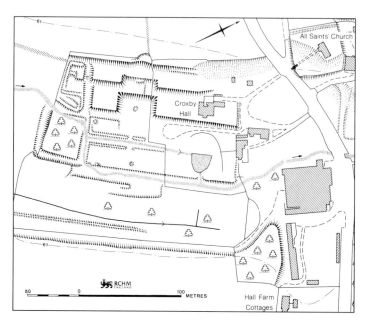

73 *Croxby (Lincolnshire): extract from field survey plan showing gardens; original scale 1:1000.*

74   *Low Ham*
      (Somerset).

Early post-medieval gardens

The best archaeological survival of such remains often correlates with the short life and early destruction of the associated house. In these circumstances, the site of the house usually forms part of the earthworks. It may appear as a distinctive, tight jumble of relatively massive earthworks with stone or brick core, as at Wakerley or Harrington (Northamptonshire) (RCHME 1975, plate 20; Wilson 1991, fig 3.5) or may be difficult to locate with certainty at all, as at Low Ham (Somerset) (**fig 74**) or Quarrendon (Buckinghamshire) (see p83). There is a tendency for peripheral structures — garden buildings, stables, gateways, mills, curtilage walls — to survive through some form of practical re-use. This is especially so when the site has an on-going use at a reduced social level as a tenanted farmstead, for example. Such isolated stylish survivals — even just recycled architectural fragments — can therefore be useful markers and clues. But re-use can entail relocation, too, like the porch from the great later sixteenth-century house at Gerards Bromley that was removed to form an eyecatcher in the eighteenth-century park at Batchacre (Staffordshire: SJ 750 260), where it remains as a forlorn survivor of the destruction of that parkland in its turn.

All such features are intimately and essentially part of the archaeology of garden sites. For typically, house and gardens — the built and the earthwork elements — formed parts of integral and contemporary designs. Even when gardens were added to a pre-existing house, their location and organisation were related to arrangements for approach and access, and to location of public and private rooms, and to such special facilities as long galleries (eg Wilson-North 1989; Coope 1986). Though the historic interplay between house and garden has as yet been little explored in detail, these matters are reflected crudely in the terminology of 'entrance front' and 'garden front'.

Choice of site was important and its manipulation could entail substantial earth movement. Terraces were most readily positioned on slopes, ornamental water features in or close to valley bottoms; but the designers also exploited natural springlines, used reservoirs that survive as earthwork dams, valley contour leats and distant conduit houses for piped supplies. With the exception of especially elevated locations like Howley Hall (West Yorkshire) (Ainsworth 1989) or Throwley Hall (Staffordshire) (Everson 1995b), supply and management of water bulks large in the archaeological evidence both within and outside the garden site (Currie 1990). Elevation for the house and a south-facing aspect for the gardens are common, but not invariable. All are well illustrated at Chipping Campden (see **fig 72**).

Few were new sites, however, and their inherited components will be a relevant matter (Wilson-North 1989; Booth and Everson 1994). A special and numerous category are sites re-using dissolved medieval monasteries. Here conscious choices about the retention and remodelling of monastic buildings and other elements of the precinct are varied and significant. Resulting earthworks, commonly representing several phases superimposed on a monastic original, can be complex and difficult to disentangle (Everson 1996a; Wilson-North and Porter 1997).

An impact of garden design and construction can often be seen on the local church, through refurbishment, rebuilding or relocation. At Chipping Campden the parish church formed a backdrop both to the access route and to the gardens (**fig 75**); at Low Ham (Somerset) it was rebuilt in an ornate and outdated style; at Knaith and Stainfield (Lincolnshire) churches were notably altered for visual effect (Everson *et al* 1991, 112–17, 176–7); at Kirby (Northamptonshire) (Dix *et al* 1995, 292–300) and Woodham Walter (Essex) (Ainsworth *et al* 1991), it was removed. It could fulfil an enhanced role as family burial place, as notably at Warkton (Northamptonshire: SP 893 797); tombs and monumental inscriptions therefore stand as another form of field evidence and marker. A family chapel created on the side of the church facing the garden could provide a viewpoint of special symbolic significance almost amounting to a garden building, as at Kirtling (Cambridgeshire: TL 686 576). Other public buildings, such as almshouses, could result from big-house patronage and be located to emphasise that (see **fig 75**).

Because a house and gardens formed a substantial land-use entity, their creation could distort pre-existing land-use and communication patterns (eg Dix *et al* 1995, 292–300) and create new ones that, as at Chipping Campden, are a legacy to the present. For many, their cost was such that specific occasions, such as an advantageous marriage, may lie behind their creation. Several examples are known where the incomplete and higgledy-piggledy state of surviving earthworks themselves demonstrate that an ambitious scheme failed to reach its intended conclusion, as (in different degrees) at Lyveden (Northamptonshire) in the 1590s or Low Ham (Somerset) and Gawsworth (Cheshire: SJ 892 698) a century later.

Early garden remains are known from a range of social levels: royal, courtier and county. The social aspirations and connections they represent, their conspicuous consumption of wealth and their ability to sustain religious and cultural symbolism all make them of wider

75   *Chipping Campden: the church of St James with almshouses to the left and lodge gates to the right.*

historical moment (eg Johnson 1996). The extent to which such aspirations penetrated down the social scale is an outstanding question. Evidence of fragmentary regular or ornamental adjuncts to quite minor houses undoubtedly exist within earthwork complexes. Though unprepossessing and difficult to interpret or date, they may be the raw material for such an enquiry.

The source material that can be drawn into the study of gardens alongside the physical remains is varied: much of it is very accessible and of traditional local historical interest. It includes genealogy and family history, estate plans, architects' plans and designs, topographical drawings, visitors' and travellers' accounts, letters and family diaries and estate accounts. The richness of resulting integration affords an exceptionally rewarding field for non-excavational study.

It remains the case, however, that frequently it is the recognition of the distinctive earthwork remains that forms the catalyst and focus for such a study or even the sole evidence to work with.

Residual planting

For such early formal gardens, the weight of field evidence is heavily biased to plan-form and structure, as represented by earthworks, rather than planting. Residual survival of planting schemes of that age is rare, whether as trees or stumps, but therefore worth special attention. From gardens more than 250–300 years old, relevant species are more likely to be the inconspicuous and unimpressive, like holly, yew and thorn, than standard trees. In either case, there is value in recording planting 'as found', as part of the physical remains, to promote detection of organised planting — in rows, in avenues, in geometrical blocks, and by spacing to indicate grown-out hedges or intended original appearance. Coupled with this is the potential of the archaeology of trees themselves, for example in the evidence they preserve of their former management by coppicing, pollarding and so on (Rackham 1980, esp 3–6; Phibbs 1991). Guidance on dating may be available from tree-ring counts, or estimates of girth and canopy. For early gardens dating by introduction of species (see Rackham 1986, 52–61) may prove more relevant, as with blocks of *Tilia europaea* at Gawsworth (Cheshire), which are unlikely to pre-date the 1680s.

Such interpretation of planting demands specialist knowledge and experience not routinely to be expected of those engaged in archaeological fieldwork. This can be found in individual scholars and in professional practices specialising in landscape design and interpretation, whose on-site co-operation or advice should be sought. Nevertheless, recognition by fieldworkers of the potential of residual planting, stumps and tree-holes as legitimate items for accurate recording is in itself an important step that provides a platform of field record for further work.

Parkland landscapes

Recording and interpretation of planting is routine practice for landscape architects and garden historians studying eighteenth-century and later parkland (Phibbs 1983). This process creates reports that are valuable records 'as found', backed by historical information and interpretation. The beginning of a national collection of such reports exists at the Centre for the Conservation of Historic Parks and Gardens in the Institute for Advanced Architectural Studies, University of York. Such recording can, in appropriate circumstances, be undertaken in a fully archaeological way by planning even extended parkland landscapes (by air and/or ground survey) and combining recording of earthwork and residual features with surviving planted material and hard detail — location of statuary, steps and so on — to the same standard to form the basis for co-ordinated interpretation (Pattison 1998). Species identification, assessment of age of planting and design intention is a specialist activity here too, that in a local context would benefit from engaging the skills and interest of members of a relevant County Garden Trust or similar body in a co-operative undertaking.

Designed parkland landscapes also contain typical earthworks of parkland — ha-has, sites of buildings, water features, drives, tree-rings, boundaries — all capable of change, adaptation and abandonment. Some of their most essential features, such as lawns, graded slopes, views and vistas, on whose creation most money was spent, present difficulties of recording archaeologically because of their sheer scale and success in looking natural (Phibbs 1998).

Parks also encapsulate and fossilise pre-existing landscapes (Brown 1998). These are typically worthy of record in their own right. They may also, either at large (Rackham 1986, 129) or as individual features (Bowden 1998), be deliberately retained, re-used or adapted in the parkland context.

Urban, suburban and recent

Gardens and parks of the nineteenth and twentieth centuries are exceedingly numerous as features of the English landscape and are diverse in form (Elliott 1986). The category's potential extends to gardens of suburban villas and terraces (Muthesius 1982, 74–8; Galinou 1990, 122–33, 180–97), to the curiosity (eg Turner nd), to municipal parks (Conway 1991) and even to urban cemeteries. Detailed archaeological recording of this totality is not possible or desirable, and even identification and basic documentation is far from complete. Choices and priorities are necessary against an assessment of importance on national, regional and local scales. A framework is provided by EH's selective, non-statutory *Register of Historic Parks and Gardens*, organised by county. The network of County Garden Trusts, now practically complete across the country, is active in drawing together information on a county basis, and county surveys by local authorities and others have not only increased the body of information available as record, but in several instances produced a publication that characterises the potential (eg Hedley and Rance 1987; Williamson and Taigel 1990; Hall 1995; Stamper 1996).

Records of even the most important of individual gardens of recent date can certainly prove to be surprisingly inadequate. For example, archaeological fieldwork at Gertrude Jekyll's own garden at Munstead Wood has shown the potential, in such exceptional instances, of treating a combination of hard details and residual planting of a modern garden as the subject for recording 'as found' (Everson 1995c) (see **plate 10**).

Medieval gardens

The focus of archaeological fieldwork on gardens has been and remains on the abandoned formal layouts of the early post-medieval period, with some forays into later contexts. Characterisation and identification of medieval gardens as field remains is a matter of current academic research, with results that are both exciting and problematic (Everson 1998). The small-scale, enclosed garden closely integrated with residential buildings — the type that figures principally in our traditional conception of medieval gardens — has proved difficult to identify as abandoned field remains (Everson *et al* 1991, 129–31). More common, at least in their survival in a recognisable state, may be a form of medieval designed landscape, more akin to eighteenth-century creations but commonly exploiting ponds and meres to create a contrived setting and carefully organised access (Taylor 1989b; Everson *et al* 1991, 184–5). A notable example is Bodiam Castle (East Sussex) (Everson 1996b) (see **fig 49**). As was the case when formal garden earthworks first came to attention, recognition of such designs is more a change of perspective, involving a re-focusing of expectation and perception, than a matter of outright new discoveries.

RECORDING AN INDUSTRIAL COMPLEX
THE ROYAL GUNPOWDER FACTORY, WALTHAM ABBEY (ESSEX)

Within its boundary, the 75-hectare site of the Royal Gunpowder Factory encapsulates the history of over 300 years of explosives manufacture and research. At the time of the survey, the site comprised nearly 250 roofed and ruined buildings, and over 200 former buildings represented by floor slabs or buried archaeological remains linked together by an extensive canal network. The security afforded to the site by Ministry of Defence ownership contributed to a remarkable level of preservation, including runs of steam heating pipes and dated electricity poles and tramlines, providing the physical evidence for relationships in the landscape, which elsewhere have been so easily destroyed by casual vandalism.

The challenge this survey presented to the RCHME was to record the diversity of the field remains (RCHME 1994; Cocroft 1996). Fortuitously, the Ministry of Defence had commissioned a detailed 1:500 topographical electronic survey of the site. Outline plan sheets were provided to the archaeological surveyors at a scale of 1:1000 onto which archaeological detail was added using standard graphical methods. From the field this detail was digitised into the surveyor's CAD file, allowing the archaeological information to be held as a distinct data set within the civil engineer's drawing file.

Running in parallel with the topographic survey, selected buildings were chosen for full written analysis. The survival of many contemporary architectural drawings dispensed with the need to produce an original drawn record. However, a detailed

Aerial photograph of the northern part of the site.

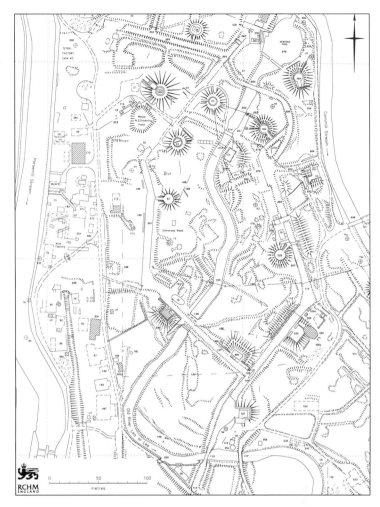

Extract from CAD-based survey drawing.

photographic record was made of these buildings and all notable structures on the site, supplemented by low-level aerial photography.

In addition to the wealth of field remains, a bewildering amount of documentary material exists in scattered repositories. This includes historic maps, architectural drawings, technical manuals, historic photographs and more rarely published descriptions. The very richness and diversity of this material in itself threatened to become overwhelming and incomprehensible. The solution devised was to use what were termed 'component sheets' to record every building and significant feature on the site. This system, based on conventional archaeological excavation context sheets, was flexible enough to record all the different types of physical remains on the site and relate them to any known documentation. Fixtures and fittings could also be correlated with these sheets, vital in providing a context for artefacts retained for future museum use. In total, over 600 sheets were compiled.

The unusual completeness of the documentation supporting the survey of the RGPF allowed something of the dynamism of this complex landscape to be reconstructed. This was revealed in the addition of new process buildings and in extensions to the canal and tramway systems. Most large industrial plants are subject to constant renewal and modification, as new processes are introduced. This was most dramatically illustrated in 1898, when many of the gunpowder buildings were converted to manufacture the new chemical explosive cordite. At this date, the old south to north flowline through the factory was reversed. New relationships were created, as buildings were converted to house novel processes and new structures were shoe-horned into this established landscape.

THE ROYAL GUNPOWDER FACTORY - WALTHAM ABBEY

NUMBER S31	OLD SERIES 93	RCHME NUMBER	N.G.R. TL 37600 01844

NAME/FUNCTION	START DATE	END DATE
Press House No.4	1879	by1886
No.1 Moulding House	by1886	1898?
Cylinder Cutting House	1898?	by 1908
Cordite Blending House	by1908	1917?
CE Packing House	1917?	by 1940
CE Store No.1	by 1940	1945

CARTOGRAPHIC DEPICTION		DOCUMENTARY REFERENCES	
1886	WASC 900/38 + SUPP5 975 ; No 1 Moulding House	Plan and elevation	
1886	WASC 900/41A	date?	No.1 Moulding House- shows timber framed building in centre of traverse, small rooms on south elevation west side Shoe Room east room Store, both lit by circular slights RCHME Neg. BB92/26362
1886	WASC 900/42		
1886	WASC 900/41A No1 Moulding House		
1897	WASC 900/53C		
c1900	WASC 900/79 Cylinder Cutting House	1908	RGPF Ledger WASC 1509 + WASC 1764 ; Blending House and Shoe Room built 1879 p9
c1910	WASC 900/65		
c1910	WASC 900/79	c1925	RGPF Ledger WASC 1680
1917	WASC 900/70	c1945	RGPF Ledger WASC 1508 ; Blending House and Shoe Room
1917	WASC 900/72		
1919	WASC 900/74		
c1920	WASC 900/80	1972	ERDE List ; Asbestos Hut
1923	WASC 900/84 ; CE Packing House	1991	Mott McDonald survey
>1940	WASC 900/91A	1992	RARDE List ; Demolished gunpowder store/retaining walls only
1940	Proc Court Inquiry 20-Apr-1940 appendix I CE Store No.1		
1954	A - B.34 ; S31		
c1960	WASC 900/94 ; S31		
c1963	WASC 900/97 ; S31		
1972	WASC 900/102 ; S31		
1972	WASC 900/104 ; S31		
1976	WASC 900/113 ; S31		

Component sheet for the Gunpowder Press House.

10 Buildings in the landscape

Buildings form an important, sometimes a dominant, part of historic landscapes, either as standing structures (with or without roofs) or as vestigial buried remains. The old idea that the study of buildings is somehow separate from other archaeological disciplines has now largely been superseded by the recognition that buildings provide another form of evidence for the evolution of the historic landscape. Archaeologists undertaking landscape studies will now wish to examine buildings for what they can reveal about the social and economic development of their region, setting this evidence alongside that provided by other archaeological and documentary sources.

Despite this new emphasis on integrating different types of evidence, it has to be stated that, as in other specialist fields, the analysis of buildings has its own dynamic and its own internal agenda. Like other sources, buildings can be studied entirely for their own sake, and considerable energy is expended on aspects such as structural evolution, the use of cast iron in early industrial buildings for example, or the development of style and plan, such as the chronological and geographical incidence of different plan forms in vernacular houses. For the landscape historian, there are some limited inferences to be drawn from such studies, but the primary use of buildings for landscape studies will be for more general purposes. There are many excellent books in print about both the recording of buildings (eg Wood 1994) and about the development of different building types; to take the example of farm buildings, studies range from the national and documentary-based (Harvey 1984), through the national with strong regional and methodological emphasis (Wade Martins 1991), to local studies of different types (Peters 1969; Jones and Bell 1991). This chapter is not concerned with buildings as architecture, but with those aspects of the study of buildings which have a more direct relevance for an examination of the changing landscape.

Different types and Levels of survey will prompt different questions. A general and broad-ranging landscape history of a large area — a county, a region defined by its topographical character (the Vale of York or the Tyne valley, for instance), a group of parishes with either some type of unity (tenure in historic times, for example) or clear contrasts (upland and lowland, gentry and yeoman) — will demand analysis of the chronological, social and geographical distribution of different building types, and, if sufficient numbers of buildings are recorded, then general conclusions may be drawn from the evidence and used to inform wider discussions of social and economic evolution. Such work may show how buildings reflect economic and social development within a county (eg Pearson 1994), or a smaller region (eg Machin 1978) or just two parishes (Alcock 1993). Surveys of particular site types (for example, industrial, agricultural or

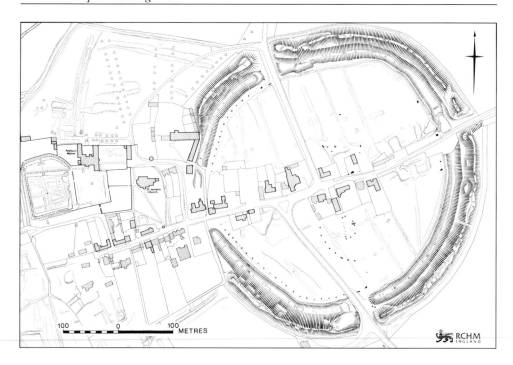

76   *Avebury (Wiltshire): extract from field survey plan, showing henge, church and manor house; original scale 1:1000 (Modern detail reproduced from Ordnance Survey mapping with the permission of the Controller of Her Majesty's Stationery Office © Crown Copyright. RCHME Licence GD03133G/4/98).*

ecclesiastical landscapes) will require a different approach, more closely related to the development of individual building types. Two good illustrations of the contribution of buildings to studies of industrial landscapes are Palmer and Neaverson (1992) and Muter (1979). Studies of single sites demand a third approach, with greater stress on the particular characteristics of the buildings which form part of the site and with discussion of how an individual monument relates to other monuments of the same type or period (Bold 1988; Wade Martins 1980).

The essential questions which must be addressed by the landscape historian are the links, in terms of cause and effect, between buildings and other aspects of the environment. The presence, sometimes also the form, of buildings may explain and be explained by other features of the landscape, for the associations between elements which we observe today are rarely the result of accident and, if we can recognise it, have significance. The issue is one of relationships — chronological, functional and spatial — between evidence of different types.

The *chronological* relationship between buildings and other elements of the landscape is one of the starting points in any inquiry. It will often be the case that standing buildings date from a much later period than any other aspect of the observable archaeology; for example, a farmstead, with house and farm buildings built piecemeal over the course of the nineteenth century, may overlie part of a medieval field pattern (Beresford and St

77   *Rievaulx Abbey (North Yorkshire) from the air. The church and claustral buildings form*
the nucleus of a complex landscape. The precinct included farm buildings, fields, meadows,
water courses for latrines, mills, a tannery and all the service buildings which allowed the
community to function (Coppack 1990, 100–101). Not all these elements survive well,
but earthworks reveal their former presence.

Joseph 1979, 117–36), or a medieval church may lie within an earlier enclosure (Ryder
1993, 17–18). In these circumstances, the discrepancy in date must, of course, be noted,
and it must be asked whether the association has significance from other standpoints.
More rarely, standing buildings can comprise the earliest form of evidence in a particular
landscape. Such is the case where a medieval house of high status forms the nucleus of a
country park laid out in the eighteenth or nineteenth century. And it is often the case that
standing buildings and other archaeological remains date from broadly the same period.
The buildings and landscape of the extractive industries, such as lead and coal mining, are
good examples of this contemporaneity.

The assessment of relative dates leads into an inquiry into the *functional* relationship
between buildings and other aspects of the historic landscape. Again, there are a number
of possible associations. At one extreme, there may be no link, probably because the
buildings date from a totally different era, the intervening period bringing dramatic
change to the nature of the landscape. The medieval or post-medieval mansion lying
adjacent to a henge monument, as at Avebury, may be an example of this lack of
connection. The more powerful association at Avebury is that between the mansion and
the parish church, and indeed between the parish church and the henge (**fig 76**). All sorts
of questions are raised by these juxtapositions, and clearly not all of them can be answered
from archaeological evidence alone.

78   *Oats Royd, Midgeley (West Yorkshire). In the foreground is a substantial vernacular house*
     of 1645, built by the Murgatroyd family, probably on the profits of the textile industry.
     Two hundred years later, the family built the first part of the steam-powered worsted
     spinning mill, seen in the background. The mill was extended in many phases in the mid-
     and late nineteenth century.

On many sites, however, there is a clear association between different types of monument. A monastic complex may have remains not only of buildings of the church and cloister, but also earthworks associated with water-management systems, including fishponds and sewerage (Coppack 1990, 81–99) (**fig 77**). Many industrial sites have contemporary architectural and archaeological remains relating to the same process; the ruined engine houses and the spoil heaps, tramways and water-management systems of the tin and copper mining industries in Devon and Cornwall clearly all result from the same economic activity and require to be considered together (Palmer and Neaverson 1994, 67–87).

Many sites may have remains related to the same function but built in different eras. Topographic advantage or strategic location gave some sites a military importance over a long period. A well-known case is Portchester Castle (Hampshire), where a Roman fort was adapted as the bailey of the medieval castle, and there are many other examples where the military use of a site demonstrably stretches from antiquity into the modern era. At Pendennis Castle (Cornwall), the site is made up of many layers of defensive earthworks and buildings from the Henrician through to the Second World War (**plate 21**). Industrial sites can provide similarly related evidence of different dates: many of the grinding wheels and forges of the Sheffield region have water-powered systems developed first in the early post-medieval period, but have surviving buildings of a later age (Crossley 1989). Some textile regions have remains of water-powered fulling mill sites established in the medieval period, clothier houses of the post-medieval era, weavers' cottages of the nineteenth century and great factories of the steam age (Giles and Goodall 1992, 76–122) (**fig 78**). All

79   *Hackthorn (Lincolnshire). This aerial view shows the country house landscape centred on the mansion and church, surrounded by parkland which includes an ornamental lake. To one side of the nucleus are the walled kitchen gardens and the estate village, the latter replacing the earlier village revealed still by earthworks in the park. Beyond the park lie the rectangular fields of the enclosed landscape; the medieval fields can still be seen in ridge-and-furrow (foreground).*

these monuments provide important evidence for different phases in the development of cloth production.

Functional associations may not be as obvious as the examples cited above. The classic image of the Potteries is that of Josiah Wedgwood's mansion, Etruria, blackened by smoke and set against a backdrop of the local chaos that characterised the pottery industry, with conical spoil heaps and mine headgear (Hoskins 1955, plate 51). The house built by the great potter was originally surrounded by a park, and its design, size and setting reflected his elevated position in local society. Time and commercial pressures, however, dealt harshly with this ordered environment, for soon the park became part of the industrial landscape which Wedgwood had helped to create, coal tips dominating the scene around the house. The link can be extended beyond the immediate surroundings, for the swathes of workers' housing which lay around such nuclei represent another manifestation of the same process of industrial development (Baker 1991, 29–35, 42–5). It is interesting to record that recent developments have largely removed the remains of coal mining from Etruria, and now it is difficult to imagine the close linkage which existed between different monuments making up the industrial scene. In other areas too, twentieth-century decline in traditional industries, together with changes in demography and standards of living, have swept away much of the landscape of England's industrial areas, but where these elements survive — as they do in some northern textile regions (Giles and Goodall 1992,

166–99; Calladine and Fricker 1993, 136–59) — they merit study as part of a long story of industrial change.

Functional interrelationships are also evident in rural settings, in particular in and around the country house and its park (**fig 79**). This landscape may be viewed as a demonstration of the power of the landed interest in some parts of the English countryside. The centre of the park will be the country house, a potent symbol of temporal authority, perhaps grouped with the parish church, lending spiritual weight to the scene. In the park there may be buildings and monuments — a grotto, obelisks, triumphal arches, temples, a mausoleum — all set within an artificial landscape, with plantations of trees, roads and bridges, water features, a ha-ha, formal or informal gardens according to the fashion of the age, and some at least planned to be viewed from specific rooms within the house (see pp147–8). Around the house are the offices — laundries, stables, coach house, kennels, kitchen gardens, builder's yard and so on — which provided the facilities needed by aristocratic families. Close by will be a home farm, sometimes built in model form by an improving landlord. Beyond the park, bounded by a high wall and with access controlled by gate lodges, lies the estate infrastructure which supported the aristocratic way of life. Accommodation for a workforce was provided in an estate village, often rebuilt on model lines, or simply removed from sight of the main house. The village may replace an earlier settlement in the park, now evident only in earthwork remains. An inn may have been built to house visitors, there may be estate offices, a school and a village hall. There may also be a small, elaborately detailed railway station, feasible only because it served the country house. And around the village, possibly extending for many parishes, is the farming landscape, one perhaps dominated by tenant farms laid out by private or public enclosure awards. The landscape might include woods for timber and game, mills for grinding corn, perhaps even modest experiments with crafts and small-scale industry. Viewed in one sense, all these features are related, for they all contribute to the type of hierarchical social organisation and dominantly agricultural economy which characterised large parts of rural England.

Functional links produce *spatial* relationships between monuments of different types, for proximity and distance are often the result of deliberate planning. The example of the estate village moved to clear a view from a country house is one of the more obvious types of planning requiring dissociation between monuments; the earlier spatial proximity at Hackthorn (**fig 79**) is still evident in the earthwork remains of the village. Another aspect of dissociation concerns the way in which monuments express patterns of influence over time. In many upland areas of England, the Established Church was poorly represented by places of worship and, as these areas grew in population in the eighteenth and nineteenth centuries, this vaccuum was filled by non-conformist sects, which built numerous chapels, many in lonely places serving a dispersed upland community (**fig 80**). Proximity between monuments results from a number of considerations. The presence of good transport facilities, in the pre-1830 period primarily connected with navigable rivers or canals, acted as a magnet for industries or commercial ventures which required bulk transport: York retained river-front warehouses until recent decades, Leeds has a number on both river and canal (**fig 81**), and Ellesmere Port developed as a town around warehouses built at the point where the Ellesmere and Chester Canal linked with the River Mersey (Roberts 1995).

80   *Baptist chapel, Pole Moor, Colne Valley (West Yorkshire). First built in 1790 and extended in 1858–9, this remote chapel served the hill communities to the west of Huddersfield.*

81   *The River Aire in Leeds (West Yorkshire), lined on the north bank with nineteenth-century warehouses with loading bays for the movement of goods into and out of barges.*

Just as a facility such as transport spawned new industry, manufacturing activity itself stimulated new satellite trades giving rise to a complex web of linked activities: in textile regions one finds machine makers and chemical plants, and quarrying can be linked to explosives manufacturing. Similarly, the woodland region of Furness (Cumbria) with its iron ore deposits hosted a group of related industries, ironworking, charcoal burning and gunpowder manufacture being the principal ones (see **figs 64, 83**). The spatial relationship between these landscape features is not, therefore, the result of accident.

Understanding a building or complex

Landscape students need to come to an understanding of the architectural remains within their area. This understanding, essential in the assessment of the type of relationships considered above, will be provided by a more or less detailed examination of the buildings. The depth of study will be determined by the requirements of the survey, and by the relevance of the architectural evidence to the chosen themes. Clearly, it is not necessary to probe too deeply into the development of a post-medieval country house, if the focus of study is the *medieval* agricultural landscape, but if the *evolving* landscape itself is the main subject of attention then the house's phasing and its relationship to other elements in the landscape will be more important.

There are certain basic questions which the archaeologist will wish to address to all monuments. The answers may establish that the buildings have no relevance to the enquiry, belonging perhaps to a different period or to a type that lies beyond the scope of the survey in question. More probably, however, the answers will show that buildings have a role to play and will demonstrate the essential links to be made with other aspects of the landscape. The *date or dates* at which a building or complex was erected will self-evidently be an important starting point, since by establishing this with confidence the chronological relationship with other evidence will become clear. Decisions on dating are famously difficult (Mercer 1975, 6; Pearson 1994, 3; Wade Martins 1991, 78–86). The date of some buildings is well known, or at least thought to be beyond question, and dendrochronology can be applied in some cases to provide precision. However, most buildings — the vast majority of vernacular or early buildings, for example — are not precisely datable, through either scientific or documentary research. Even datestones are open to suspicion in some cases, for they can be moved and re-used with ease. Styles and structural forms have a long currency in many types of building, and, while there may well be a typological evolution, it may be unsafe in a particular instance to claim one building as absolutely later or earlier than another. Good dating tends to be based not upon a single feature of a building, but rather upon a combination of factors, including structural and stylistic features and, almost equally important, a consideration of the building's social status. When accurate dating is not possible, general and relative dating can provide important information about the evolution of different parts of the landscape.

The second essential in the consideration of buildings concerns *function*. Most functions are self-evident — a house for living in, a church for worship and so on — but others are more obscure. A mill may certainly be industrial, but it will be important to determine whether it was used to grind corn or to house fulling stocks and other textile machinery

82   *Newstead Abbey*
      (Nottinghamshire)
      illustrates the way in
      which the changing
      use of buildings is
      reflected in the
      landscape. The
      medieval abbey was
      partly converted into
      a country house,
      with the church
      retained ultimately
      as a gothic ruin.
      The abbey precinct
      was laid out in
      different phases as
      parkland and formal
      gardens.

or processes, since both these functions will relate to other archaeological evidence in the area. Industrial buildings thus reveal the range of economic activities practiced in an area at different periods. So too do farm buildings, although conclusions drawn from the presence and absence of barns, cowhouses and so on need to be hedged around with caveats concerning the changing way in which farming was practiced over a long period. Military or defensible buildings, too, may have associated monuments, and their presence tells a great deal about conditions of life at the time of their construction. The student must also be alive to changes of use, some as dramatic as the transition from monastery to country house (**fig 82**), others less blatant, for example the conversion of part of a barn to accommodate livestock. Industrial buildings can change function too: the blast furnace at Low Nibthwaite (Cumbria), built in 1735, became in turn a bobbin mill, a sawmill and then a private dwelling (**fig 83**). Whatever the case, the reasons underlying these new uses may be significant indicators of change in the historic landscape and should be recognised as such.

The date and function of buildings are determined by the examination of each structure. The archaeologist should, however, at the same time consider the relationship between a single monument and other monuments in the area, for patterns of great significance can emerge from the analysis of large numbers of buildings. When analysed in bulk, buildings of many types provide important evidence for change or continuity and for social and economic evolution. They can raise many questions which, even if not answerable using architectural evidence alone, at least provide a vital framework for the examination of other related sources.

The rarity or typicality of a building can only be assessed in a broad context, and this

83   *Low Nibthwaite (Cumbria): the lower part of the eighteenth-century blast furnace survives as the right-hand end of the main range, with the top storey of the nineteenth-century bobbin mill built across it. In the early twentieth century, the site became a saw mill.*

84   *The Luddenden valley, Calderdale (West Yorkshire). The landscape seen by Daniel Defoe in the 1720s. Defoe remarked that there was 'hardly a house standing out of a speaking distance from another, and … almost at every house there was a tenter, and almost on every tenter a piece of cloth … look which way we would, high to the tops, and low to the bottoms, it was all the same; innumerable houses and tenters, and a white piece upon every tenter'.*

164

assessment plays a vital role in determining the significance of a particular building. Significance, it should be noted, lies not just in the pioneering, the innovative, the earliest, the latest and other such superlatives: typicality is vitally important, and the establishment of what is common is the foundation of area building surveys. Judgement of significance emerges only from wide knowledge, either of the national setting of monuments of major importance, or of the local or regional character of buildings of more parochial character. All buildings proclaim themselves by their presence and make statements. Clearly conclusions must be drawn from the presence of a major country house or large medieval church in a landscape, since this tells us something of the patronage and influences at play in the region at the time of construction. The presence of a number of churches in a region of study provides the potential for important questions to be asked about the dates of the major building periods, the evidence for contraction, and the patronage underlying the pattern of building. And, to take a third example, the careful and judicious analysis of industrial complexes, such as textile mills, allows one to determine stages in the progress from domestic to factory working, a change which has many implications for the landscape.

For minor buildings, say of vernacular status, the analysis of large numbers will yield important evidence about the evolution of the landscape. There are many aspects of bulk analysis which require caution and must be considered when weighing the value of the architectural evidence (Johnson 1993, 7–14). Present-day remains may offer a good indication of previous distribution, but changes wrought by pressures such as mining or urban expansion can produce a very skewed pattern of survival. Some sensitivity will, therefore, be required in the comparison between areas or between types of building in the same area. If, however, one can with some confidence establish the validity of the surviving patterns, a number of very important issues may be addressed. The date and character of the different waves of house construction since the middle ages will determine which levels of society were able to build at different times and to different standards, and this will provide vital evidence for the dominant influences on the development of the area. Sometimes aristocratic, gentry and yeoman houses are found together in the same region, sometimes the presence of one precludes the others, or conversely the absence of one permits the others. The West Yorkshire dales, in particular Calderdale, were distantly administered by absentee owners, and in this power vacuum there developed a prosperous society of minor gentry and yeomen, able to build good houses from the late Middle Ages (**fig 84**). The local wealth was based on the textile industry, and this permitted the subdivision of holdings into small plots, each, however, with a substantial house of early date (RCHME 1986, 106–32). If the study area is sufficiently large, bulk analysis is a vital tool in determining the social stratigraphy and economic and chronological development of a landscape, and the implications for other aspects of archaeological inquiry cannot be overstated.

Recording a building

The purpose in recording a building or group of buildings will vary according to the nature of the study of which this exercise forms a part. In a general survey of a large area, only superficial detail may be required, but a closer focus will be needed, when the area of study is small and when buildings form a significant element in the landscape. There is, therefore, no single way to record a building, and the approach selected will be determined by the type of study and the available resources. Descriptions of different Levels of architectural recording have been provided by the RCHME (1996b) and need not be repeated here. It suffices to note that four Levels of record are identified as most commonly applicable, ranging from simple identification and a photograph to a fully measured and documented survey.

In a survey of a large area, or in a holistic study of a landscape with many different building types, various stages in recording can be identified. Given that a need for a particular survey has been demonstrated, the first stage in any research will be the definition of the questions to be addressed of the material. This will determine the Level of record — detailed or general — needed to recover the relevant evidence. The next stage is always to determine that relevant records do not already exist, in private or public repositories, for it is difficult to envisage a situation which would justify re-survey where usable material exists. The gathering of background material, from documents and other archaeological sources, will help to provide the context for the study of the buildings, for the more that is known from other sources the more one can address pertinent questions to the architectural material. It might be useful to express a caveat here, for while taking account of the evidence of other sources, one must retain an open mind about potentially contradictory material presented by architectural evidence. One must not, therefore, be so led by the other sources that one overlooks dissentient evidence provided by buildings, even if this is uncomfortable. Experience suggests that it is precisely through such conflicts that one reaches a better and closer understanding of the validity of different sources, and therefore of the true pattern of landscape change.

The fieldwork stage of recording may itself have different phases. Detailed knowledge of the architectural subject matter will help to inform the approach to survey, and some intensive recording of a limited number of buildings may highlight how further work should proceed. This might be followed by a Rapid survey, perhaps collecting basic information and recording with photographs; this will allow the total material to be assessed at an elementary level and provide material on which to base decisions on what to record and at what level of detail. Selection will often be the only way of dealing with large numbers of monuments, and the best selection will include good examples of typical monuments together with those which depart from the norm. It is important, therefore, to record the significant because typical and the significant because atypical. A programme of detailed fieldwork will follow selection, and the results of the fieldwork will then, if necessary, be prepared as an archive. The type of record produced will, as stated above, be determined by the nature of the inquiry, but the destiny of the record may well have an influence in this respect. If the intention is to produce archives which may be used by other people for other purposes, then questions of presentation and consistency clearly play a greater part than in the case of records produced purely for internal research purposes. The careful and systematic collection of information is, however, increasingly part of archaeological method, and potential use by other people should be considered in the design of any record format.

PART III: PRODUCTS

11 Illustration and the written report

In archaeology, as in other field sciences, illustrations and written reports are two sides of the same coin. A piece of text without a plan is as unthinkable as a plan without any explanatory text: the text explains and qualifies the plan.

ILLUSTRATIONS

Having applied best practice to an analytical earthwork survey to produce an accurate and comprehensive plan, it is essential that the same standards are achieved at the drawing-up stage; a good survey can lose its impact, and to some extent its credibility, through being badly drawn. It is the draughtsman's aim to present the graphical results of a survey as clearly as possible, to be understood by specialists and non-specialists alike. The illustrations should carry forward the analytical processes of the survey itself and clarify arguments put forward in the accompanying text.

Preparation

Field drawings
At the completion of fieldwork, the product should be a well-drawn and complete pencil field drawing or, if using digital methods, an annotated computer plot. Ideally, the field surveyor should be the draughtsman, because the plan should attempt to portray the character as well as the dimensions of the site, and only someone with an intimate knowledge of the site can do this. However, where this is not possible the draughtsman should fully understand the field drawing and be familiar with the site or landscape. Before commencing work on the final version, the illustrator should be satisfied that the drawing is complete and that no information is missing or unclear. Even if the draughtsman undertook the survey, a delay between completion of the fieldwork and drawing can result in some of the site's subtleties being forgotten, if they were not recorded clearly.

Objective

Before beginning the drawing the objectives should be clear: publication, a working or management plan, or an archive drawing? There must always be an archive drawing, at full survey scale and including all survey information, whether the survey is to be published or not.

Equipment

The finished plan is essentially a penned version of the field drawing, and polyester drawing film is the best medium for this. It is easy to draw on with pens and pencil. Alterations are made easily and the material itself is durable, maintaining its stability indefinitely. A suitable grade for penned drawings is 125 micron.

When using film, the best results are achieved with modern technical pens. These pens come in a range of sizes, but only a limited selection is needed. The 0.18mm is the main workhorse, for both hachures and linework. A 0.13mm or 0.10mm is useful for smaller hachures; however, both should be used with caution for basic linework. Other useful sizes are 0.25mm, for linework and stipple, and 0.35mm and 0.5mm for heavier lines. Special ink, designed for use on film, must be used as normal inks for use on paper are totally unsuitable for film. Alterations may be made using a film ink eraser, or a razor blade or scalpel for careful scratching out. The only other drawing instruments and materials needed are standard technical drawing items.

Drawing techniques

Earthwork depiction - the hachured plan, basic techniques

The hachured plan remains the most effective means of depicting earthworks. Although unfairly criticised in some quarters for being over-complicated and confusing to the non-specialist, no better system has yet been developed. It is the very capacity to manage complex sites as well as simple ones which make the hachure such a flexible means of depiction. Perhaps the most important virtue of hachures, however, is that they portray clearly chronological relationships between features (see **fig 34**). Even if plans are simplified for wider dissemination, the hachured earthwork plan is still the best starting point and the basis for the archival record.

Hachures are elongated delta-shaped symbols which, when arranged in arrays, convey the positions of the top and bottom of a slope accurately, where the wide end (head) represents the top and the narrow end (tail) the bottom. Variations on this basic convention may be used to depict a diversity of subtle differences in earthwork forms and gradients (**fig 85**).

The most important basic principle in drawing hachures is the uniformity of spacing, size and alignment within each array. If this principle is not followed, the result is an untidy mess. Secondly, the different gradients or 'weights' of slopes must be shown and this is achieved by varying hachure thickness and spacing between arrays. Without using this variation all slopes will appear the same, giving a misleading impression of the site. If possible, the hachures should be drawn freehand, spaced by eye and without the use of a straightedge. This may seem a daunting prospect to the beginner, but with practice most people can achieve an acceptable standard, and one which is superior to that drawn by mechanical means.

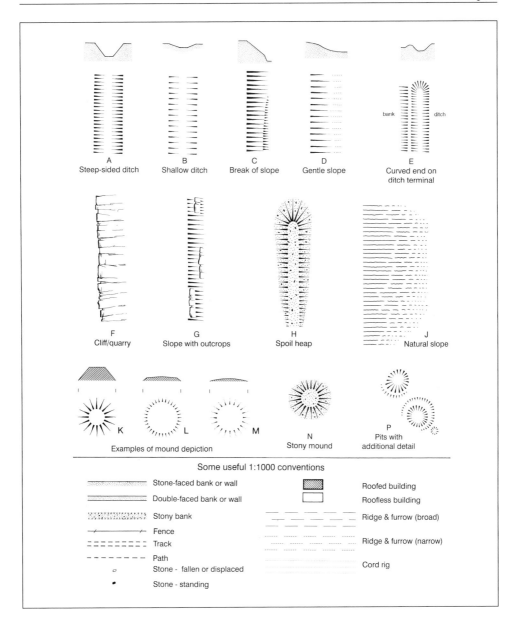

85   *Conventions: hachure depictions of earthworks and associated features. For a full list of conventions, see RCHME (forthcoming).*

Spacing and weight

Although steep slopes will have very closely spaced hachures, it does not follow that those for gentle or shallow slopes will be very widely spaced, as there is a limit at which too great a spacing will cause the form of the slope to be lost. A balance has to be drawn between thickness and spacing to achieve a visible variation in the depicted slope. **Figure 85 (A** and **B)** shows two parallel ditches of different profiles, where differing thickness and spacing of hachures gives a contrasting density and makes these subtleties visible to the eye. This effect is very useful to illustrate the prominence of one feature over another and can help to demonstrate chronological sequences.

When drawing linear features such as ditches or ramparts, it is important that the hachures of opposing sides of the feature are similarly spaced and opposite each other. Failure to do this results in an untidy plan which is difficult to read. Similarly for curving or rounded features, any changes in spacing must be gradual to maintain the continuity of the array (**fig 85**).

Break of slope
Some slopes do not have even gradients and may steepen or flatten out gradually, to blend with the natural topography. If the steepening is so pronounced that there is a break of slope, this should be surveyed and depicted by drawing the slope as two gradients, with the tails of the upper hachures touching the heads of the lower (**fig 85, C**). Where a slope starts to level out and has no clearly defined base, the tail of the hachure can be broken to depict this (**fig 85, D**). Through a combination of all these effects, it is possible, with practice, to depict quite subtle changes in gradient.

Natural slopes
Where natural slopes form an important element of a site, such as at hilltop locations, they should if possible be surveyed and depicted, using contours or the natural hachure convention. When using the latter technique, it is important that the plan does not become unduly cluttered with natural slopes, detracting from the archaeological detail. The convention is a slightly wavy line radiating to show the form of the slope and breaking up as it descends (**fig 85, J**). The heads may be thickened and rounded for the more precipitous gradients, though this should be kept to a minimum so as not to dominate the drawing or cause confusion with the earthwork hachures.

Additional drawing methods

Contours
Although contours are an important and long-established means of depicting gradients, they are not generally suitable for recording the earthwork elements of an archaeological site (see p66). However, contours are a useful method of indicating the nature of the terrain in which the earthwork is sited. If for example an earthwork site is positioned at the foot of a steep slope, or at the head of a small coombe or valley, subtle use of contours at an appropriate interval can convey this well, though the contours should not interfere with the hachured areas. Similarly, where there is a change in levels on the interior of a hillfort or other enclosure, contours can portray this very effectively. Contours should, like the natural hachure, be used with caution, so as not to over-complicate parts of a drawing which are already heavily detailed with earthworks. A careful decision has to be made on the appropriate vertical interval.

86   *Setta Barrow on the Devon– Somerset border: plan and profile.*

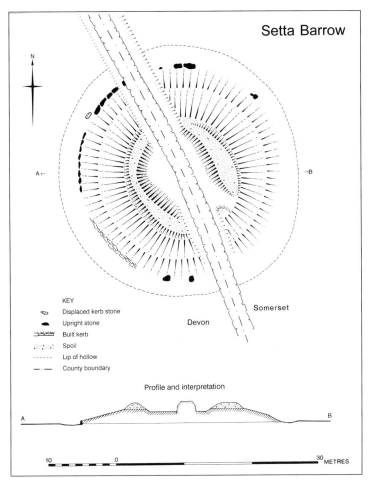

Setta Barrow

KEY
- Displaced kerb stone
- Upright stone
- Built kerb
- Spoil
- - - - - - Lip of hollow
— · — County boundary

Somerset

Devon

Profile and interpretation

10   0   30 METRES

Profiles

Profiles are valuable to illustrate the shape of earthworks, particularly on defensive sites, and to record current heights and angles of slopes where erosion is a problem.

The positions of profiles should be accurately plotted on the plan, and the profile itself should be conventionalised, so that it is clear what features the section cuts through (**fig 86**). It is sometimes necessary, where gradients are slight, to exaggerate the heights of a profile by varying the vertical/horizontal scale ratio by 2 to 1. This scale difference must be clearly stated on the drawing.

Maps & smaller scale plans

Large dispersed sites such as field systems, or multi-period archaeological landscapes, need to be drawn at smaller scales, if all relevant features are to be included on one plan. These plans can be surveyed at the intended scale or may be made up of several larger-scale plans accurately reduced, simplified and re-drawn. Often they are a combination of both. The most suitable scales to use are 1:2500, 1:10,000 and occasionally 1:5000, the advantage of

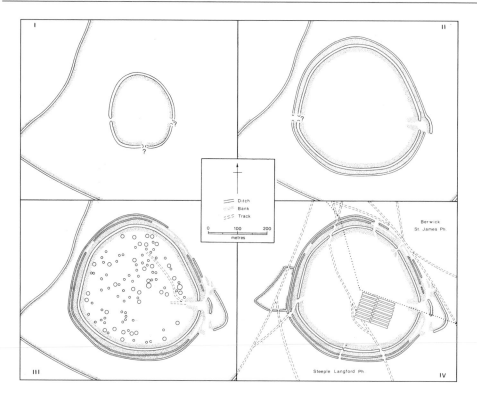

87   *Yarnbury (Wiltshire): interpretative phase diagram.*

the former two being that OS coverage exists at these scales, giving a very good basis for tying surveys together. This is particularly useful when preparing maps digitally using CAD.

When using these scales, fine detail has to be omitted, although a 1:2500 scale plan can still include a surprising amount of detail. Hachures may be used for larger features, and stony banks and cairns may be depicted using stipple. However, some features such as leats, buildings and hut circles need to be conventionalised. At 1:10,000 scale, the main aim is to show geographic location and site type and nearly all features have to be conventionalised.

Annotation

Annotation of illustrations needs to be neat, unobtrusive and minimal. However, all archive plans should contain a metric scale bar and a north point as well as a title box containing locational and other information (see **fig 64**). Publication drawings should, if possible, be oriented with north approximately to the top, and appropriate grid intersections should be shown where necessary. A key must be included for any conventionalised features. Text placed within the drawing should be avoided. For archive drawings of very complex detail, such as industrial landscapes, it is sometimes best to place annotations on a separate overlay.

There are several means of adding annotation to the drawing. Hand-lettering is best used only by those with the appropriate skills. Stencils and electronic stencilling machines can give a very satisfactory result and have the added advantage of permanence and durability essential for archive plans. For publication a more aesthetically pleasing appearance is required. This can be achieved by using rub-down lettering or computer generated paste-ups on either paper or sticky-back film; the advantage of this latter technique is that several 'dry runs' can be attempted, using different layouts and font sizes before a final version is chosen. However, stick-down lettering is fragile and only suitable for preparing camera-ready copy; it should not be used on drawings intended for the archive.

Beyond the earthwork plan

While plans and maps remain as the basic means of depicting and recording earthwork sites, it is often necessary to develop the ideas and interpretations which result from the survey into a form which may convey them more readily to others. By selective simplification and conventionalising of significant features, it is possible to convey phases of activity or distinctly different types of evidence which have been brought to light as a result of survey (**fig 87** and **plate 22**).

The inclusion of colour, if available, is by far the best method of highlighting differing elements or phases of an earthwork plan. In its most straightforward form, the hachures themselves can be coloured, using different colours for the separate phases. At very complex sites, several versions of the same basic plan may be necessary, each highlighting separate features. At smaller scales, such as 1:2500, a multi-phase field system, for example, may be understood at a glance when reproduced in colour. This technique is also useful for combining information from differing sources, eg earthwork survey, geophysical survey and air photographic transcription, where all three produced in monochrome on the same plan could be confusing, and if prepared separately the impact would be lost.

Although colour is sometimes available when producing one-off reports for limited circulation, archive plans and for exhibition or display work, its use in publications is still very restricted, due to cost. The best alternative therefore is the use of grey shades. Such plans may be produced by conventional means, preparing the plan in separate layers and instructing the printer on the percentage of tint or, more usually, using a computer graphics program. Although more limiting than colour, grey shades can still effectively break down a site into its component parts. Line weight is another alternative for linear monuments, where different elements can be highlighted by a combination of heavier and lighter lines.

Reconstruction drawings are a useful method of interpreting archaeological features and have been used most successfully, particularly at sites where good physical evidence exists as a basis, or where standing or ruined buildings remain, or information from excavations, or contemporary photographic evidence is available. For earthworks, however, extreme caution must be exercised as few sites of this type will yield sufficient information from field survey alone for an adequate reconstruction and the results may be academically questionable, if not almost total fabrication.

One option which is available to some is the Digital Terrain Model (DTM; see p69 and **figs 23, 31**), which allows suitably surveyed archaeological features to be presented as a three-dimensional model, either on screen or on paper. The earthworks may then be viewed from any angle and their form may become more readily understandable. This is particularly useful, where aerial photographs of a site are not available, due to tree coverage for instance, and a ground survey can provide the first 'view' of the earthwork features as a whole.

Computer graphics

Many of the methods of interpretive depiction described here can be effectively carried out using computer graphics programs and the results of geophysical survey and air photographic transcription, for instance, are routinely plotted or drafted using computers. The advantages of computer graphics are that data can be easily manipulated and assembled, and laborious hand drawing routines, such as hatching, stippling and shading can be performed accurately and with speed. Drawings may be altered easily, and many different versions of the same basic drawing can be produced. Computers also handle colour with much greater ease than can be achieved using traditional draughting methods. Unfortunately, the production of hachured plans to high enough standard using a computer is not yet a reality, though this will without doubt change in time. It must also be noted, however, that digital media are not archivally stable.

Survey data may be input to a computer environment by scanning hand drawn images and editing them using a graphics package or, if using CAD, field survey data may be downloaded directly from a data capturing device, or hand digitized using a tablet. CAD is particularly useful as it can enable data from differing accurately gathered sources to be combined into one drawing, as long as proper provision has been made for its use at the survey stage and common points of reference are established within each data set. In CAD, different types of information may be kept on separate layers, using different colours, symbols and line types; for example, a ground survey could be overlaid onto an aerial photo plot, together with geophysical, fieldwalking and excavation data, or for management plans the position of footpaths and erosion, vegetation and animal burrows, or planned future encroachments at the site.

Once prepared in this way, the range of options for a finished product is wide. The material may be retained in its digital format and transferred to a suitable GIS system, where it may be viewed and contrasted with a vast array of other geographical data, or it may be plotted onto paper or film in its CAD format for management and archive plans and, if suitable plotting equipment is available, for publication. However, publication quality is often better produced by transferring the drawings into a graphics program, specifically designed to produce high-quality illustrations. Within such software, colour, grey shading, annotation and lettering can all be incorporated and reproduced through suitable printing equipment to an extremely high standard.

The finished product

The final report resulting from a piece of fieldwork should contain a balanced selection of relevant illustrations, drawn to a consistent standard. By using a variety of drawings of differing scales, it is possible to convey not only highly detailed plans of the archaeological features, using data from a variety of sources, but also the geographical context and relationships with the landscape and with other monuments. The inclusion of interpretative plans can in addition convey many of the thoughts and conclusions regarding the chronology and nature of the site which come about as a result of the survey.

REPORTS

The principal written product resulting from a survey will be the *archive* report. This is distinct from the *publication* report, which will be described in Chapter 12.

Producing a coherent written description that integrates the available evidence is a particular skill. Upon its success and its sensible integration with the graphical elements of the field recording depends the communication of understanding by those involved in the fieldwork, who have had privileged access to the field remains, to their readers now or at any time in the future who may not have that access.

Length is not the difficulty. Even the shortest account has to choose what to include, in what order to present information and what weight to give any part. The short monument descriptions in the published Royal Commission *Inventory* volumes were a good discipline in that respect. Blandness and failure to grapple with the interpretative consequences of fieldwork can be a danger. There are, indeed, instances of field recording, where no new insights or understanding emerges and a brief, straightforward description suffices, but in the majority of cases new fieldwork produces new information and new understanding sometimes amounting to a complete revision of what is known, and this needs to be conveyed clearly and systematically.

Complete objectivity is not a valid aim. It *cannot* be in the light of the necessary choices about inclusion, order and weighting and *should* not be because of the imperative to allow the understanding resulting from fieldwork to be developed and conveyed. Yet, at the heart of the activity lies the observation and recording of field remains, and similarly at the heart of the resulting report must be a description of those remains, sometimes even a catalogue of features, including observations of relationships, out of which grows the interpretation.

All reports are likely to require bibliographical references and most will need to include acknowledgements. More substantial reports will need a list of contents or even an index.

An unpublished archive report might therefore have several elements, but the amount of detail to be included will depend to a large extent on the Level of survey (see Appendix I).

Reports for different types of survey

Rapid survey

The report of a Rapid survey may be very brief and contain no more than the reasons for survey, the methodology, a short resumé of the findings and any conclusions, and recommendations for future work. Information on individual sites may be presented in tabular form.

Landscape survey

The report of a Landscape survey would include: an introduction saying when and how the fieldwork was done, with what specific objectives and in what circumstances; a description of location, soils and geology; documentary evidence; a summary of previous archaeological work; associated buildings or finds; the field remains recorded; and interpretation and synthesis on the development of the landscape including comparative material. In the section on field remains, individual sites or groups of sites would be treated separately, with perhaps one or two paragraphs of description and discussion to each. Recommendations for further research might be added.

Large-scale survey

All the elements listed above for Landscape survey would be included. At Level 3 the unit of description moves from the site to the individual feature, so that the report might be up to ten times longer or even, in the case of a complex industrial site, twenty times. A full discussion, bringing in consideration of comparative sites elsewhere, and possibly recommendations for future research and management, would form a conclusion.

POWER AND PERSISTENCE
HEREFORDSHIRE BEACON

The design of fortifications has constantly evolved to counteract improvements in weaponry and tactics, while new materials, such as masonry, brick, concrete and steel, have been adopted as they became available. Fortification has also embodied elements of symbolism and prestige, making emphatic statements of power, as in the dramatically massive hillfort ramparts of the Herefordshire Beacon (or British Camp), Malvern or the sheer brutality of the keep at Conisbrough (South Yorkshire). Arguably nothing before the Henrician forts of the mid-sixteenth century is uniquely military; for the medieval period, at least, the balance of much recent thinking has tipped away from a militaristic understanding of castles towards an emphasis on their role as expression of power and status (eg Stocker 1993).

Herefordshire Beacon or British Camp, Malvern: the medieval ringwork and other defences lie within massive prehistoric ramparts.

The fieldworker should be aware of this, and of the re-use of naturally defensive positions, sometimes over many periods, which is a frequent occurrence, as at Pendennis (**plate 21**). Prehistoric hillforts, and indeed Roman forts, were sometimes re-used in the medieval period to accommodate mottes, ringworks and baileys. The Herefordshire Beacon is a good example of this too. The investigative archaeologist should always be alive to the possibility of an earlier defensive work underlying a medieval castle or later fortification.

Stone castles often have outer earthen defences, though these are frequently overlooked by castellologists, a striking example of the way in which upstanding masonry structures draw attention to themselves at the expense of slighter remains. Orford Castle (Suffolk), for example, has extensive and spectacular outworks (Higham and Barker 1992, 196). Earth and timber castles as a whole have been neglected, despite the work of Higham and Barker and the RCAHMW (1991). Also neglected are stone-built castles which, because of their state of preservation, resemble earthwork castles, such as Wark-on-Tweed (Northumberland) (Welfare *et al* 1998).

Few earthwork castles have any documentary history, so field archaeology is a prime means of research. Occasionally, evidence for assaults on castles, otherwise undocumented, survives archaeologically in the form of siege castles, as at East Chelborough (Dorset), for instance (Lewis 1989).

Several specialist organisations, such as the Hillfort Studies Group and Fortress Studies Group, provide a core of knowledge on fortifications of different periods; their members can be consulted to the benefit of the non-specialist field archaeologist.

12 Making it all available

Archaeology depends upon a fragile and finite resource. It is the archaeologist's duty to conserve this resource and to make the results of a fieldwork project, including the original archive, available to the public.

Many of the points considered below are covered by guidance notes, codes of conduct and standards, and as such they enjoy broad agreement within the discipline. Although these documents are often drawn up to cover specific archaeological situations, such as planning-related tasks or government-funded projects, when taken together they define 'best practice' and can be applied with equal validity across the whole range of archaeological field recording. This chapter points to that best practice.

The sequence of events is that *arrangements* for publication come first, then the assembly and deposit of the archive and then the preparation for the publication.

ARCHIVING PRINCIPLES

Why the archive should be deposited in a public record

The archive should be deposited in an appropriate and accessible public record within a reasonable period of the end of the project. This remains the case, even if the project has been fully published (ACAO 1993, 10.1; IFA 1997, 4.2).

The current philosophy, which has in turn influenced government policy (eg DoE 1990), recognises the irreplaceability of archaeological deposits and evidence and so favours their 'preservation *in situ*'. Where destructive intervention (such as excavation) is necessary, the concept of 'preservation by record' is applied. In this latter case, the archive replaces the deposits which have been destroyed and assumes the role of primary archaeological evidence. For non-destructive fieldwork, such as analytical survey, future public access to the archive created may appear less critical, but there are still strong reasons for its public deposition:

(a) The archive created by a survey is a point-in-time record of the condition of a site or landscape. If the site is subsequently destroyed or eroded, or even restored for display, the archive remains an invaluable source of evidence for what has been lost.

(b) Public access to the archive will help disseminate any interpretative or academic insight gained by the fieldwork. This is especially true if the project remains unpublished, but holds true even after formal publication.

(c) Publication media usually impose limitations of scale. A survey plan may have to be reduced to A4 or smaller format, with corresponding loss of detail. The full-size plan will only be available as archive.

(d) Publication should be at a level appropriate to the importance of the results (EH 1991, A7.2.1.i). Much detail will therefore remain unpublished. Deposition of the archive gives the opportunity to include the unedited report, supporting text, interpretation/phase drawings and perhaps also other media.

Archive users

The archive created by archaeological activities is of interest to those responsible for managing the heritage and to everyone working in archaeology, whether fieldworkers or desk-based researchers. The archive and the information it contains are highly relevant to the local SMR, the planning archaeologist, other professional and amateur fieldworkers (particularly those organising fresh projects) and other researchers.

The information contained in the archive may be used, among other things, to enhance the SMR, enable the planning archaeologist to deliver good advice, inform site managers and those organising fieldwork projects, avoid unnecessary duplication of work on a site and inform academic research and other study.

How the creator's rights are protected

The project director or creator of the archive has the right to be identified as the originator of that work and has rights of primacy. All archive, both text and artwork, is protected by copyright and is subject to the legal controls of 'fair dealing'. Repositories will strictly monitor the copying of archive and will draw users' attention to their legal responsibilities. Where archive is used, it should be duly acknowledged, as with published sources.

If an archive is deposited before publication, most repositories are willing to hold it on restricted access for a limited and pre-arranged period to allow time for publication.

Where and when archive should be deposited

The archive should be deposited in an accessible public archive with the facilities to curate the material at least to minimum standards (IFA 1997, 2.1; ACAO 1993, 10.1), such as an MGC-registered museum with a relevant collecting policy (SMA 1993, 2.4.2). In some cases, a County Record Office may be more appropriate, if the local museum is unable to curate documentary archive. Few SMRs have the facilities to curate documentary archive or to make it available for study.

Where possible, discussion should be held with the intended repository at the outset of the project to confirm that it is willing to accept the archive and to ensure that any requirements it may have regarding the format of the material are accommodated (IFA 1994, 3.6.1, 3.6.2; EH 1991, 4.10; MGC 1992, 1.4, 2.12). Some museums levy a storage charge for archive from developer-funded projects, in which case this needs to be established at an early stage.

The integrity of the archive should be maintained: it should not be divided between different repositories (ACAO 1993, 10.2a; MGC 1992, 2.1; SMA 1993, 2.4.1, 4.5.4). If several organisations require access to the documentary archive, copying should be considered. Any finds and documentary archive should be deposited in the same museum, wherever possible; if they are separated, a copy of the archive should be lodged with the finds.

The results of fieldwork should be disseminated, including deposition of the archive, without 'undue delay' (IFA 1997, 4.2). There is no agreed statement of the maximum acceptable delay between the completion of a project and its dissemination, which will depend in part upon the scale and resourcing of the project. The IFA (1997, 4.5) mentions an upper figure of 10 years, while the ACAO (1993, 11) proposes 6 months. The assumption is, however, that dissemination will follow promptly upon the completion of the project.

Notification of other bodies

To aid access, the local SMR should be notified that the fieldwork has taken place, including the location of the archive and any finds (ACAO 1993, 10.2d; EH 1991, 8.3; SCAUM 1997, 1.3), and informed if the archive is subsequently transferred. A published account should note where finds and documentary archive are deposited (EH 1991, A7.1.1.v; IFA 1994, Appendix 5).

What should be deposited

The archive must be able to stand on its own as a self-explanatory and comprehensible record. For excavations, EH (1991, Appendix 3 & 6) has defined the 'site archive' and the 'research archive'. The site archive represents the original record of the project, including the primary field record; the research archive is derived from work done at the analysis phase, particularly post-excavation study. This distinction may be less helpful for field survey projects, for which the archive can be regarded as a single entity.

Original records and appropriate contextual material should be kept as part of the archive. Ideally, originals should not be altered or amended, but if they are then any changes should be clearly indicated and dated. The archive should include the following, where relevant: project brief/specification, correspondence (unless confidential), field drawings and final drawings, full report, field notebooks, pro formas, photographic materials (prints and negatives), supporting documentation, finds (where present) and an index. The following material should not be deposited: multiple drafts of text or illustrations, unless differing significantly from the final version, page and galley proofs, printed matter or personnel records.

The way in which data held in digital formats is handled will depend upon the ability and readiness of the repository to accept it. Digital *capture* is easy, digital *archiving* is not, and this has an adverse effect on the maintenance of digital data in the long term. There is little point in a repository accepting records in a format it cannot access. The option of depositing a hard copy of digital data, either in addition to or in place of the digital format, should always be considered (MGC 1992, 2.13.vii; SMA 1995, 9.5d).

Transfer of ownership

A public repository should not be expected to accept and curate material that it cannot make available. The MGC (1992, 2.11; followed by SMA 1995, 5.1) recommends that a museum should not accept material, unless copyright is formally assigned or a licence to use the material is granted.

Note on differences of law and practice within the United Kingdom

Whilst the above principles are widely accepted, the legislation and accepted practice surrounding archaeological fieldwork differs in different parts of the United Kingdom, as well as across international boundaries. Consequently, the situation regarding the ownership and deposition of archaeological archives is complex.

In order to ensure public access in perpetuity, only repositories recognised as places of deposit under the Public Records Act, such as a County Record Office, should be approached. A licence is required for archaeological fieldwork in Northern Ireland: this will include archive issues. In Scotland and Wales, discussion with the NMR (or with the DoE Environment & Heritage Agency in Northern Ireland) in advance of a proposed project is strongly recommended. This will include advice regarding archive deposition. For Scotland, the NMR is the primary repository for archaeological archive.

The Treasure Act 1996 has replaced the common law of treasure trove. The Act extends the definition of treasure to cover, effectively, all gold and silver objects over 300 years old, all coins over 300 years old found in hoards, and associated objects, as well as objects that would previously have been regarded as treasure trove. It excludes objects whose owner can be traced, unworked natural objects (including human and animal remains) and objects from the foreshore, which are wreck. Under the Act, all treasure must be reported to the coroner of the district in which it was found within 14 days of finding or identification; this obligation applies to archaeologists as well as other finders. The *Code of Practice* on the Treasure Act (DNH 1997) contains guidance for finders, sets out guidelines on rewards, gives advice on the care of finds and lists useful addresses.

ASSEMBLING THE ARCHIVE

This section considers the correct materials to be used in order to create a permanent record of a survey; all primary field archive will form part of the permanent record. Long-term storage requirements are not discussed, as they are the responsibility of the repository (see British Standard 1978 (BS 5454); MGC 1992, especially Appendix C).

From the outset of a project, due consideration must be given to recording methods, to permanence (using the correct materials) and to arrangements for access. Access is an intellectual, as well as a physical concept: combining the public deposition of an archive with intelligibility to other researchers.

Archival materials

Published guidance on the preparation and storage of archaeological documentary archives is available (Ferguson and Murray 1997; Walker 1990). In addition to these general statements, many repositories have their own specific requirements for the format of the archive and the materials used and may be reluctant to accept material which does not conform to their standards. It is advisable to discuss any requirements with the intended repository before the project begins, as mistakes may prove costly to rectify later (IFA 1994, 3.6.3, 3.6.5).

Paper
Much modern paper has a short life-span. Recycled and copier paper is particularly poor. Paper used in the course of field recording or for any final document which will form part of the deposited archive should be of good quality. A number of manufacturers produce 'archival paper' (Ferguson and Murray 1997, Appendix 5), though this tends to be expensive.

Drawing film
Polyester-based film is an approved medium for archive drawings, being chemically and physically very stable, and should be used for all drawings intended to form part of the permanent archive. The use of standard-sized sheets, no larger than A0 or smaller than A4, is recommended for ease of handling and storage. However, it is sometimes unavoidable, for extensive sites or landscapes, to use sheets of film larger than A0. Ideally the minimum thickness of film should be 125 microns to resist stretching.

Adhesives and clips
Where possible, the need for adhesives should be avoided. Pressure-sensitive adhesives and non-drying adhesives should not be used due to the risk of damage to the paper. They also perish over time. Adhesives used for mounting drawings or attaching labels should be free from staining materials and possess a neutral pH. Methylcellulose and starch-based adhesives are recommended (Ferguson and Murray 1997, Appendix 5).

Only brass or plastic-coated paper-clips should be used. Steel paper-clips, staples and rubber bands will rust or perish and mark the material. Ring binders are not recommended for the same reason. Metal spiral-bound notebooks are unsuitable as the binding becomes rusty; hardback notebooks with sewn pages are more suitable.

Pencils
A sharp pencil with a hard lead (2H–6H) should be used on drawing film, but only a soft pencil should be used for writing on the reverse of photographic prints. Colour pencils are less permanent. All documents upon which pencil has been used should be kept in the dark. Fixatives should not be used, as they are unstable in the long term.

Pens and inks
A water-based permanent black film ink should be used for all drawings. Felt-tip pens should not be used. The use of ink and pencil on the same document may cause problems

of contrast, if it is subsequently copied.

Dry lettering and tones

Dry-transfer lettering and tones are not archivally permanent; over time the adhesive is lost and its deterioration can lead to rotting of the medium to which it has been attached. Some fixing agents contain unspecified plasticisers which may discolour and become brittle with age. As an alternative, the use of stencils is recommended for lettering.

Photographic materials

Only black-and-white film can be regarded as archivally permanent. Colour film and transparencies will fade over time, resulting in a loss of colour balance and even complete loss of the image. Colour photographs and transparencies are valuable for lecture, exhibition and publication purposes, but only black-and-white film is suitable for recording purposes. Film and prints should be stored separately, in case of fire and water damage. All film and prints intended to be deposited as part of the archive should be hand-processed to ensure archival quality. After suitable processing and meticulous washing to remove unwanted chemical residue, negatives should be stored in suitable enclosures and handled as little as possible to avoid damage to the emulsion. Stability of temperature and humidity is better than frequently changing conditions. Prints last longer with minimum exposure to light, particularly bright sunlight which bleaches the image.

Video is becoming increasingly common as a means of on-site recording. While it is useful for giving presentations, it has only a limited life. It should not therefore be used as a replacement for black-and-white photography or for other recording methods.

Magnetic media

Digital methods, such as digital survey recording, digital cameras, databases, word-processed text and computer-aided draughting systems, have many advantages for data capture and manipulation and for desk-top publishing. However, digital media are not suitable for long-term storage. These media are not archivally permanent, and the obsolescence of both software and hardware can render them unreadable. Also, many repositories lack the facilities to access documents in the infinite variety of these formats.

Enclosures

Enclosures must be of archival quality, and a repository will usually specify acceptable standards. Brown paper envelopes should not be used, as they are highly acidic; acid-free envelopes are available (Ferguson and Murray 1997, Appendix 5).

Labelling

All items in the archive must be clearly labelled as part of a single coherent sequence to allow future consultation. It is recommended that each plan or drawing should include a standard information box to present this information clearly and consistently (see **fig 64**). Whether or not an information box is used, the following details should appear on each plan/drawing: organisation, names or initials of personnel, date of survey, project name,

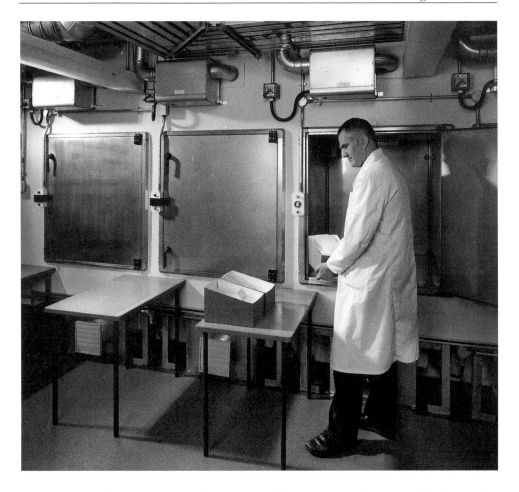

88   *National Monuments Record Centre, Swindon: using the acclimatisation chambers in the archive building.*

site name, project number or code, site location — administrative, site location — National Grid Reference, scale of survey (written and as a bar), north arrow and key to conventions used.

Storage

Long-term storage in the correct environment is the responsibility of the repository (**fig 88**). The project director is responsible for ensuring that the correct materials are used from the outset, and that the archive is maintained in good condition while in his or her charge prior to its deposition (IFA 1997, 3.5). This requires attention to a number of simple house-keeping issues:

> (a) masking tape must be peeled off drawing film as soon as possible to avoid marking it

(b) do not store or use the archive in areas prone to damp or water damage (eg a basement or garage)

(c) do not store the archive in areas of fluctuating temperature or humidity; sharp changes are more detrimental to archive material than absolute values

(d) do not store or use the archive in dusty or dirty areas or on the floor: dirt may stain the archive and can harbour pests

(e) do not leave the archive in strong natural or artificial light, as this can cause fading; store the archive in a dark place (eg a plan press or cupboard)

(f) do not expose the archive to risk from food, drink or tobacco

(g) do not use steel paper-clips, staples, pressure-sensitive adhesive tape or rubber bands to keep material together

(h) do not fold or roll the archive unnecessarily (it may be necessary to roll outsize plans/drawings); where possible, store the archive flat

(i) always handle documents with care; wash your hands.

Copying

Any requirements for copying the archive should be considered at the start of the project (ACAO 1993, 10.1). Archive may be copied for a variety of reasons:

(a) as a condition of acceptance some repositories require that a security copy of the archive is deposited with the original material (SMA 1995, 9.5)

(b) a working copy may be required by the repository to protect original material from wear (MGC 1992, 15.3)

(c) copies of the documentary archive may be required for deposition with the finds, if deposited separately

(d) various interested parties may require access to the archive, and copying may provide the most practical solution

(e) in England, a microfilm copy of any excavation archive should be offered to the NMR (IFA 1994, 3.6.4; MGC 1992, 15.5; SMA 1995, 9.5); the same condition should apply to survey archive. For microfilming, see Handley (1998).

Photo-mechanical transfer (PMT) is a suitable method for copying maps and plans, particularly where accuracy is essential. However, it can only deal with images up to a certain size (A2) and is bulky to store.

PUBLICATION

Publication should always be considered whenever a survey has produced significant amounts of new material or new information. Decisions therefore have to be taken as to what should be published and the most appropriate form of publication: careful planning and consideration of the target audience (before anything is written) are essential. The temptation is often to describe everything that was found; this laborious trotting out of every last detail is usually quite unnecessary and may well deaden the impact of the insights gained through the recording process. It is the *insights* that readers are hungry for.

In the presentation of surveys, the greater part of the descriptive side may be dealt with in two ways: by the compilation of an archive report (including items like the height of each scarp, the inclusion of which would overburden most textual reports), and by the publication of a plan, or plans, suitably labelled and captioned; an extended caption can be a very useful device. This leaves the final crucial element as the focus for publication: the synthesis. This is the presentation of distilled conclusions: the succinct expression of what was learnt and the considered view of the context in which the information should be seen. Here it is insight, new and received, that dominates. The complexity of a site should be indicated by the illustrations; the text should focus on getting the important messages across. Any detailed information that really is *essential* to the arguments put forward should be set out as briefly as possible; the remainder belongs in the archive.

The publication of survey information must include a number of essential elements:

(a) All the information for the geographical location of the site or landscape, a National Grid Reference of 6 or 8 figures, as appropriate, and a location map. Unless the site is well known to the target readership, an inset should be used to indicate its regional and national context. If an OS map has been used as a base, it is necessary to check with the OS that their copyright has not been contravened.

(b) The text must also include an explanation of why the site was chosen for survey and a brief description of the recording method. The second item is important, because it provides the reader with a basis from which to assess the metrical accuracy of the planning.

(c) A topographical summary should also be included, not forgetting the underlying geology; all this provides essential background.

(d) Thereafter, the text should present description and, crucially, interpretation.

Especially when dealing with a medieval or post-medieval site, due consideration must be given to the historical sources available. Exactly how these documentary sources are woven into the text is a matter of choice. The golden rule is that each source must be clearly given, so that others may consider it too.

In advancing arguments and in providing comparisons, it is necessary to refer to other publications. Full details of these bibliographical references must be given in the appropriate form, conforming to the 'house style' of the appropriate journal or publisher. Guidance on this and many other topics related to publication is included in *Signposts for Archaeological Publication* (CBA 1991). If in doubt, give more information rather than less on each reference. High standards have been maintained in many journals, particularly the major national archaeological periodicals, and recent volumes offer examples of best practice. It is important to indicate where any related archive can be consulted.

Before either the text or the illustrations are finalised, the ideal place of publication should be identified. In Britain, this often means a choice between a county or regional journal, or a national specialist journal. At this stage, the editor should be contacted to confirm their interest in an article on this particular subject, indicating its approximate length and the number of illustrations, and enquiring about the deadline for submission. No draft should be sent until it is asked for. If the reply from the editor is encouraging, the text should be revised according to the written instructions that most journals provide for contributors. If these guidelines are followed, along with all the current practice of the journal (especially in the form of bibliographical references, the provision of an abstract and the design of the captions), the paper will probably be accepted. If this is not done, the inevitable rejection will be deserved.

Then (and only then) the next step is to prepare the illustrations. The illustrations should be designed to the proportions of the printed area. The clarity that may be required for the depiction of details must be borne in mind: drawings should be prepared to a larger size than the printed area, as they tend to improve by being reduced to about two-thirds of the original. It is vital to ensure that any lettering is at the correct size, so that it is not too large or too small on reduction. It is useful to check what level of reduction a trial portion of the detailed drawing will sustain by testing a sample area on a reducing photocopier. A 'window' at a larger scale may be required to show intricate details of a landscape survey. Framing the survey plan should focus on what needs to be shown: unless the editor gives express permission, 'fold-outs' — which are prohibitively expensive — should not be considered; a split across two facing pages may be a good alternative for a large plan. Captions should not be included within the drawing: they waste space and can dominate and detract from a drawing. (For further advice on preparing drawings, see pp167–75.)

A reader of sound judgement can be asked to read the draft in order to check that it is clear and that it has a sound, logical flow, and that all the necessary evidence (but no more) has been presented. *Everyone* benefits from being edited and from constructive criticism. On submission, the paper should be complete and in the exact form demanded (usually a disk and a hard copy). Reduced versions of plans and photographs should be provided; original drawings should not be sent, until the paper has been accepted. The editor may ask for some revisions, but this should not discourage as it usually implies acceptance. Once the paper has been formally accepted for publication, the next time that you will see it will be as a printer's proof: revisions at this stage can be expensive so must be confined to the correction of errors only. Careful planning and preparation ensure that the arrival of a survey in print is a real thrill and an appropriate reward for hard work.

Appendix I — Levels of archaeological survey

This appendix is summarised from *Recording Archaeological Field Monuments: a descriptive specification* (RCHME forthcoming), which should be consulted for matters of detail and for drawing conventions.

The purpose of records

At any Level a record of an archaeological feature is a varying mix of description and interpretation, providing information on the monument's form, construction, function, condition, and how it has been affected by later development and use. Its context, relationships, associations and significance must all be recorded appropriately.

In the production of records some guiding principles should be borne in mind:

- a record must describe and interpret the site or landscape, with supporting evidence, and should chart its development and chronology, explaining what is significant
- a record should aim to be accurate; the Level of record should be clearly stated the record (text and graphics) must be clear and concise; sources used must be cited in full
- the record should be produced on media that can be copied and which are archivally stable
- a security copy of the record should be made as soon as possible; it is advisable to retain hard copy of all digital data
- no fieldwork project is complete until all necessary records have been entered in the appropriate database and archive; adequate time must be set aside for this.

The methods by which survey data are assembled have changed radically, but the hachured plan, with contours where necessary, and a complementary text remain at the core of the work.

These guidelines are not intended to be definitive. Circumstances will arise where those involved with the conservation, management and understanding of an archaeological site or landscape will require records with an emphasis or content which differ from those described here. However, this specification will fulfil most requirements for the recording of field monuments.

Forms and Levels of recording

In defining Levels of recording, the intention is:

- to enable an estimate of required resources to be made before the beginning of a project
- to give clear guidance about working practices
- to provide check-lists of what may be included in the record of a site or landscape
- to enable users of the record to appreciate the intensity of recording and to understand the basis upon which conclusions have been reached.

In addition to 'core' data (see Level 1, and Items 1–3 of the Written Account, below), most records of archaeological field monuments will combine a written description and analysis with a visual record made by a metrically accurate survey drawing and, where appropriate, photographs.

Four Levels of recording have been identified. It is, however, not possible to prescribe forms and Levels of record for all circumstances. Objectives, time and resources vary from case to case. Furthermore, initial aims must be flexible to allow subsequent modification where necessary.

The following description of the four Levels is followed in each case by a specification of the elements (Items) that may be included as mandatory or recommended components in an archaeological record; these Items are set out under three headings:

> The Written Account
> Survey drawings
> Photography

An Item from this list may be included or omitted in any record, where it is not appropriate, but any substantial departure should be noted.

Ground photography of field monuments must be regarded as complementary to a survey and not as a substitute.

Level 1 The provision of non-analytical essential information ('core' data), including structured indexes of the location, period, type and condition of a monument, which would result from Rapid investigation (see Items 1–5 of the Written Account, below). This will be accompanied by a 1:10,000 cartographic record of the location and extent of the site. There may be consultation of easily available background information, including previous surveys, buildings records, archives, aerial and ground photography, excavation records and other local sources.

> A Level 1 record would typically consist of:
> The 'core' monument record
> The Written Account: Items 1–5 and 12 (see below)
> A cartographic record: an annotated 1:10,000 map indicating location and extent (Items 13–14).

Level 2 The provision of a basic *descriptive and interpretive* record of a monument resulting from field investigation. This record would aim to provide qualitative information beyond the scope of Level 1, but it must include the 'core' data. The information provided at Level 2 should be able to satisfy broad academic and management requirements. A survey at a scale that will represent the form of the monument will normally form part of the record. A statement of method, of accuracy and of the quality of investigation and survey will normally be included. Background information consulted at this Level will be the same as at Level 1.

A Level 2 record would typically consist of:

The 'core' monument record

The Written Account: Items 1–5, 8–12

Survey drawings: accurate cartographic location and extent of the monument and a site plan at a scale of up to 1:2500 (Items 13–14, 18; also 15 in exceptional cases)

Photography: as appropriate.

Level 3 A detailed and *fully analytical* record of a monument resulting from field investigation. This record will provide a quality of description, interpretation, graphical depiction and analysis beyond the scope of Level 2, though it must include the 'core' data. An accurately located, measured survey (map-based or divorced) at an appropriate scale (1:1250 or larger), to represent adequately the form and complexity of the monument, will always form part of the record; additional cartographic material may be generated. To some extent Level 3 investigation is 'open-ended', with specifications tailored individually to suit a variety of requirements, but it always requires a detailed descriptive and analytical approach complemented by accurate survey. A statement of method, of accuracy and of the quality of investigation and survey will always be included. All related and readily accessible background information should be consulted at this Level.

A Level 3 record would typically consist of:

The 'core' monument record

The Written Account: Items 1–12

Survey drawings: accurate cartographic location and extent of the monument and a site plan at a scale of 1:1250 or larger (Items 13–21)

Photography: as appropriate.

Level 4 An *integrated, multi-disciplinary* record of a monument resulting from field investigation and other activities. This record will have all the characteristics of Level 3 investigation but will be enhanced by additional specialist research or fieldwork which might take the form of: detailed historical research; geophysical or geochemical survey; palynological or pedological survey; survey and analysis of residual planting; 'fieldwalking' programmes; assessment of artefacts or reassessment of excavation collections; analytical recording of standing structures; and excavation. In many cases, such enhancements would result from contracted-out arrangements or negotiated partnerships. The distinguishing characteristic of this Level is that the enhancement will be included in the project design and will form part of the record and analysis, rather than being simply an information set which has been consulted, or a separate event.

A Level 4 record would typically consist of:

The 'core' monument record and all the Items listed for Level 3, plus additional specialist survey or investigation.

The Written Account

Whether the information is presented as text or in tabular format, the introductory material should always include Items 1–3. Item 4 may prove adequate for the description at Level 1, and item 5 for Level 2. In Levels 3 and 4, Item 6 is mandatory. Exactly how the information is given may vary depending on the type of monument. Unnecessary descriptions and dimensions that can readily be obtained from the survey drawings should be avoided. Where complex relationships exist, the use of interpretative drawings is to be encouraged.

1   The type/classification and period of the monument. The *Thesaurus of Monument Types* (RCHME/EH 1998) should be used.

2   The exact location; National Grid Reference (up to 8 figures); identifying numbers (eg NMR, SMR, SAM); local authority details (eg Parish, District, County).

3   The name of the compiler, date of investigation and reason(s) for survey, with details of site ownership and current land use.

4   The key source (eg aerial photograph or principal publication).

5   A summary description of the salient features; this is particularly important for monuments with lengthy and complex reports.

6   A *concise* description of the site, including information on plan, form, area, function, age, development sequence and past land use.

7   A *detailed* description of the site, including the same information as in Item 6, plus a full analysis and interpretation with the supporting evidence presented.

8   Consideration of the topographical setting of the monument and its relationship to other sites and landscapes, and to neighbouring historic buildings.

9   The potential for further investigation and other forms of survey should be assessed and recommendations made. Any finds made during investigation should be noted.

10   Relevant information from other sources, including published or unpublished accounts and oral information; the location of unpublished records must always be given. Relevant bibliographical references must be included, but an inclusive bibliography need not be assembled.

11   A brief assessment of the local, regional and national significance of the site with regard to its origin, purpose, form and status.

12   A brief 'Event Record'; this is a succinct description of the activities that were necessary for the compilation of the monument record, which may be coupled with the information provided in Item 3.

Survey drawings

The scale of a survey drawing must be appropriate to the Level of recording, the nature and extent of the site, the amount of detail that exists and the use which will be made of the survey. A Level 1 survey will require only a locating symbol on a map or a pecked line indicating the extent of the site. Level 2 surveys will normally be drawn at scales up to 1:2500, and at Levels 3 and 4 1:1250 or larger. The same scale should, if possible, be used throughout a project to facilitate comparisons.

Complex relationships within a site or landscape may need to be drawn at a larger scale and this can be done as an inset or 'window'. Profiles should be drawn, where it is necessary or helpful to do so. For insets and profiles, the scale, position and orientation of the supplementary drawing must be clearly shown.

All drawings must include a metric scale-bar and north arrow and be clearly labelled with the site name, surveyor(s) and date of survey. Drawings in a set must be clearly cross-referenced to each other.

A set of drawings may contain:

13   A diagrammatic plan showing the location or extent of the monument or landscape.

14   A metrically accurate site plan, typically at 1:1000, 1:1250 or 1:2500, showing the form of the site or landscape. The plan should be related to topographical features and to modern detail. The use of larger scales (eg 1:500 or 1:250) may occasionally be justified, where intricate detail should be shown (usually where masonry elements are present).

15   Profiles illustrating salient vertical and horizontal differences in ground surface. Their position must be marked on the plan and their orientation distinguished by means of a reference letter and arrow at each end.

16   Interpretative diagrams showing successive phases; phase plans must be accompanied by a copy of the survey from which the interpretation has been derived.

17   Reconstruction drawings may be used, where there is a fair degree of certainty; such drawings must be accompanied by copies of the surveys from which they are derived.

18   Copies of aerial photographic transcriptions.

19   Copies of earlier plans which throw light on the history and interpretation of the monument. This includes any excavation plans which contribute to an understanding of the visible remains.

20   Copies of plans derived from geophysical or geochemical survey. The limits of survey, or common points, must be shown.

21   Copies of plans showing the extent of artefact distributions found by 'fieldwalking'.

Photography

Photography has an important application in recording the general topography and setting of a monument. It can rarely convey the extent or form of sites and landscapes and may be appropriate only for well-defined sites of limited extent, such as standing stones or castle mounds, or in recording sites where standing structures survive, such as military and industrial remains. Black-and-white photography is preferable for archive purposes. Each print should be clearly labelled with the subject, orientation and date and cross-referenced to its negative.

Appendix II — Survey equipment

This appendix is a guide to the general categories of surveying equipment which a field archaeologist might consider using when preparing to undertake a survey project. Some antiquated (but still usable) items have been included, as these are often all that is available and these items are still referred to in surveying textbooks.

Tape measures

The most basic item of equipment which should be in any fieldworker's kit; it is important to develop good taping practice and understand differences between slope measurements (measurements along the ground surface) and horizontal measurements (used in map and plan making). For most fieldwork, 20m or 30m plastic-coated (fibron) tapes are the most useful and portable. Tapes which are graduated in metres, decimetres and centimetres on both sides are easy to read in the field. Tape measuring by one person can be achieved by using a spike, such as a tent peg or surveying arrow, at the zero end of the tape to fix it in the ground. Generally, tapes are cheaper when bought from specialist survey supplies companies, rather than on the high street. Always budget for spares, as tapes frequently break or tear. If increased accuracy is required, steel tapes are available, but these are more expensive and cumbersome. On large, open, flat sites, 100m tapes are useful, but can be unmanageable in high winds.

Surveying chain (or land chain)

For many years metal chains were the only type of 'tape' which would provide any degree of accuracy when measuring survey lines. These are very rarely used today, tapes being used in their place. They are heavy and cumbersome (more so than steel tapes) and need two people to use them. They should be avoided (though some specialist survey suppliers still stock them). The term 'chaining' or 'chain survey' is still frequently found in surveying textbooks and surveying dialogue, although now these terms refer to the technique (more correctly 'tape-and-offset'), rather than the equipment.

Prismatic compass

A basic surveying tool which should always be acquired if possible. It is one of the simplest ways of measuring bearings (angles related to magnetic north) available to the surveyor. It is hand-held and easily used by one person. As well as its use for orientation, it can be used as a low-order theodolite to measure relative angles. Therefore, a compass is most useful for 1:10,000 scale mapping and sketch surveys, as it can be used for resectioning and traversing at this scale. For the methodology for accurate surveying with prismatic compass, see Farrar (1987) and Brown (1987, 54). A Silva compass is a cheaper, but less accurate and robust alternative.

If a prismatic compass is not available, a pocket sextant, originally designed for maritime navigation in small craft, can be used to measure horizontal angles for 1:10,000 and 1:2500 survey when working alone.

Optical square

Although models vary, this extremely useful instrument is essentially two pentagonal prisms mounted one above the other in a plastic or metal housing, allowing the user to view with reasonable accuracy 180° alignments and 90° offsets. Its main function therefore is to establish and check alignments and right-angles within map-based surveys and for taping-and-offsetting during detail survey; it can also be used for setting out grids. With this small hand-held instrument (and some practice in its use), two ranging rods, two tape measures and a drawing board, a fieldworker can undertake accurate large-scale surveys of small monuments (Brown 1987, 50–1).

Ranging poles

These are usually of wood or metal, 1m or 2m in length. Lightweight plastic ones are also available, but are liable to snap. They are painted red and white in divisions of 0.1m, 0.2m or 0.5m and usually slot into one another to build up longer lengths. They have many functions, but are mainly used for marking ends of lines to be measured, identifying targets and as photographic scales; they can also be used as rigid measuring poles. These are desirable for most surveys, but can be home-made from broom handles. For low budget surveys or where large numbers are required, bamboo canes with a strip of fluorescent tape attached make excellent markers.

Ground markers

It is essential to mark the ground positions of control points. The type of marker used will depend on the expected duration of the survey and the type of site. Long-duration surveys demand more permanence (metal, wooden or plastic pegs, or paint marks on rocks or masonry), whilst temporary markers (survey arrows, bamboo canes, chalk marks and golf-tees) may suffice on surveys unlikely to last more than a few days. The degree of public access on a site must be borne in mind, as experience shows that if a marker is removable, it will be removed. Permanent markers such as alloy ground anchors should be used for very long-term surveys and for monitoring tasks. Where possible, utilise existing fixtures such as hydrant covers or drain frames. Discrete brass rivets and survey nails can be knocked into gaps in kerbstones and tarmac and with the aid of a hand-drill can be fixed into concrete plinths or rocks. Survey supply companies can provide a long list of useful markers, although with ingenuity many can be home-made.

Field notebooks

A notebook is essential for making general notes, recording measurements when using tape-and-offset techniques, booking angles and distances when using optical instruments; also, sketches should be made of the location of survey stations. It is essential therefore that a personal or site notebook or booking sheets are maintained. Any notebook with good quality paper will suffice, but durable and well set out surveying notebooks can be obtained from survey suppliers. Additional items, such as an A4 weathersealed clipboard, are useful for working on map extracts or diagrams.

Field drawing boards

A drawing board, light enough to carry on a shoulder-strap and big enough to allow an OS 1:2500 map, 1:10,000 map or a plot of your own survey for field completion to be taped onto it, is an invaluable item of survey equipment, particularly for map-based rapid survey. Maps can be covered with a sheet of plastic drawing film keyed to the underlying map; this facilitates plotting of detail, construction lines and erasures, notes, etc without marking the map and also keeps dirt and rain off the map (this is essential, if a paper map is being used). Such boards can easily and cheaply be made from marine 3-ply covered with Papyroboard. Purpose-made field drawing boards can be mounted on a lightweight tripod.

Drawing film

Although it is expensive, drawing film (125 micron thickness) is essential for field drawings. It is more stable than paper, easier to draw on, rainproof and allows erasures to be made. It is also more suitable for archiving.

Field drawing and plotting equipment

The surveyor should have:

Scale/Ruler: this should be of one single appropriate scale and about 15cm/6" in length as longer ones tend to be unwieldy and difficult to pocket. The 'toblerone' type containing several scales should be avoided, as these can be very frustrating and often lead to errors in plotting as they are invariably picked up with the wrong scale showing. The scale should also have one flat side, as bevelled rules will not lie flat on the plan and are therefore unsuitable for laying off right angles in conjunction with a set square.

Straightedge: In addition to a short scale, it may be helpful to have a longer steel straightedge (450mm/18") as this is advantageous for drawing baselines, etc.

Set Square: Used for laying off right angles or offsets with a scale, this should be a 60°/30° one about 15cm/6" long; larger ones are awkward to use and difficult to pocket.

Pencil: A well-sharpened quality drawing pencil of the adjustable 'clutch' type is best; a 6H lead is recommended.

Eraser: This should ideally be of the 'pencil' type which is easier to hold and sharpen, and enables erasing of small precise areas without rubbing out too much surrounding detail.

All this equipment, apart from the straightedge, is best kept together in a small pencil-case with a few spare leads, pens, masking tape, etc.

Level

The principal use of a level is for measuring differences in height when used with a levelling staff. Levels are categorised as to their accuracy, falling into three classes: Class I (precise), Class II (general purpose) and Class III (construction or builders). The greater the accuracy, the greater the cost. *Dumpy, tilting* and *automatic* levels are the ones most likely to be encountered by archaeological fieldworkers, and a Class II automatic level will serve most needs in terms of accuracy and ease of use. A level would only be used, if an accurate knowledge of heights, whether related to height datum above sea level via the system of OS Bench Marks, or a site datum from which to measure relative heights over a small area, is required; this is more often of value in excavation than in field survey. Levels can be used to height a matrix of points, the plan positions of which are known, from which ground contours can be interpolated.

Almost all levels can be used as optical tape measures. This factor is often ignored. Readings up to a distance of around 60m to an accuracy of around 0.2m are possible with most levels by reading between the horizontal hairs on the telescope and multiplying by the stadia constant (which is given in the instrument handbook, but is usually 100). If the level has a horizontal circle (which many have), then horizontal angles and distances can be measured as well as heights, so this type of level can be a low-order theodolite/Optical Distance Measurement (ODM) device. Small, flat sites with low accuracy requirements could be surveyed at medium scale (1:2500) with this type of level. If a staff was unavailable or the linear accuracy by this method was unacceptable, tapes could be used to measure the distances instead.

Pocket levels, plane-tables with clinometers, self-reducing alidades, theodolites/EDM and GPS can also provide height information with varying degrees of accuracy. A pocket level is a hand-held level which can read heights on a staff to a level of accuracy acceptable for profiling most earthworks and can also be used economically for measuring the heights of substantial slopes: 'if one knows the height of one's eye from the ground [the vertical distance] can be taken as one climbs up the bank, by first fixing upon some stone or tussock of grass at the eye's level as one stands in the ditch, and then going up to it and taking another level, and so on to the top' (Williams-Freeman 1915, 331).

Abney level
A small, hand-held instrument for measuring angles of inclination (slope); while useful for quantifying gradients, its main use is for measuring angles of slope when measuring with tapes, to enable horizontal distances to be calculated. Although an approximate level line can be estimated with this instrument, it is *not* a level and should not be used for measuring heights. These are still obtainable from survey supply specialists. Some modern hand-held clinometers perform the same function.

Plane-table
This equipment allows a survey to be plotted as it progresses in the field and is a cost-effective method of accomplishing detail survey of archaeological earthworks. It can also be used for control survey at small scale (1:10,000). The plane-table (collective term for a number of components) consists of:

    (a) A tripod.

    (b) A drawing table, mounted on the tripod, which can be rotated and clamped in the horizontal plane.

    (c) An alidade (or sight rule). The simplest type is a straight-edge with siting vanes which allows a line to be drawn on the plan in exactly the same direction as the object being sited on. Alidades can be plastic rulers with vertical sights (the cheapest), brass with sliding arm mechanisms (traditional, better than plastic, but very difficult to obtain) or telescopic (a magnifying telescopic sight mounted on the alidade — the most accurate and most expensive). A popular variant of this is the self-reducing alidade which when used with a levelling staff allows horizontal distances to be observed regardless of ground slope, as well as allowing heights to be calculated (ODM). With the self-reducing alidade, distances can be read to an accuracy of 0.1m at 50m (acceptable for 1:1000 or 1:500 scale survey), or 0.5m at 150m (acceptable for 1:2500 survey). Alternatively, some modern telescopic alidades have a small EDM mounted for distance measurement.

(An instrument known as an Indian clinometer, which is used with a plane-table, is sometimes confused with an alidade because of its physical similarities, but is used purely for measuring height differences, usually in connection with small-scale mapping.)

(d) A spirit level, usually a small circular 'pond' bubble, is used to ensure that the drawing table is level. Many alidades incorporate a pond bubble.

(e) A plumbing fork and plumb-bob are necessary for large-scale survey. They allow the surveyor to ensure that the ground position as represented on the drawing board is vertically above the actual ground position. For small-scale work plumbing the centre of the table suffices.

Theodolite

There is often confusion about the terminology and differences between theodolites, ODM, EDM, theodolite/EDM and 'total-station'.

A theodolite is an instrument with a rotating telescope for measuring horizontal and vertical angles. Today, theodolites fall into two distinct categories, *optical/mechanical* (angles manually read from the graduated circles) and *electronic* (angles read and displayed by electronic components). Optical/mechanical theodolites are being superseded by electronic varieties, but are still available. All theodolites fall into four classes:

Class I — Precision. Designed for high-precision surveying, such as first-order national triangulation, they normally measure angles to 0.1 - 0.5 seconds of arc and have high magnification telescopes. They are extremely expensive. It is unlikely that any archaeological survey project would require this class of theodolite.

Class II — Universal. Designed mainly for second- and third-order national triangulation and high-accuracy engineering work, they measure angles direct to one second of arc and are often referred to as 'one second' theodolites. Telescope magnification is only marginally less than Class I instruments. Slightly less expensive than Class I theodolites, they are good all-round instruments, particularly if control is to be put over a large area or ties made over long distances into the National Grid. For smaller archaeological survey projects, there is little need for this class of instrument.

Class III — General Purpose. Designed mainly for general survey and construction work, where very high accuracy is not required, these instruments have an angle accuracy by direct reading up to 20 seconds of arc. Telescope magnification is lower than in Class II. Cheaper than Class I and II items, this class of theodolite can cope with even relatively large archaeological landscape surveys.

Class IV — Builders. Used mostly in the construction industry for site-based survey, accuracy is in the order of 1 – 10 minutes of arc. Usually they have low telescope magnification. These are often very sturdy, cheap and easy to use. For most archaeological surveys of small to medium-sized sites, this class of theodolite is more than adequate.

The main advantages of electronic theodolites over optical/mechanical ones are that they are generally easier to use, more consistently accurate and can be linked to data loggers to store and process data automatically. Conversely, optical/mechanical ones tend to be more robust and long-lived, although to ensure consistent results they have to be regularly tested and maintained more methodically than electronic ones.

Optical Distance Measurement (ODM)

The principal purpose of the theodolite is to measure angles only, but, when used with other equipment, they can be used to calculate distances as well. This is achieved by using fixed graduations on the optics of the telescope (the stadia hairs) and a levelling staff: almost all theodolites, including electronic ones, can be used in this way. Some theodolites use variable distance stadia hairs to compensate automatically for slope and to produce direct horizontal distances (diagram tacheometers). ODM can be rather specialised and tends to demand some knowledge of basic trigonometry and theodolite technique. Training for this is only usually acquired through survey courses at various colleges and universities, or through on-site training with a surveyor.

Electromagnetic Distance Measurement (EDM)

An EDM unit measures *distances* only. The higher the accuracy and greater the range, the higher the cost. Most will achieve an accuracy on measuring a line of 5mm ± 5ppm (parts per million, ie 5mm over 1000m) and ranges vary from 200m to 1500m, using a single prism, to over 3km with multiple prisms. Variations in temperature and atmospheric pressure have to be compensated for. An EDM unit by itself is fairly limited in use: to get the most benefit it should be used in combination with a theodolite or with a telescopic alidade. With the majority of EDMs, distances are measured by sending a beam (on the infra-red spectrum) from the EDM unit to one or more reflecting glass prisms, although now a number of reflector-less EDM devices are available, albeit with somewhat limited range. All EDMs require a power source, usually ni-cad batteries.

Theodolite/EDM

Most theodolites (including the majority of modern optical/mechanical and almost all electronic theodolites) can be fitted with an adaptor to enable an EDM to be mounted on them. It is usually possible to 'mix and match' EDM units with theodolites regardless of manufacturer via these theodolite adaptors. Because of the number of different components and adaptors, however, this combination can be difficult to use and prone to mechanical failure. Most EDMs will calculate horizontal as well as slope distance, difference in height and some will perform co-ordinate calculations. With optical/mechanical theodolites, angles have to be manually read and fed into the EDM unit for those calculations to take place; with electronic ones, the information can be transferred automatically, and these usually have the advantage that they can be linked to an electronic data-logger, so that all data are recorded automatically and can either be processed on site or transferred to a computer. Adding an EDM to an old optical/mechanical theodolite can be a cost-effective way of upgrading survey capacity to undertake large area control surveys, but it must be borne in mind that to conform to the principles of survey the range of an EDM and the class of theodolite it is used with (in terms of angle accuracy) should be compatible. Therefore it would be ineffective (and would lead to planimetric errors) to combine a long range (*c* 3km) EDM with a Class IV theodolite reading angles only to 5 minutes of arc. A Class III theodolite and medium range (*c* 1km) EDM is the most flexible combination and will cope with most survey requirements of archaeologists from small sites to large landscapes. However, if funds are available a total-station should be considered.

Total-station

To make the process of EDM and angle measurement simpler, manufacturers have produced electronic theodolites with the EDM unit built in; these are known as *co-axial* EDMs, but are now frequently, if somewhat misleadingly, referred to as *total-stations*. These are easy to use and are ideally suited for those without a specialist survey background. In general, a Class III equivalent instrument with up to 1km range is suitable for most archaeological purposes. Most also display on-board calculations such as horizontal distance, height difference, co-ordinates, etc (which can be booked and plotted by hand), or can be connected to electronic data-loggers for automated recording. Some allow input of feature codes which can then be interpreted by surveying software on computers to produce electronically generated drawings and 3D ground models via printers and plotters. This combination is ideal for the majority of survey requirements, particularly the provision of control over most sites and landscapes, and is particularly cost effective for recording and plotting large amounts of data quickly.

This total-station combination is probably the most desirable for archaeologists who undertake all types of survey on a regular basis, and on a long-term basis it may be cheaper to buy than hire. If survey is undertaken infrequently, it may be more cost effective to hire as needed. EDM kit of any kind demands peripheral equipment, such as tripods, targets, prisms, poles, batteries and cables; the cost of these should not be underestimated, as they can add a third to the overall price. In addition, two-way radios are desirable for communicating between observer and the person holding the prism on large sites. A number of survey equipment hire companies exist, but to ensure that the right combination is hired be prepared to spend some time explaining the operational requirements and final products. Lack of computer or plotting facilities need not be a barrier to automated recording and processing, as there are many bureaux who will undertake this work at very reasonable cost and most survey hire companies can advise on this.

Global Positioning System (GPS)

One of the most recent technologies which has a direct impact on methods of archaeological survey is the GPS. This is a system developed by the US Department of Defense, comprising 24 satellites orbiting the earth and a number of ground stations. Its primary purpose is to enhance the effectiveness of military operations by the US and its allies, by simplifying accurate navigation. Methods of exploiting its potential for precise positioning have been developed by several survey equipment manufacturers. GPS equipment receives data from the satellites and allows ground positions to be computed.

While *navigational* GPS, using a single receiver, achieves positional accuracy of within about 50 metres from truth, *differential* surveying with GPS, using two receivers simultaneously and coupled data-loggers (one static at a known point and one free to fix new points, or 'rover'), allows points to be surveyed within 1cm of their true position. Because of the large amounts of data collected, a high-specification computer and special processing software are required to produce co-ordinates and plan/map positions.

GPS is suited to large open areas such as moorland, where large amounts of data have to be collected and where map detail is sparse. Navigational GPS has a role in rapid surveys at small scale on open moorland landscapes for estimating map references, but it is not a surveying tool.

The main advantage of surveying with differential GPS is that movement is not constrained by considerations of ground intervisibility; once a base station has been established on a known point, the surveyor can move freely over a large area, fixing features with accuracy. GPS is an extremely successful means of fixing the position of archaeological features, where sites have unobstructed, open-sky visibility, but at present it is less successful in wooded or built-up areas. Specialist training is needed to operate and process data efficiently. For infrequent use, the task can be contracted to a survey company.

References

Adam, N J, Adams, J, Allen, M J, Draper, S, Fontana, D, Gardiner, J and Watson, K 1995 *The Langstone Harbour Archaeological Survey Project: Second Interim Report 1994* Hampshire County Council.

Ainsworth, S 1989 'Howley Hall, West Yorkshire: field survey' *in* M C B Bowden, D A Mackay and P Topping (eds) 1989, 197–210.

Ainsworth, S forthcoming 'Bronze Age settlements on the Derbyshire moorlands' *Derbyshire Archaeol J*

Ainsworth, S, Everson, P L, Cocroft, W D and Ryan, P 1991 'A fragmentary grave cover and the site of Woodham Walter church', *Essex Archaeol Hist* **22**. 170–3.

Alcock, N 1993 *People at Home: living in a Warwickshire village 1500–1800* Phillimore. Chichester.

Aldhouse-Green, S H R, Whittle, A W R, Allen, J R L, Caseldine, A E, Cuilver, S J, Day, M H, Lundquist, J and Upton, D 1993 'Prehistoric human footprints from the Severn Estuary at Uskmouth and Magor Pill, Gwent, Wales' *Archaeol Cambrensis* **141**. 14–55.

Alfrey, J and Clark, K 1993 *The Landscape of Industry: patterns of change in the Ironbridge Gorge* Routledge. London.

Allen, M J, Fontana, D, Gardiner, J and Pearson, A 1994 *The Langstone Harbour Archaeological Survey Project: the Assessment 1993* Hampshire County Council.

Andrews, J and Dury, A 1773 *Map of Wiltshire* (Wiltshire Archaeol Natur Hist Soc, Records Branch **8** (1952))

Armstrong, L 1978 *Woodcolliers and Charcoal Burning* Coach Publishing House/Weald and Downland Open Air Museum. Sussex.

Ashbee, P 1960 *The Bronze Age Round Barrow in Britain* Phoenix. London.

Ashbee, P 1974 *Ancient Scilly* David and Charles. Newton Abbot.

ACAO 1993 *Model briefs and specifications for archaeological assessments and field evaluations* Association of County Archaeological Officers.

AIA 1993 *Index Record for Industrial Sites Recording the Industrial Heritage: a handbook* Association for Industrial Archaeology.

Aston, M 1983 'Deserted farmsteads on Exmoor and the Lay Subsidy of 1327 in West Somerset' *Somerset Archaeol Natur Hist* **127**. 71–104.

Aston, M 1985 *Interpreting the Landscape* Batsford. London.

Aston, M (ed) 1988 *Medieval Fish, Fisheries and Fishponds in England* Brit Archaeol Rep Brit Ser **182**. Oxford.

Atterbury, J 1995 'Saving industrial records: is there progress?' *in* M Palmer and P Neaverson (eds) 1995, 9–15.

Ayscough, S and Caley, J 1802 *Taxatio Ecclesiastica Angliae et Walliae, auctoritate Papae Nicholai IV c AD 1291* Record Commission. London.

Baker, D 1991 *Potworks: the industrial architecture of the Staffordshire Potteries* RCHME. London.

Bannister, A and Raymond, S 1977 *Surveying* (4 edn) Pitman. London.

Baradez, J 1949 *Vue-Aérienne de l'organisation Romaine dans le Sud-Algérien* Arts et Metiers Graphiques. Paris.

Barker, K and Darvill, T (eds) 1997 *Making English Landscapes* Bournemouth University School of Conservation Sciences Occas Pap **3** (Oxbow Monogr **93**).

Barley, M 1974 *A guide to British topographical collections* Counc Brit Archaeol. London.

Barrett, J 1987 'The Glastonbury lake village: models and source criticism' *Archaeol J* **144**. 409–23.

Batey, M 1968 'Nuneham Courtenay: an Oxfordshire eighteenth-century deserted village' *Oxoniensia* **33**. 108–34.

Bell, M G 1990 *Brean Down: Excavations 1983–1987* Engl Heritage Archaeol Rep **15**

Bell, M G 1993 'Intertidal archaeology at Goldcliff in the Severn Estuary' *in* J Coles, V Fenwick and G Hutchinson (eds) *A Spirit of Enquiry* Wetlands Archaeological Research Project Occas Pap **7**. Exeter. 9–13.

Bell, M G 1995 'Intertidal archaeology and the Severn Estuary' *in* G Barber and T Barnett (eds) *Water in Archaeology* Wessex Water and Bristol University. 31–41.

Bender, B (ed) 1993 *Landscape: politics and perspectives* Berg. Oxford.

Benson, D and Miles, D 1974 *The Upper Thames Valley: an archaeological survey of the river gravels* Oxford Archaeological Unit Survey **2**. Oxford.

Beresford, M 1971 *History on the ground* Methuen. London.

Beresford, M and St Joseph, J K S 1979 *Medieval England: an aerial survey* (2 edn) Cambridge University Press.

Bergh, S 1995 *Landscape of the Monuments – a study of the passage tombs in the Cúil Irra region* Central Board of National Antiquities. Stockholm.

Bettess, F 1984 *Surveying for Archaeologists* Univ Durham Excav Comm.

Bettess, F 1992 *Surveying for Archaeologists* (rev edn). University of Durham.

Bewley, R H 1993 'Aerial photography for archaeology' *in* J Hunter and I Ralston (eds) 1993, 197–204.

Bewley, R H 1994 *Prehistoric and Romano-British settlement in the Solway Plain, Cumbria* Oxbow Monogr **36**.

Bewley, R H, Cole, M, David, A, Featherstone, R, Payne, A and Small, F 1996 'New features within the henge at Avebury, Wiltshire: aerial and geophysical evidence' *Antiquity* **70**. 639–46.

Blood, N K and Bowden, M C B 1990 'The Roman fort at Haltonchesters: an analytical field survey' *Archaeol Aeliana* 5 ser **18**. 55–62.

Boismier, W A 1997 *Modelling the Effects of Tillage Processes on Artefact Distributions in the Ploughzone: a simulation study of tillage-induced pattern formation* Brit Archaeol Rep Brit Ser **259**. Oxford.

Bold, J 1988 *Wilton House and English Palladianism* HMSO. London.

Booth, P and Everson, P L 1994 'Earthwork survey and excavation at Boys Hall moat, Sevington, Ashford', *Archaeol Cantiana* **114**. 411–34.

Boutwood, Y 1996 'Roman Fort and *vicus*, Newton Kyme, North Yorkshire' *Britannia* **27**. 340–344, pl. 13.

Bowden, M C B 1991 *Pitt Rivers: the life and archaeological work of Lieutenant-General Augustus Henry Lane Fox Pitt Rivers DCL, FRS, FSA* Cambridge University Press.

Bowden, M C B 1996a 'The medieval park at Kemsing' *Archaeol Cantiana* **116** (1997). 329–32.

Bowden, M C B 1996b 'Recent archaeological fieldwork in the Howgill Fells by the RCHME' *Trans Cumberland Wesmorland Antiq Archaeol Soc* **96**. 1–11.

Bowden, M C B 1998 'The conscious conversion of earlier earthworks in the design of parks and gardens' *in* P Pattison (ed) 1998. 23–6.

Bowden, M C B and Blood, N K 1991 'The Roman fort at Rudchester: an analytical field survey' *Archaeol Aeliana* 5 ser **19**. 25–31.

Bowden, M C B and Blood, N K forthcoming 'A re-assessment of two late prehistoric sites in the Yorkshire Dales' *in* White, R (ed) *Recent Archaeological Research in the Yorkshire Dales National Park* Yorkshire Dales National Park.

Bowden, M C B, Ford, S and Gaffney, V L 1994 'The excavation of a Late Bronze Age artefact scatter on Weathercock Hill' *Berkshire Archaeol J* **74** (1991–3). 69–83.

Bowden, M C B, Mackay, D A and Blood, N K 1989 'A new survey of Ingleborough hillfort, North Yorkshire' *Proc Prehist Soc* **55**. 267–71.

Bowden, M C B, Mackay, D A and Topping, P (eds) 1989 *From Cornwall to Caithness: some aspects of British Field Archaeology: papers presented to Norman V Quinnell* Brit Archaeol Rep Brit Ser **209**. Oxford.

Bradford, J S P 1957 *Ancient Landscapes: studies in field archaeology* Bell & Sons. London.

Bradley, R 1989 'Herbert Toms — a pioneer of analytical field survey' *in* M C B Bowden, D A Mackay and P Topping (eds) 1989. 29–47.

British Standard 1978 *Recommendations for storage and exhibition of archival documents* (BS 5454)

Brookes, I P, Hunt, C O, Dorning, K J, Harding, J L, and Jones, A M 1990 *The Lindsey Coastal Survey 1989–1990* Lincoln.

Brown, A 1987 *Fieldwork for Archaeologists and Local Historians* Batsford. London.

Brown, A (ed) 1991 *Garden Archaeology* Counc Brit Archaeol Res Rep **78**.

Brown, A and Taylor, C C 1973 'The gardens at Lyveden, Northamptonshire', *Archaeol J* **129**. 154–60.

Brown, G 1998 'Parklands as guardians of early landscapes: Highclere Castle, Hampshire' *in* P Pattison (ed) 1998. 7–12.

Buchanan, R A 1972 *Industrial archaeology in Britain* Penguin. Harmondsworth.

Buchanan, T 1983 *Photographing Historic Buildings* HMSO. London

Bullen, R A 1930 *Harlyn Bay and the Discoveries of its Prehistoric Remains* Padstow.

Caley, J and Hunter, J 1810–34 *Valor Ecclesiasticus, temp. Henrici VIII auctoritate regia institutus* Record Commission.

Calladine, A and Fricker, J 1993 *East Cheshire Textile Mills* RCHME. London.

Campbell, J 1977 *The Upper Palaeolithic in Britain* (2 vols) Oxford University Press.

Cantor, L 1983 *The Medieval Parks of England: a gazetteer* Department of Education, Loughborough University of Technology.

Capper, J E 1907 'Photographs of Stonehenge as seen from a war balloon' *Archaeologia* **60** part 2. 571.

Cardwell, P 1995 'Excavation of the hospital of St Giles by Brompton Bridge, North Yorkshire' *Archaeol J* **152** (1996). 109–245.

Charlton, B and Day, J 1984 'Henry MacLauchlan: surveyor and field archaeologist' *in* Miket, R and Burgess, C (eds) *Between and Beyond the Walls: essays on the prehistory and history of North Britain in honour of George Jobey* John Donald. Edinburgh.

Clark, A 1957 'The transistor as the archaeologist's latest tool' *Illus London News* **230**. 900–1.

Clark, A 1990 *Seeing Beneath the Soil* Batsford. London.

Clark, C M 1987 'Trouble at t'mill: industrial archaeology in the 1980s' *Antiquity* **61**. 169–79.

Clarke, H 1984 *The Archaeology of Medieval England* British Museum Publications. London.

Cocroft, W D 1994 *Oare Gunpowder Works, Faversham, Kent* Faversham Papers **39**. Faversham.

Cocroft, W D 1996 'A methodology for recording complex industrial/military sites; the example of RCHME's survey of the Royal Gunpowder Factory Waltham Abbey, Essex' *in* M Coulson and H Baldwin (eds) *Pilot study on defence environmental expectations* University of Wales Swansea NATO CCMS Rep **211**.

Cocroft, W D, Everson, P L, Jecock, M and Wilson-North, R 1989 'Castle Ditch hillfort, Eddisbury, Cheshire reconsidered: the excavations of 1935–38 in the light of recent field survey' *in* M C B Bowden, D A Mackay and P Topping (eds) 1989, 129–35.

Coles, B and Coles, J 1986 *Sweet Track to Glastonbury: the Somerset Levels in prehistory* Thames and Hudson. London.

Coles, J 1972 *Field Archaeology in Britain* Methuen. London.

Coles, J and Goodburn, D 1991 *Wet Site Excavation and Survey* Wetlands Archaeological Research Project Occas Pap **5**.

Coles, J and Hall, D 1997 'The Fenland Project: from survey to management and beyond' *Antiquity* **71**. 831–44.

Colt Hoare, R 1812 *The Ancient History of Wiltshire* (2 vols) William Miller. London. (rep 1975 EP Publishing/Wiltshire County Library)

Conway, H 1991 *People's Parks* Cambridge University Press.

Conzen, M 1969 *Alnwick, Northumberland: a study in town plan analysis* Inst Brit Geogr **27**. London.

Coope, R 1986 'The "Long Gallery": its origins, development, use and decoration', *Architect Hist* **29**. 43–84.

Coppack, G 1990 *Abbeys and Priories* Batsford. London.

Corney, M, Gaffney, C and Gater, J 1995 'Geophysical investigations at the Charlton Villa, Wiltshire, England' *Archaeol Prospection* **1:2**. 121–8.

CBA 1991 *Signposts for Archaeological Publication* (3 edn) Counc Brit Archaeol. London.

Cranstone, D 1990 'The excavation of industrial sites' *Fld Archaeol* **13**. 231–3.

Crawford, O G S 1924a 'The Stonehenge Avenue' *Antiq J* **4**. 57–9.

Crawford, O G S 1924b *Air survey and Archaeology* Ordnance Survey Professional Pap, n ser **7**.

Crawford, O G S 1929 *Air Photography for Archaeologists* Ordnance Survey Professional Pap, n ser **12**.

Crawford, O G S 1954 'A century of air photography' *Antiquity* **28**. 206–10.

Crawford, O G S 1955 *Said and Done* Weidenfeld and Nicolson. London.

Crawford, O G S and Keiller, A 1928 *Wessex from the Air* Oxford University Press.

Crawshaw, A J G 1995 'Oblique aerial photography: films' *Aerial Archaeol Res Group News* **10**. 23–7.

Crossley, D (ed) 1989 *Water Power on the Sheffield Rivers* Sheffield Trades Historical Society/Sheffield University. Sheffield.

Crossley, D 1990 *Post-Medieval Archaeology in Britain* Leicester University Press.

Crossley, D 1994 'Early industrial landscapes' *in* B Vyner (ed) *Building on the Past* Roy Archaeol Inst. London. 244–63.

Crow, J and Hill, S 1995 'The Byzantine fortifications of Amastris in Paphlagonia' *Anatolian Stud* **45**. 251–65.

Crump, B and Wallis, S 1992 'Kiddles and the Foulness fishing industry' *Essex J* **27**. 38–42.

Crutchley, S 1994 *Assessment of the Potential of Aerial Photographic Survey in examining England's Intertidal Archaeological Resource* RCHME (unpubl internal report).

Cunliffe, B 1994 'The Danebury environs project' *in* A Fitzpatrick and E Morris (eds) *The Iron Age in Wessex: recent work* Association Française D'Etude de L'Age du Fer/Trust for Wessex Archaeology Limited. 38–42.

Cunnington, M E 1927 'Prehistoric timber circles' *Antiquity* **1**. 92–5, pl I and II.

Cunnington, M E 1933 'Excavations in Yarnbury Castle Camp, 1932' *Wiltshire Archaeol Natur Hist Mag* **46**. 198–213.

Currie, C K 1990 'Fishponds or garden features, *c* 1550–1750' *Garden Hist* **18/1**. 22–46.

Currie, C R J and Lewis, C P (eds) 1994 *English County Histories: a guide* Alan Sutton. Stroud.

Daniel, G E 1986 *Some Small Harvest* Thames and Hudson. London.

Darby, H C 1971 *The Domesday Geography of Eastern England* (3 edn). Cambridge University Press.

Darvill, T C 1993 'Working practices' *in* J Hunter and I Ralston (eds) 1993, 169–83.

Darvill, T C 1996 *Prehistoric Britain from the Air* Cambridge University Press.

David, A 1995 *Geophysical Survey in Archaeological Field Evaluation* English Heritage Research and Professional Services Guideline **1**.

Davies, W and Astill, G G 1994 *The East Brittany Survey: fieldwork and field data* Scolar Press. Aldershot.

DNH 1997 *The Treasure Act 1996: code of practice (England and Wales)* Department of National Heritage. London.

DoE 1990 *Planning Policy Guidance 16: Archaeology and Planning* Department of the Environment. HMSO. London.

DoE 1992 *Planning Policy Guidance 20: Coastal Planning* Department of the Environment. HMSO. London.

DoE 1994 *Documentary Research on Industrial Sites* Department of the Environment: Contaminated Land Research Rep.

Deuel, L 1969 *Flights into Yesterday* Macdonald. New York.

Dix, B, Soden, I and Hylton, T 1995 'Kirby Hall and its gardens: excavations in 1987–1994', *Archaeol J* **152**. 291–380.

Dunbar, J 1992 'The RCAHMS: the first eighty years' *Trans Ancient Monuments Soc* **36**. 13–77.

Dunn, C J 1988 'The barrows of East Central Powys' *Archaeol Cambrensis* **137**. 27–42.

Dyer, C 1991 *Hanbury: settlement and society in a woodland landscape* Department of English Local History Occas Pap **4** ser 4. Leicester University Press.

Dymond, C W and Hodgson, T H 1901 'An ancient village near Threlkeld' *Trans Cumberland Westmorland Antiq Archaeol Soc* **2** (1902). 38–52.

Edis, J, MacLeod, D, and Bewley, R H 1989 'An archaeologist's guide to the classification of cropmarks and soilmarks' *Antiquity* **63**. 112–26.

Elliott, B 1986 *Victorian Gardens* Batsford. London.

EH 1991 *Management of Archaeological Projects* (2 edn). English Heritage. London.

EH/RCHME 1996 *England's Coastal Heritage: a statement on the management of coastal archaeology* Engl Heritage. London.

Evans, J G 1975 *The Environment of Early Man in the British Isles* Paul Elek. London.

Everard, C E 1980 'On sea-level changes' *in* F H Thompson (ed) *Archaeology and Coastal Change* Soc Antiq London Occas Pap (n ser) **1**. 1–23.

Everson, P L 1988 'What's in a name? "Goltho", Goltho and Bullington' *Lincolnshire Hist Archaol* **23**. 93–9.

Everson, P L 1989a 'Lost and Found in Lincolnshire: two problems in archaeological inventorizing' *in* M C B Bowden, D A Mackay and P Topping (eds) 1989, 55–64.

Everson, P L 1989b 'Field Survey by the RCHME on the gritstone moorlands of the Derbyshire Peak District: Stanton Moor' *in* A Gibson (ed) *Midlands Prehistory* Brit Archaeol Rep Brit Ser **204**. 14–26.

Everson, P L 1989c 'The gardens of Campden House, Chipping Campden, Gloucestershire' *Garden Hist* **17/2**. 109–21.

Everson, P L 1991 'Three case studies of ridge and furrow: 1. Offa's Dyke at Dudston in Chirbury, Shropshire: a pre-Offan field system?' *Landscape Hist* **13**. 53–63.

Everson, P L 1995a 'The earthworks at Shenley Brook End' *in* R Ivens, P Busby and N Shepherd, *Tattenhoe and Westbury: two deserted medieval settlements in Milton Keynes* Buckinghamshire Archaeol Soc Monogr Ser **8**. 79–84.

Everson, P L 1995b 'Earthworks of the post-medieval garden associated with Throwley Old Hall' *in* F Cleverdon *Survey and Excavation in the Manifold Valley* Staffordshire Archaeol Stud **5**. 26–30.

Everson, P L 1995c 'The Munstead Wood survey 1991: a methodology for recording historical gardens by the RCHME' *in* M Tooley and P Arnander (eds) *Gertrude Jekyll: essays on the life of a working amateur* Michaelmas Books. Witton-le-Wear. 71–82.

Everson, P L 1996a 'The after-life of monastic houses: the earthwork evidence' *in* C Sturman (ed) *Lincolnshire People and Places: Essays in Memory of Terence R Leach (1937–1994)* Soc Lincolnshire Hist Archaeol. Lincoln. 13–17.

Everson, P L 1996b 'Bodiam Castle, East Sussex: castle and its designed landscape' *Chateau Gaillard* **17**. 79–84.

Everson, P L 1998 '"Delightfully surrounded with woods and ponds": field evidence for medieval gardens in England' *in* P Pattison (ed) 1998. 32–8

Everson, P L, Richmond, H and Stocker, D in prep 'The Premonstratensian Abbey of St Mary at Barlings and its grange at Lings, Lincolnshire'

Everson, P L and Stamper, P 1987 'Deserted Settlements in Shropshire: Berwick Maviston and Attingham Park' *Trans Shropshire Archaeol Soc* **65**. 64–9.

Everson, P L, Taylor, C C and Dunn, C J 1991 *Change and Continuity: rural settlement in north-west Lincolnshire* HMSO. London

Everson, P L and Wilson-North, R 1993 'Fieldwork and finds at Egerton, Wheathill', *Shropshire Hist Archaeol* **68**. 65–71.

Farrar, R 1987 *Survey by Prismatic Compass* Counc Brit Archaeol Practical Handbook **2**. London.

Fawn, A J, Evans, K A, McMaster, I and Davies, G M R 1990 *The Red Hills of Essex: salt-making in antiquity* Colchester Archaeol Group. Colchester.

Featherstone, R 1994 'Aerial reconnaissance in England 1994' *Antiquity* **68**. 812–15.

Featherstone, R, Horne, P, Macleod, D, and Bewley, R H 1995 'Aerial reconnaissance in England, summer 1995' *Antiquity* **69**. 981–8.

Ferguson, L M and Murray, D M 1997 *Archaeological documentary archives: preparation, curation and storage* Inst Fld Archaeol Pap **1**.

Fisher, P F 1991 'The physical environment of Cranborne Chase' *in* J Barrett, R Bradley and M Hall (eds) *Papers on the Prehistoric archaeology of Cranborne Chase* Oxbow Monogr **11**. Oxford. 11–19.

Fleming, A 1988 *The Dartmoor Reaves: investigating prehistoric land divisions* Batsford. London.

Fleming, A 1997 'Towards a history of wood pasture in Swaledale (North Yorkshire)' *Landscape Hist* **19**. 57–73.

Forestry Commission 1995 *Forests and Archaeology Guidelines*. Edinburgh.

Foster, S and Smout, T C (eds) 1994 *The History of Soils and Field Systems* Scottish Cultural Press. Aberdeen.

Frere, S S and St Joseph, J K S 1983 *Roman Britain from the Air* Cambridge University Press.

Fulford, M G, Champion, T and Long, A (eds) 1997 *England's Coastal Heritage: a survey for EH and the RCHME* Engl Heritage Archaeol Rep **15**.

Gaffney, C and Gater, J with Ovenden, S 1991 *The Use of Geophysical Techniques in Archaeological Evaluations* Inst Fld Archaeol Techn Pap **9**.

Gaffney, V and Tingle, M 1989 *The Maddle Farm Project: an integrated survey of prehistoric and Roman landscapes on the Berkshire Downs* Brit Archaeol Rep Brit Ser **200**. Oxford

Galinou, M (ed) 1990 *London's Pride. The glorious history of the capital's gardens* Anaya Publishers. London.

Giles, C and Goodall, I H 1992 *Yorkshire Textile Mills 1770–1930* HMSO. London.

Glasscock, R (ed) 1975 *The Lay Subsidy of 1334* British Academy Records of Social and Economic History, n ser **2**.

Glasscock, R (ed) 1992 *Historic Landscapes of Britain from the Air* Cambridge University Press.

Godbold, S and Turner, R C 1994 'Medieval fishtraps in the Severn Estuary' *Medieval Archaeol* **38**. 19–54.

Good, G L, Jones, R H and Ponsford, M W 1991 *Waterfront Archaeology* Counc Brit Archaeol Res Rep **74.**

Goulty, N R, Gibson, J P C, Moore, J G and Welfare, H G 1990 'Delineation of the Vallum at Vindobala, Hadrian's Wall, by a shear wave seismic refraction survey' *Archaeometry* **32**. 71–82.

Goulty, N R and Hudson, A L 1994 'Completion of the seismic refraction survey to locate the Vallum at Vindobala, Hadrian's Wall' *Archaeometry* **36**. 327–35.

Griffith, F M 1990 'Aerial reconnaissance in mainland Britain in the summer of 1989' *Antiquity* **64**. 14–33.

Haigh, J G B 1991 'The AERIAL program, Version 4.1' *Aerial Archaeol Res Group News* **3**. 31–3.

Hall, D and Coles, J 1994 *Fenland Survey: an essay in landscape and persistence* Engl Heritage Archaeol Rep **1**. London.

Hall, E 1995 *The Garden of England* Kent County Council.

Hampton, J N 1989 'The Air Photography Unit of the Royal Commission on the Historical Monuments of England, 1965–85' *in* D L Kennedy (ed) *Into the Sun: essays in air photography in archaeology in honour of Derrick Riley* J R Collis Public.. Sheffield. 13–28.

Handley, M 1998 *Microfilming Archaeological Archives: standard and guidance* Inst Fld Archaeol Pap.

Harding, P A and Lewis, C R 1997 'Archaeological investigations at Tockenham, 1994' *Wilts Archaeol Natur Hist Mag* **90**. 26–41.

Harley, J B 1972 *Maps for the Local Historian* Standing Conference for Local History.

Harley, J B 1975 *Ordnance Survey Maps: a descriptive manual* Ordnance Survey. Southampton.

Harley, J B 1979 *The Ordnance Survey and Land-Use Mapping: Parish Books of Reference and the County Series 1:2500 maps, 1855–1918* Hist Geogr Res Ser, **2**.

Harley, J B and Phillips, C W 1964 *The Historian's Guide to Ordnance Survey Maps* Standing Conference for Local History.

Hart, C R 1981 *The North Derbyshire Archaeological Survey to AD 1500* North Derbyshire Archaeol Trust. Chesterfield.

Hart, C R 1993 'The ancient woodland of Ecclesall Woods, Sheffield' *in* P Beswick (ed) *Ancient Woodlands: their archaeology and ecology* Landscape Conservation Forum. Sheffield. 49–66.

Harvey, N 1984 *A History of Farm Buildings in England and Wales* (n edn) David and Charles. Newton Abbott.

Haselgrove, C, Millett, M and Smith, I (eds) 1985 *Archaeology from the Ploughsoil: studies in the collection and interpretation of field survey data* Department of Archaeology and Prehistory, University of Sheffield.

Hedley, G and Rance, A 1987 *Pleasure Grounds: the gardens and landscapes of Hampshire* Milestone Publications. Horndean.

Hendry, G, Bannister, N and Toms, J 1984 'The earthworks of an ancient woodland' *Bristol Avon Archaeol* **3**. 47–53.

Higham, M C 1996 '*Aergi* names as indicators of transhumance: problems of the evidence' *in* HSA Fox (ed) *Seasonal Settlement* Vaughan Paper **39**. Leicester University. 55–60.

Higham, R and Barker, P 1992 *Timber Castles* Batsford. London.

Hill, J D 1995 *Ritual and Rubbish in the Iron Age of Wessex: a study on the formation of a specific archaeological record* Brit Archaeol Rep **242**. Oxford.

Hindle, B 1988 *Maps and Local History* Batsford. London.

Horsley, J 1732 *Britannia Romana* John Osborne and Thomas Longman. London. (rep 1974 Frank Graham. Newcastle upon Tyne.)

Hoskins, W G 1955 *The Making of the English Landscape* Hodder and Stoughton. London.

Hudson, K 1984 *Industrial History from the Air* Cambridge University Press.

Hunter, J and Ralston, I (eds) 1993 *Archaeological Resource Management in the UK: an introduction* Inst Fld Archaeol/Alan Sutton. Stroud.

IFA 1994 *Standard and Guidance for Archaeological Field Evaluations* Inst Fld Archaeol.

IFA 1997 *By-laws of the Institute of Field Archaeologists: code of conduct* (rev edn) Inst Fld Archaeol.

Jacobi, R M, Tallis, J H and Mellars, P A 1976 'The Southern Pennine Mesolithic and the ecological record' *J Archaeol Sci* **3**. 307–20.

Johnson, M 1993 *Housing Culture* Smithsonian Institution Press. Washington DC, USA.

Johnson, M 1996 *An Archaeology of Capitalism* Blackwell. Oxford.

Johnson, N and Rose, P 1994 *Bodmin Moor: an archaeological survey vol 1: The human landscape to c 1800.* Engl Heritage/RCHME. London.

Johnson, S 1979 *The Roman Forts of the Saxon Shore* (2 edn) Paul Elek. London.

Johnson, S 1989 *Hadrian's Wall* Batsford. London.

Johnston, D E (ed) 1977 *The Saxon Shore* Counc Brit Archaeol Res Rep **18**. London.

Jones, G and Bell, J *Oast Houses in Sussex and Kent: their history and development* Phillimore/Hop Industry Research Survey. Chichester.

Jones, M 1993 *Sheffield's Woodland Heritage* (rev edn) Green Tree Publications. Rotherham.

Kelley, D W 1986 *Charcoal and Charcoal Burning* Shire. Princes Risborough.

King, D J C 1983 *Castellarium Anglicanum* (2 vols) Kraus International. New York.

Kirby, K J 1984 *Inventories of Ancient Semi-natural Woodland* Focus on Nature Conservation Series **6**.

Knowles, D and Hadcock, R 1971 *Medieval Religious Houses of England and Wales* Longman. London.

Lambert, D, Goodchild, P and Roberts, J 1995 *Researching a Garden's History: a guide to documentary and published sources* Landscape Design Trust and Institute of Advanced Architectural Studies, University of York.

Langford, M J 1997a *Basic Photography* (6 edn) Focal Press. London.

Langford, M J 1997b *Advanced Photography* (6 edn) Focal Press. London.

Langmuir, E 1995 *Mountaincraft and Leadership* (3 edn) Scottish Sports Council/Mountain Leader Training Board.

Lee, G 1995 'Forestry management and archaeology' *in* A Q Berry and I W Brown (eds) *Managing Ancient Monuments: an integrated approach* Clwyd Archaeology Service. 97–104.

Lewis, C R 1989 'Paired mottes in East Chelborough, Dorset' *in* M C B Bowden, D A Mackay and P Topping (eds) 1989. 159–71.

Long, A and Roberts, D 1997 'Sea-level change' *in* M G Fulford *et al* (eds) 1997. 25–49.

Lowry, B (ed) 1995 *20th Century Defences in Britain* Counc Brit Archaeol Practical Handbook **12**. York.

Macdonald, G 1917 'General William Roy and his *Military Antiquities of the Romans in North Britain*' *Archaeologia* **68**. 161–228.

Machin, R 1978 *The Houses of Yetminster* Bristol University Department of Extra-Mural Studies.

Mackay, D 1990 'The Great Chesters aqueduct: a new survey' *Britannia* **21**. 285–9.

Macready, S and Thompson, F H (eds) 1985 *Archaeological Field Survey in Britain and Abroad* Soc Antiq London Occas Pap (n ser) **6**.

Marren, P 1990 *Woodland Heritage* David and Charles. Newton Abbott.

Marshall, J D and Davies-Shiel, M 1977 *The Industrial Archaeology of the Lake Counties* Michael Moon. Beckermet.

McAvoy, F 1994 'Marine salt extraction: the excavation of salterns at Wainfleet St Mary, Lincolnshire' *Medieval Archaeol* **38**. 134–63.

McDonnell, R 1995 *Bridgwater Bay: a rapid preliminary assessment of Gore Sand and Stert Flats* RCHME (unpubl survey report).

McOmish, D S, Brown, G and Field, D forthcoming *The Archaeology of Salisbury Plain*

Megaw, J V S, Thomas, A C, and Wailes, B 1961 'The Bronze Age settlement at Gwithian, Cornwall' *Proc W Cornwall Fld Club* **2** pt 5 (1960–1). 200–15.

Mercer, E 1975 *English Vernacular Houses: a study of traditional farmhouses and cottages* HMSO. London.

Milne, G and Hobley, B (eds) 1981 *Waterfront Archaeology in Britain and northern Europe* Counc Brit Archaeol Res Rep **41**. London.

Milne, G, McKewan, C and Goodburn, D 1998 *Nautical Archaeology on the Foreshore: hulk recording on the Medway* RCHME. Swindon.

Morris, E L 1985 'Prehistoric salt distributions: two case studies from western Britain' *Bull Board Celtic Stud* **32**. 336–79.

Morris, E L 1994 'The organisation of salt production and distribution in Wessex' *in* A P Fitzpatrick and E L Morris (eds) *The Iron Age in Wessex: recent work* Assoc Française d'Etude de l'Age du Fer/Trust for Wessex Archaeology. Salisbury. 14–16.

MGC 1992 *Standards in the Museum Care of Archaeological Collections* Museums and Galleries Commission.

Muskett, J 1988 *Site Surveying* MacDonald & Evans. London.

Muter, W G 1979 *The Buildings of an Industrial Community: Coalbrookdale and Ironbridge* Phillimore. Chichester.

Muthesius, S 1982 *The English Terraced House* Yale University Press. London.

NERC 1997 *Guidance Note: Safety in Fieldwork* Natural Environmental Research Council. Swindon.

Nesbit, R C 1996 *Eyes of the RAF* Alan Sutton. Stroud.

Northumbrian Surveys 1997 *Report on Ground Penetrating Radar at Harbottle Castle, Upper Coquetdale, for Northumberland National Park* Northumbrian Surveys. Catton.

Oliver, R 1993 *Ordnance Survey Maps: a concise guide for historians* Charles Close Society. London.

Olwig, K R 1993 'Sexual cosmology: nation and landscape at the conceptual interstices of nature and culture: or, what does landscape really mean?' *in* B Bender (ed) 1993. 307–43.

OS 1965 *Textbook of Topographical Surveying* Ordnance Survey. HMSO. London.

OS 1968 *An Introduction to the Projection for Ordnance Survey Maps and the National Reference System*. Ordnance Survey. HMSO. London

Ovenden, S 1994 'Application of Seismic Refraction to archaeological prospecting' *Archaeol Prospection* **1:1**. 53–63.

Owen, D 1975 'Medieval chapels in Lincolnshire', *Lincolnshire Hist Archaeol* **10**, 15–22.

Owen, T and Pilbeam, E 1992 *The Ordnance Survey: map makers to Britain since 1791* HMSO. London.

Palmer, M 1990 'Industrial archaeology: a thematic or a period discipline?' *Antiquity* **64**. 275–85.

Palmer, M and Neaverson, P 1992 *Industrial Landscapes of the East Midlands* Phillimore. Chichester.

Palmer, M and Neaverson, P 1994 *Industry in the Landscape, 1700–1900* Routledge. London.

Palmer, M and Neaverson, P (eds) 1995 *Managing the Industrial Heritage* Leicester Archaeol Monogr **2**.

Palmer, R 1984 *Danebury: an aerial photographic interpretation of its environs* RCHME Suppl Ser **6**. HMSO. London.

Palmer, R 1995 'Trying Kodak Technical Pan' *Aerial Archaeol Res Group News* **11**. 13.

Parfitt, K and Fenwick, V 1993 'The rescue of Dover's Bronze Age boat' *in* J Coles, V Fenwick and G Hutchison (eds) *A Spirit of Enquiry* Wetlands Archaeological Research Project Occas Pap **7**. Exeter. 77–80.

Pattison, P (ed) 1998 *There by Design: field archaeology in parks and gardens. Papers presented at a conference organised by the RCHME and the Garden History Society* RCHME. Swindon./Brit Archaeol Rep Brit Ser **267**. Oxford.

Pearson, S 1994 *The Medieval Houses of Kent: an historical analysis* HMSO. London.

Peters, J E C 1969 *The Development of Farm Buildings in Western Lowland Staffordshire up to 1880* Manchester University Press.

Phibbs, J 1983 'An approach to the methodology of recording historic landscapes', *Garden Hist* **11** no 2, 167–75.

Phibbs, J 1991 'The archaeology of parks — the wider perspective' *in* A Brown (ed) 1991. 118–22.

Phibbs, J 1998 'Recording what isn't there: three difficulties of 18th-century landscapes' *in* P Pattison (ed) 1998. 27–31.

Piggott, S 1985 *William Stukeley: an eighteenth-century antiquary* (rev edn) Thames and Hudson. London.

Poidebard, A 1934 *La trace de Rome dans le désert de Syrie* Bibliothèque Archéologique et Historique **18**. Paris.

Pryor, F M M 1991 *Flag Fen: prehistoric Fenland centre* Batsford. London.

PRO 1967 *Maps and Plans in the Public Record Office, I: British Isles c 1410–1860* Public Record Office. HMSO. London.

PRO 1899–1921 *Inquisitions and assessments relating to Feudal Aids, with other analogous documents, 1284–1431* Public Record Office. HMSO. London.

Pugh, J C 1975 *Surveying for Field Scientists* Methuen. London.

Pybus, D 1983 'The alum hole at Sandsend' *Trans Scarborough Dist Archaeol Hist Soc* **25**. 31–5.

Rackham, O 1975 *Hayley Wood, its History and Ecology* Cambridge and Isle of Ely Naturalists Trust. Cambridge.

Rackham, O 1976 *Trees and Woodland in the British Landscape* Dent. London.

Rackham, O 1980 *Ancient Woodland: its history, vegetation and uses in England* Edward Arnold. London.

Rackham, O 1986 *The History of the Countryside* Dent. London.

Rackham, O 1989 *The Last Forest: the story of Hatfield Forest* Dent. London.

Ratcliffe, J and Parkes, C 1989 *Fieldwork in Scilly: March 1989* Cornwall Archaeol Unit.

Renfrew, C and Bahn, P 1996 *Archaeology: theories, methods and practice* (2 edn) Thames and Hudson. London and New York.

Richards, J 1990 *The Stonehenge Environs Project* Engl Heritage Archaeol Rep **16**. London.

Riden, P 1987 *Record Sources for Local History* Batsford. London.

Riley, D N 1944 'The technique of air-archaeology' *Archaeol J* **101**. 1–16.

Riley, D N 1987 *Air Photography and Archaeology* Duckworth. London.

Riley, D N 1996 *Aerial Archaeology in Britain* Shire. Princes Risborough.

Riley, H 1995 'Brean Down, Somerset: interim report on a new survey by the RCHME' *Archaeology in the Severn Estuary* **6**. 13–21.

Ritchie, W, Tait, D A, Wood, M and Wright, R 1977 *Surveying and Mapping for Field Scientists* Longman. Harlow.

Roberts, B K 1987 *The Making of the English Village* Longman. Harlow.

Roberts, G, Gonzalez, S and Huddart, D 1996 'Intertidal holocene footprints and their archaeological significance' *Antiquity* **70**. 647–51.

Roberts, T W 1995 *Ellesmere Port 1795–1960* Privately published. Gisborne, New Zealand.

Rodger, E 1972 *The Large Scale County Maps of the British Isles 1596–1850: a union list* Bodleian Library. Oxford.

RCAHMS 1990 *North-East Perth: an archaeological landscape* Royal Commission on the Ancient and Historical Monuments of Scotland. HMSO. London.

RCAHMW 1991 *An Inventory of the Ancient Monuments in Glamorgan* vol 3 pt 1a *Medieval secular monuments: the Early Castles from the Norman Conquest to 1217* Royal Commission on the Ancient and Historical Monuments of Wales. HMSO. Cardiff.

RCHME 1960 *A Matter of Time* HMSO. London.

RCHME 1968 *An Inventory of Historic Monuments in the County of Cambridge* vol 1 *West Cambridgeshire*. HMSO. London.

RCHME 1975 *Archaeological Sites in North-East Northamptonshire* HMSO. London.

RCHME 1976 *Ancient and Historical Monuments in the County of Gloucester: Iron Age and Romano-British Monuments in the Gloucestershire Cotswolds* HMSO. London.

RCHME 1979a *Stonehenge and its Environs* Edinburgh University Press.

RCHME 1979b *Long Barrows in Hampshire and the Isle of Wight* HMSO. London.

RCHME 1982 *An Inventory of the Historical Monuments in the County of Northampton* vol 4 *Archaeological Sites in South-West Northamptonshire.* HMSO. London.

RCHME 1986 *Rural Houses of West Yorkshire* HMSO. London.

RCHME 1994 *The Royal Gunpowder Factory, Waltham Abbey, Essex: an RCHME Survey, 1993* RCHME. London.

RCHME 1996a *The National Inventory of Maritime Archaeology for England* RCHME. Swindon.

RCHME 1996b *Recording Historic Buildings: a descriptive specification* (3 edn). RCHME. Swindon.

RCHME forthcoming *Recording Archaeological Field Monuments: a descriptive specification* RCHME. Swindon.

RCHME/EH 1998 *Thesaurus of Monument Types: a standard for use in archaeological and architectural records* (2 edn) RCHME/English Heritage. Swindon.

Ryder, P 1993 *Medieval Churches of West Yorkshire* West Yorkshire Archaeological Service. Wakefield.

SCAUM 1997 *Recording information about archaeological fieldwork* Standing Conference of Archaeological Unit Managers

Schofield, A J (ed) 1991 *Interpreting Artefact Scatters: contributions to ploughzone archaeology* Oxbow Monogr **4**. Oxford.

Scollar, I, Tabbagh, A, Hesse, A and Herzog, I 1990 *Archaeological Geophysics and Remote Sensing* Cambridge University Press.

Simmons, I G and Innes, J B 1981 'Tree Remains in the North York Moors' *Nature* **294**. 76-78.

Simmons, I G and Innes, J B 1988 'Late Quaternary vegetational history of the North York Moors: X. Investigations on East Blisdale Moor' *J Biogeography* **15**. 299–324.

Sinclair, C 1994 *Tracing Scottish Local History: a guide to local history research in the Scottish Record Office* HMSO.

SMA 1993 *Selection, Retention and Dispersal of Archaeological Collections: guidelines for use in England, Wales and Northern Ireland* Society of Museum Archaeologists.

SMA 1995 *Towards an Accessible Archaeological Archive: the transfer of archaeological archives to museums: guidelines for use in England, Northern Ireland, Scotland and Wales* Society of Museum Archaeologists.

Smith, N in prep 'The archaeology of enclosure in the New Forest' *Hampshire Stud.*

Soffe, G and Clare, T 1988 'New evidence of ritual monuments at Long Meg and her Daughters, Cumbria' *Antiquity* **62**. 552–7.

Sparkes, I G 1977 *Woodland Craftsmen* Shire. Princes Risborough.

Spoerry, P (ed) 1992 *Geoprospection in the Archaeological Landscape* Oxbow Monogr **18**. Oxford.

Stamper, P 1996 *Historic Parks and Gardens of Shropshire* Shropshire Books. Shrewsbury.

St Joseph, J K S (ed) 1966 *The Uses of Air Photography: nature and man in a new perspective* John Baker. London.

Stocker, D 1993 'The shadow of the General's armchair' *Archaeol J* **149**. 415–20.

Sumner, G H 1913 *The Ancient Earthworks of Cranborne Chase* Chiswick Press. London. (rep 1988 Alan Sutton/Wiltshire County Library).

Swan, V G 1984 *The Pottery Kilns of Roman Britain* RCHME Suppl Ser **5**. HMSO. London.

Tate, W and Turner, M 1978 *A Domesday of English Enclosure Acts and Awards* Reading University Library.

Taylor, C C 1974 *Fieldwork in Medieval Archaeology* Batsford. London.

Taylor, C C 1983 *The Archaeology of Gardens* Shire. Princes Risborough.

Taylor, C C 1989a 'Whittlesford: the study of a river-edge village' *in* M Aston, D Austin and C Dyer (eds) *The Rural Settlements of Medieval England: studies dedicated to Maurice Beresford and John Hurst* Basil Blackwell. Oxford. 207–27.

Taylor, C C 1989b 'Somersham Palace, Cambridgeshire: a medieval landscape for pleasure?', in M C B Bowden, D A Mackay and P Topping (eds) 1989. 211–24.

Thomas, A C 1958 *Gwithian: Ten Years' Work (1949–1958)* Camborne Printing Co. Camborne.

Tilley, C 1994 *A Phenomenology of Landscape: places, paths and monuments* Berg. Oxford.

Tilley, C 1995 'Rocks as resources: landscapes and power' *Cornish Archaeol* **34**. 5–57.

Tolan-Smith, M 1997 'Approaches to the study of ancient woodland — Horsley Wood' *in* C Tolan-Smith (ed) 1997 *Landscape Archaeology in Tynedale* Tyne-Solway Ancient and Historic Landscapes Research Programme Monogr **1**. University of Newcastle upon Tyne. 43–52.

Tomalin, D (ed) 1994 *The Wootton-Quarr Survey* Isle of Wight County Council Archaeological Unit: draft report for English Heritage.

Tooke, C S 1984 'The ballast trade in the port of Great Yarmouth' *Great Yarmouth Dist Archaeol Soc* **2:1**. 13–16.

Topping, P 1987 'A "new" signal station in Cumbria' *Britannia* **18**. 298–300.

Topping, P 1989 'Early cultivation in Northumberland and the Borders' *Proc Prehist Soc* **55**. 161–79.

TUC 1988 *Hazards at Work (TUC Guide to Health and Safety)* Trades Union Congress. London.

Trenchmann, C T 1936 'Mesolithic flints from the submerged forest at West Hartlepool' *Proc Prehist Soc* **2**:2. 161–8.

Trueman, M 1995 'The Association for Industrial Archaeology's IRIS initiative' *in* M Palmer and P Neaverson (eds) 1995, 29–34.

Turner, R C nd *Mellor's Gardens: a Victorian allegorical garden at Hough-Hole, Cheshire* Cheshire County Council.

Wade Martins, S 1980 *A Great Estate at Work* Cambridge University Press.

Wade Martins, S 1991 *Historic Farm Buildings* Batsford. London.

Walker, K 1990 *Guidelines for the Preparation of Excavation Archives for Long-term Storage* UKIC Archaeology Section.

Watkins, C 1990 *Woodland Management and Conservation* David and Charles. Newton Abbott.

Welfare, A T 1986 'The Greenlee Lough (Northumberland) palimpsest: an interim report on the 1985 season' *Northern Archaeol* **7**/2. 35–7.

Welfare, H G 1989 'John Aubrey — the first archaeological surveyor?' *in* M C B Bowden, D A Mackay and P Topping (eds) 1989. 17–28.

Welfare, H G and Swan, V G 1995 *Roman Camps in England: the field archaeology* HMSO London.

Welfare, H G, Bowden, M C B and Blood, N K 1998 'Fieldwork and the castles of the Anglo-Scottish border' *in* P Pattison, S Ainsworth and D Field (eds) *Patterns in the Past: essays in honour of Christopher Taylor* Oxbow Books. Oxford. 53–60.

Whimster, R P 1983 'Aerial reconnaissance from Cambridge: a retrospective view 1945–1980' *in* G S Maxwell (ed) *The Impact of Aerial Reconnaissance on Archaeology* Counc Brit Archaeol Res Rep **49**. 92–105.

Whimster, R P 1989 *The Emerging Past: air photography and the buried landscape* RCHME London.

White, R 1995 'A landscape of the lead industry: the Yorkshire Dales' *in* M Palmer and P Neaverson (eds) 1995. 61–6.

Whiteman, A (ed) 1986 *The Compton census of 1676, a critical edition* British Academy Records of Social and Economic History, n ser **10**.

Whittle, E and Taylor, C C 1994 'The early seventeenth-century gardens of Tackley, Oxfordshire' *Garden Hist* **22/1**. 37–63.

Whyte, W S and Paul, R E 1997 *Basic Surveying* (4 edn) Laxtons (Butterworth-Heinemann). Oxford.

Wiegand, T 1920 *Sinai: Wissenschaftliche Veröffentlichungen des Deutsch-Türkischen Denkmalschutz Kommandos* **1**. Walter de Gruyter and Co. Berlin.

Wilkinson, T J and Murphy, P 1986 'Archaeological survey of an intertidal zone: the submerged landscape of the Essex coast, England' *J Fld Archaeol* **13**:2. 177–94.

Wilkinson, T J and Murphy, P 1995 *The Archaeology of the Essex Coast, Vol 1: The Hullbridge Survey* East Anglian Archaeology **71**.

Williams-Freeman, J P 1915 *Field Archaeology as Illustrated by Hampshire* Macmillan. London.

Williamson, T 1987 'Early co-axial field systems on the East Anglian boulder clays' *Proc Prehist Soc* **53**. 419–32.

Williamson, T and Taigel, A 1990 *Gardens in Norfolk* Centre for East Anglian Studies. Norwich.

Wilson, D R 1982 *Air Photo Interpretation for Archaeologists* Batsford. London.

Wilson, D R 1991 'Old gardens from the air' *in* A Brown (ed) 1991. 20–35.

Wilson, R J P 1971 *Land Surveying* MacDonald & Evans. London.

Wilson-North, R 1989 'Formal garden earthworks at Moreton Corbet Castle, Shropshire', in M C B Bowden, D A Mackay and P Topping (eds) 1989. 225–8.

Wilson-North, R 1998 'Two relict gardens in Somerset: their changing fortune through the 17th and 18th centuries as revealed by field evidence and other sources', in P Pattison (ed) 1998. 56–64.

Wilson-North, R and Porter, S 1997 'Witham, Somerset: from Carthusian monastery to country house to Gothic folly', *Architect Hist* **40**. 81–98.

Wood, J (ed) 1994 *Buildings Archaeology: applications in practice* Oxbow Monogr **43**. Oxford.

Woodward, A B and Woodward, P J 1996 'The topography of some barrow cemeteries in Bronze Age Wessex' *Proc Prehist Soc* **62**. 275–91.

Woodward, P J 1978 'Flint distribution, ring ditches and Bronze Age settlement patterns in the Great Ouse valley: the problem, a field survey technique and some preliminary results' *Archaeol J* **135**. 32–56.

Wright, E V 1990 *The Ferriby Boats: seacraft of the Bronze Age* Routledge. London.

Yorston, R, Gaffney, V L and Reynolds, P J 1990 'Simulation of artefact movement due to cultivation' *J Archaeol Sci* **17**. 67–83.

Index

Figure and plate numbers are in **bold**

Abney level 197
accuracy 47, 48–50
aerial survey 105–15, 116–18, 132, 138
    history of 105–6
    limitations of 106, 113
    photography 28, 109–11, 141
    transcription (mapping) 27, 46, 78, 112–14, 140, **8**
alidade 58, 63, 197–8
    self-reducing 63, 64, 198, **pls 6** and **8**
Almondbury (W Yorks) 90, **42**
almshouses 148, **75**
altitude 40, 67, 133
Amasra, Turkey 17–18
annotation of plans 172–3, **64**
archive drawing 167, 192–3, **21**, **24**, **34**, **64**
archive report 175–6, 191–2
archives 30, 179–86
    copying 186
    materials 182–5
    principles 179–82
    storage 185–6, **88**
Attingham Park (Salop) 83, 86, 87
Aubrey, John 19, **3**
augering 133
Avebury (Wilts) 19, 28, 157, **3**, **76**

Bailiff Wood (Cumb) **64**
Barron's Pike (Cumb) 89
barrows 27–8, 88, **36**, **86**
baseline control scheme 54–6, **18**
Batchacre (Staffs) 147
Beckton (Greater London) **68**

Black Knoll (Salop) 83, **37**
Bodiam (E Sussex) 85, 97, 151, **49**
Bodmin Moor (Cornwall) 27, 41–2
Braunston (Northants) **35**
Brean Down (Somt) 131, **pl 17**
Bridgwater Bay (Somt) **pl 18**
Brougham (Cumb) 25, **9**
Brough St Giles (N Yorks) 93
Buckland Rings (Hants) **7**
buildings 111, 152, 155–66
Burderop Down (Wilts) **pl 4**
Burton Hall, Warcop (Cumb) **18**
Bury Castle, Brompton Regis (Somt) **31**

cairns 28, 83–4, 88, **38**
Calderdale (W Yorks) 165, **84**
cameras 97, 109
canals 80, 87, 152, 160, **35**, **81**
Carshope (Northum) **47**
castles 25, 36, 85, 97, 158, 177–8, **9**, **23**, **24**, **31**, **42**, **49**, **pl 5**
Cautley (Cumb) 88, **pl 9**
Cawfields (Northum) **50**
chain, surveying 194
chapels 36, 84, 160, **80**
checks (in survey) 50
Cherwell valley (Oxon) 112, **56**
Chipping Campden (Glos) 145, 148, **72**, **75**
chronology 24–5, 156–7 *see also* stratigraphy
churches 36, 148, 157, 160, **75**
Church Pits, Orcheston (Wilts) 85, **36**
clinometer 197

coastal change 131
Cockfield Fell (Co Durham) **14**
compass, prismatic 51, 74, 132, 194
'component sheets' 104, 153–4
Computer-Aided Drawing (CAD) 70, 152–3, 174
Conisbrough (S Yorks) 177
contour surveys 28, 65–6, 170, **22, 28**
control 48
control plot 58, **19, 20**
control stations 54–7
control survey 52–8, 77, 111, 114, 123, 139
Coombe Down (Wilts) **58**
co-ordinates 54
cord rig 71, 96, **47, 85**
county histories 19, 35–6
Crawford, OGS 21, 105, 112
cropmarks 110, **54, pl 13**
cross-head 62
Croxby (Lincs) 145, **73**

Danebury (Hants) 113
dendrochronology 40, 162
depiction 67–8, 78–9, 123–4, 128, 167–75, **62, 85**
Derwentcote (Co Durham) 33, **12**
detail control 57, 60, **20**
detail survey 50, 58–67
Devil's Dyke (Cambs) **53**
digital cameras 97
digital maps 69, 77
digital media 60, 174, 181, 184
Digital Terrain Model (DTM) 65, 69, 174, **23, 31**
'divorced' survey 46, 54ff
documents, historical 36, 137–8, 142–5, 153, 187
    research strategies for 31–2, 36–7, 93–5, 166
Dover (Kent) 131
drawing boards, field 196
drawing conventions 67, 78–9, 168–71, **85**

drawing equipment 168, 183–4, 196
drawing film 77, 168, 183, 196
Dymond, CW 19, **5**

earthworks, attributes of 24–5, 86–90
earthwork survey *see* survey, analytical
East Chelborough (Dorset) 178
electrical resistivity survey 120, **57**
Electromagnetic Distance Measurement (EDM) 132, 199–200 *see also* total-station
electronic drawing boards 60, 69–70
electronic survey equipment 15, 46, 60, 77
    see also EDM, GPS, theodolite, total-station
environmental archaeology 26, 40, 130–1
errors (in survey) 49
Etruria (Staffs) 159
'event' records 30, 192
excavation 23, 26, 71, 92–3, 128, 133, earthworks resulting from 84, 92, **44**

field drawing 167, **21, 34**
field systems 39–40, 41–2, 71, 80–1, 85, **8, 32, 36, 79, pl 4**
'fieldwalking' *see* surface artefact collection
film (photographic) 98–9, 109, 184
fish weirs 131, **pls 18 and 19**
Formby Point (Merseyside) 131
forts 25, 85, 86, 131, 158, 177–8, **9, pl 21**
Furness (Cumb) 162

gardens 25, 85, 86, 93, 145–51, 160, **9, 45, 72–4, 82, pl 10**
Gawsworth (Ches) 92, 148
geodetic survey 48, 50–1
Geographical Information Systems (GIS) 70, 174
geology 37–9, 71, 89, 121, **42**

geophysical survey 26, 28, 116–17, 119–25, 133, **57–61**, **pl 16**

Gerards Bromley (Staffs) 147, **10**, **11**

Global Positioning System (GPS) 201
    for navigation 107–8, 110
    for survey 51, 65, 68–9, 132–3, 139, **30**, **pl 19**

Goldcliff (Gwent) 129, 131

graphical survey *see* tape-and-offset

Greenlee Lough (Northum) 71–2, 90

grids 52–4

Grimes Graves (Norf) **51**

Ground Penetrating Radar (GPR) 123, **59**

Gwithian (Cornwall) 131

hachured survey 65–6, 168–70, **29**, **34**, **85**

Hackthorn (Lincs) 160, **79**

Hadrian's Wall 19, 85, **4**, **50**, **pl 1**

Haltonchesters (Northum) 93, **44**

Ham Hill (Somt) 125

Harbottle Castle (Northum) 123, **59**

'hard' detail 57–8, **20**

Harlyn Bay (Cornwall) 131

Harrington (Northants) 147

Hartlepool (Cleveland) 131

Haystacks Hill (Northum) 81–2, **8**

health and safety 43–4, 47, 133–4

Hengistbury Head (Dorset) 131

Herefordshire Beacon (Herefs) 177–8

Heronbridge (Ches) 81

High Park (Lancs) 27

High Stones (Derbys) 86

hillforts 40, 71, 90, 116–18, 125, 177–8, **42**

History of the Kings Works 35

HMS *Victory* **pl 11**

hollow ways *see* tracks

Holne Moor (Devon) **pl 22**

Honister (Cumb) **48**, **63**

Horsley, John 19, **4**

houses, polite 83, 86, 147–8, 157, 159–60, **10**, **79**
    on monastic sites 31, 83, 85, 163, **82**

houses, vernacular 159, 162, 165, **67**, **78**, **84**

Howgill Fells (Cumb) 39, **pls 2** and **9**

Howley Hall (W Yorks) 148

human remains 91

Huntingdon Castle (Cambs) 87

hunting lodges 136

illustrations 188 *see also* depiction

Indian clinometer 198

industrial landscapes 139–45, 152–4, 159–60, 162, **12**, **14**, **48**, **66–71**, **84**

industrial records 31, 33, 142, 144–5

industrial sites 33, 36, 131, 158–60, 163, **78**, **83**
    in woodland 136–7

infra-red photographs 99, 109, **pl 12**

Ingleborough (N Yorks) 40, **pl 3**

Ingram (Northum) 84

insurance 44

intersection 57

intertidal area 129–34

Kemsing (Kent) 33, **13**

Kettleby (Lincs) 85

Kinderton (Ches) 86

Kirby (Northants) 148

Kirtling (Cambs) 148

Knaith (Lincs) 148

Landscape survey 75–8, 114, 176, **8**, **33**

land surfaces, preserved 131

Langridge Newtake (Devon) 76, **33**

Large-scale survey 78–80, 176

Leeds (W Yorks) **81**

Legsby (Lincs) 84

level 196–7

level, pocket 197

Levels of survey 26, 73, 155, 166, 189–93

Lewes (Sussex) 86, **39**
libraries
    general 37, 144
    specialist 33, 106, 112, 132, 144
limestone pavement 90, **43**, **pl 3**
linear ditches **14**, **35**
Listed Buildings lists 35
Little Siblyback (Cornwall) 41–2
Local Scale Factors 51
Lockeridge (Wilts) **pl 13**
Long Meg and her Daughters (Cumb)
    pl 12
Lower Heyford (Oxon) **pl 15**
Low Ham (Somt) 93, 147, 148, **45**, **74**
Low Nibthwaite (Cumb) 163, **83**
Lyveden (Northants) 148

magnetic susceptibility 122
magnetometry 121, 124, **58**, **pl 16**
Maiden Castle, Swaledale (N Yorks) 88
Malham (N Yorks) 90
Mallerstang (Cumb) **pl 2**
maps, historical 33, 74, 116, 138 *see also*
    Ordnance Survey maps
Micheldever Wood (Hants) **65**
Middleton (Cumb) **32**
Midgeley (W Yorks) **78**
military sites 145, 158, 177–8
Milton Abbas (Dorset) 86
Minehead (Somt) **pl 19**
moats 83, 85
monastic sites 36, 91, 157–8, **57**, **77**
    later re-use of 31, 83, 85, 148, 163, **82**
morphology 81, 85, 86–8, 113
Munstead Wood (Surrey) 104, 151, **pl 10**
museums 30, 144, 180–1

National Grid 50–1, 53, 68, 126
National Monuments Records (NMR) 23,
    29–30, 106, 132, **88**

National Register of Archives 33
natural features
    and artificial features 90, **42**
    significance of 27, 37, 88
natural hachure 170, **85**
Nenthead (Cumb) **pl 20**
New Farm (Hants) **60–1**
New Forest (Hants) 136
Newland (Cumb) **67**
Newstead Abbey (Notts) **82**
North Ferriby (E Yorks) 131
notebooks 195–6
notes, field 80, 104
Nuneham Courtenay (Oxon) 86

Oare (Kent) 92
Offa's Dyke 81
Old Madeley (Staffs) 85
Optical Distance Measurement (ODM)
    199
optical square 51, 62, 74, 77, 195, **25**
Ordnance Survey maps 53, 187, **7**
    as historical documents 33, 138, 144,
        12, **69–71**
    as survey documents 46, 48, 74, 76–7,
        126, 133, 140
    digital (Superplan) 77
Orford Castle (Suff) 178

pacing 51, 74
paper 183
Park Bottom (Sussex) **6**
parks 33, 36, 86, 89, 150–1, 160, **13**, **79**
Parks and Gardens, Registers of 36
Peak District (Derbys) 85
pen computer *see* electronic drawing board
Pendennis Castle (Cornwall) 158, **pl 21**
Pevsner volumes 35
phase diagrams 173, 193, **87**
photogrammetry 114

photography 97–104, 193
    techniques 98–104, 109–11
Photo-mechanical transfer 186
Pitt Rivers, Gen AHLF 19, 128
place names 33, 36
plane survey 47, 50
plane-table 51, 58, 63–4, 77, 197–8, **pls 6–8**
Pole Moor (W Yorks) **80**
Portchester Castle (Hants) 158
private land 43, 47
profiles 28, 67, 170–1, 193, 197, **86**
publication 186–8

Quarrendon (Bucks) 83, 147

railways 80, 160, **14**, **35**
ranging poles 62, 195
Rapid survey 73–5, 166, 175, **32**
reconnaissance, aerial 107–12
reconnaissance, field 44–7, 76, 99, 139
reconstruction drawings 173, 193
recording sheet 74 *see also* 'component
    sheet'
Record Offices 30, 33, 132, 144, 180, 182
records, archaeological 26, 29, 96, 175,
    189–90
records, architectural 165–6
reports
    for archive 175–6, 191–2
    for publication 186–7
resection 52, **15**
revision (of surveys) 50
Ribblehead (N Yorks) 90, **43**, **pl 3**
ridge-and-furrow 39, 41–2, 71, 81–2, 84, **8**,
    32, **35**, **41**, **79**, **85**
Rievaulx (N Yorks) **77**
roads 80–1, **35**
Rollright Heath (Oxon) **pl 14**
Roy, Gen William 19
Royston cave (Cambs) **52**

salt production sites 131
Sandhills sconce, Newark-on-Trent
    (Notts) **28**
scale 46, 74, 76–7, 78, 171–2
Scheduled Ancient Monuments 47
Scilly Isles 129
sea-level change 130
seasonal considerations 44, 100, 110,
    125–6, 138
seismic refraction 122
Setta Barrow (Devon/Somt) **86**
settlements, 39, 41–2, 71, 82, 85, 88, 131, **8**,
    32
sextant, pocket 195
Shenley Brook End (Bucks) 95
shielings 71
Shugborough (Staffs) 86
side-scan sonar 133
single-station control scheme 54, **16**, **17**
Sites and Monuments Records (SMRs) 23,
    30, 105, 181
Sites of Special Scientific Interest 47
sketch-survey 44
small-scale survey 52
'soft' detail 58, 60, 78–9
Soil Moisture Deficit (SMD) 110
soils 39, 89, 126–7
spot heights 66–7
Stafford Castle (Staffs) **19–24**, **pl 5**
Stainfield (Lincs) 83, 148
Stanton Moor (Derbys) 83–4, 93, 135, **16**,
    17, **38**
Stanwick (N Yorks) 89
Statistical Accounts of Scotland 36
St Austell (Cornwall) **66**
Stoke-on-Trent (Staffs) **69–71**
Stonehenge (Wilts) 27
Stow (Lincs) **46**
stratigraphy 79, 80–6, **29**, **34–38**, **41**
Stumble, the (Essex) 131
Stukeley, William 19
submerged forests 129, 131
Sumner, G Heywood 21

surface artefact collection 91, 116, 125–8, **62**

survey, analytical 15–17, 23–6, 35, 37, 138–9

   aims 15, 18–19

   history of 19–21

   limitations of 24–5, 91

   personnel required 24, 52

   results of 24

survey, principles of 48–50

survey equipment 51, 194–201

   basic 51–2, 74

survey (ground) markers 57, 195

survey techniques 52–67

Sweet Track (Somt) 134

tape-and-offset 52, 58, 62–3, 77, **2**, **17**, **25**, **26**, **27**

tape measures 51, 62, 77, 194

theodolite 51, 198–200

Threlkeld (Cumb) **5**

Throwley Hall (Staffs) 148

Toms, Herbert 21, **6**

topographical drawings 33, **10**

total-station 64–5, 200, **1**

tracks 71, 83, **14**, **29**, **32**, **37**

tramways 84, **14**, **38**

traverse 52, 56–7, **19**

Treasure Act (1996) 182

trilateration 57

Tupholme (Lincs) 85

Upper Coscombe (Glos) 90

vegetational evidence 92, 134, 135, 149–50

vessels 131, 133

video 184

Wakerley (Northants) 147

Waltham Abbey (Essex) 152–4

Wark-on-Tweed (Northum) 178

Warkton (Northants) 148

weather 44, 100, 110, 120, 126

West Kennet (Wilts) 28

wetland archaeology 129

Wheathill (Salop) 95

Whin Sill, the (Northum) 39, **pl 1**

Williams-Freeman, JP 21, 105

Wimpole (Cambs) 86, 87, 114, **40–41**

Winchelsea, Lord 19

Windmill Hill (Wilts) 27–8

windmill mounds 86–7, **40–41**

Winterbourne Stoke (Wilts) 27

Witham (Somt) **57**

Woodham Walter (Essex) 148

woodland 134–9

   'ancient' 134

Wykeham Forest (N Yorks) **29**

Yarnbury (Wilts) 116–18, **62**, **87**